THE STORY OF THE RENAISSANCE

By the same author:

The Story of Ancient Egypt
The Story of Ancient Greece
The Story of Ancient Rome
The Story of the Middle Ages
The Travels of Alexander

THE STORY OF THE RENAISSANCE

by Suzanne Strauss Art

The Fay School, Southborough, Massachusetts

Pemblewick Press

Lincoln, Massachusetts

To Phynius, and to all my history
students at Fay, past and present

Acknowledgments

I am very grateful for the aid and encouragement given me by my family - my husband Bob, my son David, and my daughter Robyn. They cheered me on when I first came up with the idea of writing this book and even joined me in Tuscany, where together we analyzed first-hand the art and architecture of the fourteenth and fifteenth centuries. Bob, David, and Robyn contributed their own expertise in the areas of Renaissance history, art, and literature and helped to edit the final manuscript. This book is, in many ways, a family project.

As ever, I am indebted to my students at Fay. Their enthusiastic response to my history units and their wonderful, unbridled curiosity about all manner of things have been a major inspiration for all of the books I have written. This one is specially dedicated to them. Once again, I must thank my friend and colleague, Dick Upjohn of the Fay History Department, for tirelessly reading my manuscript and offering excellent and insightful criticisms. I am indebted to Lynn Thies for patiently and efficiently formatting my manuscript. And thank you, Phynius, for always being there.

The illustrations in this book are by the author. The statues in Figures 14, 15, 22, and 17 can be viewed in the Museum of the Bargello in Florence, those in Figure 15 and on the cover in the Academy Gallery, Florence, and the one in Figure 16 in the Museum of the Opera del Duomo, Florence.

Copyright © 1997 by Pemblewick Press

Printed in the United States

ISBN-0-9656557-0-9

TO THE TEACHER

The Renaissance was one of history's most fascinating epochs - a lavish spectacle of colorful characters, spicy political intrigues, crucial scientific discoveries, exciting overseas explorations, and unprecedented achievements in art, literature, and music. This explosion of creative activity was sparked when medieval scholars delved into the ancient past and liked what they saw. Their efforts to rekindle the intellectual brilliance of earlier times enabled European society to emerge from an age of fear and repression. Once again the needs and potentials of the individual were valued as much as universal religious beliefs, and the classical balance of reason and faith was restored. The old gloom and doom were replaced by a spirit of optimism. Man wasn't evil, he was good! And there was plenty to celebrate. During the fruitful years of the fifteenth and sixteenth centuries, an amazing number of talented people became caught up in the flurry and accomplished things that helped usher in the modern age.

The Renaissance offers something for everyone and serves as an ideal topic for an integrated unit of classroom study. The purpose of this book is to organize a rather unwieldy mass of information into manageable chunks. It focuses on such themes as the spread of humanism, the growth of the nation state, the evolving role of the artist, the reform of the Catholic Church, and the quest for distant shores, to mention but a few. Every chapter concludes with a series of review questions, related remarks and anecdotes for group discussions, and a variety of enrichment activities. This is the heart of any successful unit: the opportunity for a student, well armed with background data, to "dig deeper" into the areas that interest him most.

The book also functions as both a guide to three centuries of art history and an introduction to some of the greatest literature of the western world. It therefore requires that you gather from your library a broad collection of art books and works containing the writings (or excerpts) of such major Renaissance authors as Dante, Petrarch, Boccaccio, Machiavelli, Montaigne, and Shakespeare. It's one thing for a student to read about the life and works of Michelangelo, and quite another to visually examine the realistic figures in the frescoes of the Sistine Chapel. Nor can one really appreciate Dante or Shakespeare without reading a few sections of THE DIVINE COMEDY or a play like HAMLET. (Yes, even middle schoolers can enjoy these marvelous writers - in carefully measured doses!) And don't forget music. A wide selection of tapes and CD's of late medieval and Renaissance melodies and Masses are currently available in libraries and music stores. Imagine your students examining the Madonnas of Raphael as the notes of Palestrina are softly played in the background. Also, do take advantage of the ever-growing number of CD-ROMS and Laser Discs available for computers.

Like my other books (on ancient and medieval cultures), this one stresses the story element of history in an effort to "bring alive" the personalities and happenings of the times. I have tried to highlight the principle threads that run through the period and to make frequent connections between the main events and the major players. I have included many challenging words and expressions to pique a student's curiosity and broaden his vocabulary. Although the book is written primarily for middle school students, the interest level of the material is also appropriate for higher level history courses.

I've had great fun producing this book, and I welcome any comments or criticisms you might have that might improve the presentation of the material for your own students. All suggestions will be seriously considered as I prepare future editions of the text. (Please address your letters to Pemblewick Press, P.O. Box 321, Lincoln, Massachusetts, 0l773.)

Meanwhile, enjoy with your students THE STORY OF THE RENAISSANCE!

TABLE OF CONTENTS

TIMELINE

1305 Babylonian Captivity Begins

1306 Giotto completes the Arena Chapel frescoes,Padua

1321 Dante dies, having completed THE DIVINE COMEDY

1341 Petrarch crowned poet laureate at Rome

1348 The Black Death strikes Florence

1353 Boccaccio completes THE DECAMERON

1378 Beginning of the Great Schism

1397 The Medici bank is founded

1401 Ghiberti wins competition for design of Baptistery doors

1417 Martin V becomes Pope

1419 Brunelleschi designs dome of Florence's cathedral

1427 Masaccio paints THE TRIBUTE MONEY

1434 Cosimo de Medici becomes head of the clan

1436 Leon Battista Alberti writes treatise on painting

1440 Donatello casts DAVID

1447 Pope Nicholas V founds the Vatican Library

1450 Francesco Sforza becomes Duke of Milan

1453 Constantinople falls to the Turks

1454 The Peace of Lodi

1469 Lorenzo de Medici comes to power

1471 Sixtus IV becomes Pope

1479 Beginning of rule of Lodovico Sforza

1480 Botticelli paints THE BIRTH OF VENUS

1484 Innocent VIII becomes Pope

1484 Albrecht Durer paints his first self-portrait

1485 Henry VII crowned King of England

1492 Alexander VI becomes Pope

1492 Christopher Columbus sets out on his first voyage

1494 Charles VIII of France invades Italy

1494 Savonarola comes to power in Florence

1494 Sebastian Brant publishes SHIP OF FOOLS

1495 Leonardo da Vinci paints THE LAST SUPPER

1496 French are driven from Naples by Spanish troops

1498 Savonarola is burned at the stake

1499 Louis XII of France invades Italy, conquers Milan

1502 French and Spanish in Italy go to war

1503 Julius II becomes Pope

1503 Leonardo da Vinci paints the MONA LISA

1504 Michelangelo completes statue of DAVID

1504 Spain conquers Naples, controls southern Italy

1508 Michelangelo begins ceiling of Sistine Chapel

1509 Erasmus writes IN PRAISE OF FOLLY

1510 Raphael paints THE SCHOOL OF ATHENS

1512 Medici power is restored in Florence

1513 Machiavelli writes THE PRINCE

1513 Leo X becomes Pope

1515 Francis I of France invades Italy

1516 Thomas More publishes UTOPIA

1517 Martin Luther posts his 95 Theses

1519 Charles I of Spain is elected Emperor Charles V

1520 Henry VIII meets Francis I at the Field of Cloth of Gold

1521 Diet of Worms, Luther is declared an outlaw

1525 French defeated in Italy at Pavia

1527 Rome is sacked by troops of Charles V

1528 Publication of Castiglione's THE COURTIER

1532 Rabelais begins publishing Gartantua and Pantagruel

1534 Act of Supremacy, Henry VII head of Church of England

1536 Michelangelo begins THE LAST JUDGMENT

1540 The Jesuits become an official order

1541 John Calvin sets up his theocracy in Geneva

1543 Copernicus publishes REVOLUTIONS OF THE CELESTIAL ORBS

1543 Vesalius publishes THE STRUCTURE OF THE HUMAN BODY

1545 The Council of Trent

1547 Edward VI becomes King of England, Henry II King of France

1552 Pierre Ronsard completes his poems, AMOURS

1554 Benvenuto Cellini completes PERSEUS

1555 Mary Tudor becomes Queen of England, the Peace of Augsburg

1556 Philip II becomes King of Spain

1558 Elizabeth I becomes Queen of England

1559 Treaty of Cateau-Cambresis

1561 Mary Stuart becomes Queen of Scotland

1567 Spanish forces under Duke of Alva move into the Low Countries

1572 Massacre of Saint Bartholomew's Day, Luis de Camoes publishes THE LUSIADS

1573 Tycho Brahe publishes ON THE NEW STAR

1580 Montaigne publishes his first ESSAYS

1581 Northern Netherlands provinces proclaim their independence from Spain

1587 Mary Queen of Scots is executed

1588 The Spanish Armada

1589 Henry IV becomes King of France

1596 First four books of Spenser's FAIRIE QUEENE appear

1598 The Edict of Nantes

1599 Shakespeare becomes a partner in the new Globe Theater

1610 Galileo publishes THE STARRY MESSENGER

PROLOGUE

Petrarch was an Italian scholar of the fourteenth century who loved to read books, especially those written in the days of ancient Rome. Petrarch had a vivid imagination and could easily envision the society of those early times. He marveled at the glowing descriptions of the model Roman citizen who made the most of his opportunities and contributed his talents to the local government. Early Rome was a clean city of gleaming marble government buildings, theaters, temples, arenas, and public baths. There was even fresh running water. What a contrast the ancient world posed to medieval Europe, where no one seemed interested in self improvement, where the government was mired in political corruption, and where sewers ran down the center of the narrow city streets. And hardly anyone could read or write. Petrarch came to the conclusion that the generations who lived between the fall of the mighty Roman Empire and his own age (a mere one thousand years!) had achieved little of value. Western society seemed to have forgotten the rich heritage of the past and had fallen into a deep slumber. But now it was time to wake up!

Petrarch devoted much of his life to reviving an interest in the culture of ancient Rome. He tirelessly tracked down long forgotten books by Latin authors in the libraries of monasteries and thoughtfully read them. He also wrote his own volumes about the history and personalities of those earlier, richer times, hoping that the qualities of character and mind that made Rome a great power could be applied to improve his own society. His enthusiasm for antiquity was shared by others, and before long it spawned a new movement that slowly spread throughout much of Europe, reaching its peak in the sixteenth century. We know it as the Renaissance.

This extraordinary age glows like a bright star in the history of western literature and art. *Renaissance* is a French word meaning "rebirth." But the movement involved more than the recovery of the ideals of the past. Rather, what began as a revival of ancient values gradually evolved into a spirit of inquisitiveness about all sorts of things. People looked in a new way at the makeup of the natural world and wondered about man's place in it. Theologians consulted ancient texts and used their powers of reason to arrive at conclusions that often conflicted with the long established doctrines of the Church. Suddenly there were multitudes of questions to be asked, and the answers led to even greater intellectual challenges. One scholar joyfully remarked that he felt like a dwarf standing on the shoulders of a giant. He was raised up by the achievements of antiquity (this was the giant) and yet able to see further than his distant ancestors ever had.

The Renaissance was an exciting time to be alive. Liberated from many of the fears and superstitions of the Middle Ages, imaginative men and women became caught up in the excitement of discovery. Artists, poets, and playwrights were inspired to give form to their own visions of nature and the human condition. Scientists dramatically expanded their horizons of knowledge about the universe, philosophers wrote treatises about how society should be improved, and intrepid explorers crossed the barriers of the unknown to sail to distant shores. It was an age of genius and innovation, dominated by such legendary heroes and heroines as Michelangelo, Christopher Columbus, Queen Elizabeth I, William Shakespeare, and Martin Luther. And there were many others just as fascinating, whom you probably haven't even heard of - yet!

But it all started in ancient Italy, so it's there that our story begins.

PART I
THE ITALIAN RENAISSANCE

CHAPTER I
THE DAWNING OF A NEW AGE

The mighty Romans flexed their muscles and strutted around the ancient world for nearly a thousand years. Fearless generals like Julius Caesar managed to conquer a vast empire that eventually encircled the Mediterranean Sea. During the reign of Augustus, Roman civilization was at its peak. His subjects were governed by an intricate web of officials, guided in everyday matters by a practical system of written laws, and defended by an invincible army. Augustus rebuilt the city of Rome; its gleaming marble temples and government buildings symbolized the power and majesty of the emperor. A central feature of Roman architecture was the arch, a graceful structure that can support a tremendous amount of weight. Roman architects later discovered that by constructing a circle of arches around a central point they could create a large, open space - the dome. Remember this. It will influence the architects of the Renaissance.

Roman culture was greatly enriched by the conquest of the highly sophisticated civilization of Greece. Manuscripts by Greek authors on all sorts of subjects were translated into Latin, the official language of the Empire. And the Romans were so enamored with the Greek gods of Mount Olympus that they transformed them into Roman deities, changing their names from Greek to Latin and making up myths to connect them with the beginnings of their own society. They also liked the looks of the graceful pillars of the Greek temples, so they added them to the arches and domes of their building designs. Augustus was a great patron (supporter) of art, and he commissioned Roman sculptors to make copies of

the natural-looking statues of the Greeks. This was a good thing, too, since many of the Greek statues have been lost and only the copies survive.

The Greeks invented the theater and wrote the first plays. Does it surprise you that the Romans tried to copy these, too? Plautus, Terrence, and Seneca were Roman playwrights who wrote "up-dated" versions of Greek plays, although theirs were bloodier and more melodramatic than the originals. Greece certainly had a civilizing effect upon the ruder, cruder Romans. Even the model Roman citizen of Augustus' time was a clone of the typical Greek aristocrat: well-educated, skilled in many disciplines, including sports, and actively involved in politics. These characteristics would later define the ideal "Renaissance Man."

THE EMPIRE IS DIVIDED

But nothing lasts forever, and by the third century AD the awesome Roman Empire was in decline. There were many reasons for this, but a major factor was the hordes of barbarian tribesmen who relentlessly threatened the borders in eastern Europe. The Emperor Diocletian decided that his realm was simply too unwieldy to defend, so he divided it into two parts, each with its own ruler. The western section included much of Europe as well as the northwestern coast of Africa. Its capital was Rome and the official language remained Latin. The eastern part stretched across Greece, Asia Minor, the coast of Asia, and northeastern Africa. Its capital was Constantinople and the official language was Greek. Because Constantinople was built upon the

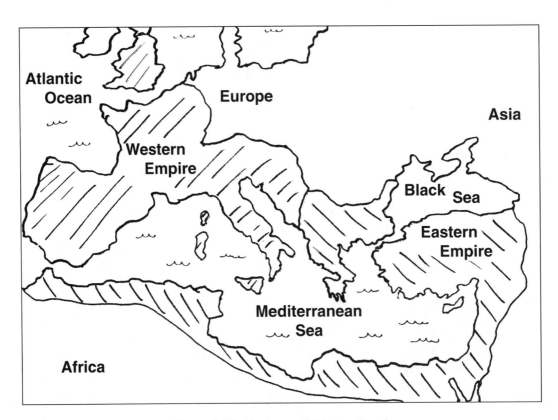

Figure 1: The Eastern and Western Empires

site of the ancient city of Byzantium, the eastern section came to known as the Byzantine Empire.

Christianity became the official religion of the Romans in 395, but eventually the Church, too, split in two. The western empire fell under the auspices of the Roman Catholic Church, headed by the Pope in Rome. People living in the Byzantine Empire were members of the Greek Orthodox Church, whose leader was the Patriarch in Constantinople.

THE FALL OF ROME

In 476 the last Roman emperor was booted off his throne by invading barbarian warriors, and the efficient Roman government bureaucracy fizzled in the West. Cities were abandoned, roads became over-

grown with weeds, and the trading network that had brought prosperity to southern Europe fell apart. Wealthy landowners built thick-walled castles and fought one another over the ownership of land. It was a dangerous era, and no one had much time to think about anything except how to survive. Most people settled in villages near the castles and exchanged their labor in the fields for protection by the knights of the local lord (and some of the crops).

This period of history is known as the Middle Ages. The term "Middle Ages" was coined by Renaissance scholars who accepted Petrarch's view that nothing much happened during the years falling "in the middle" of ancient times and their own age. It is true that during those difficult years learning and scholarship were nearly forgotten. But literacy did continue to thrive in monasteries, where monks carefully preserved the books of the past in their libraries and painstakingly made new copies of them to exchange with other monasteries. These books included the works of Roman writers like Cicero and Livy as well as those of the Church Fathers (Catholic theologians such as Saint Augustine). And, of course, the monks made plentiful copies of the Bible, which they elaborately decorated and illustrated.

In the twelfth century knights returned home from the Crusades in the Holy Land with a new taste for such eastern luxuries as silk and spices. Enterprising merchants in France, Germany, and Italy took advantage of the growing interest in imported products and gradually reestablished a trading network. Now there were opportunities for craftsmen to create materials that could be exchanged for the eastern goods. This revival of trade encouraged the settlement of new towns by artisans and merchants. Big changes were brewing, and western Europe had begun to climb out of the dark abyss.

Meanwhile, Serb and Turkish invaders gradually carved away huge chunks of the Byzantine Empire, until by the twelfth century it was reduced to the land surrounding Constantinople and a few other outposts. However, the eastern capital continued to prosper as a center of trade, art, and learning.

The Medieval Mindset

After Rome fell the Catholic Church stepped in to replace the crumbling imperial government with its own organization. This was an easy transition, because the framework of the Church administration was modeled upon the bureaucracy that had once governed the sprawling Roman Empire. And since nearly everyone in western Europe was a member of the Church, the Pope became an incredibly powerful man.

The doctrines of the Church influenced nearly aspect of daily living. According to Catholic belief, man was a miserable sinner who was condemned to struggle against all sorts of obstacles in his difficult journey through life. The one thing that sustained him was the hope that his soul might spend eternity in a heavenly paradise after he died. But to stand any chance at all in obtaining salvation (entry into heaven) he needed to carefully adhere to the rigid teachings of the Church, to faithfully participate in the seven holy sacraments (special religious ceremonies), to make a pilgrimage to a holy shrine, and to confess his sins to the local priest. Should he fail in any of these requirements, or should he be tempted to stray beyond the bounds of piety, his soul might face eternal damnation in hell (a fiery place ruled by the devil himself).

Given this great concern about the afterlife, most people did just what the Church instructed them to do. Their faith was the focus of their lives, and the local priest was their spiritual advisor. Actually, he was more than that. Not only did the priest lead the services, perform the sacraments, and collect the tithes (everyone had to give the Church one tenth of his income), but he also knew everyone's darkest secrets. And because he was often the only person in a town who could read and write, his parishioners depended upon him for advice in most practical matters - everything from interpreting a legal document to deciphering the words in a business contract.

The spire of the local church soared high above the houses and shops in every medieval city, town, and village, reminding the people of their religious obligations. The church bells served as a giant alarm clock, announcing when it was time for work, meals or prayer. (Not surprisingly, it was a monk who invented the first mechanical clock.) Parishioners gathered at the church not only for services but to celebrate such special family events as marriage and baptism. They even attended religious plays there called miracles and mysteries.

Competition had no place in a rule-ridden society like this one. Nor was there much chance of originality when anyone who was different was suspected of doing something wrong! Medieval artists were considered ordinary laborers, just like carpenters or blacksmiths. They were hired by churches and cathedrals to depict the lives of saints and to illustrate the stories of the Bible for the illiterate parishioners. They painted and sculpted the same stiff, unnatural-looking figures as their predecessors had for countless generations. Never did they consider signing their names to take credit for their efforts. Did a carpenter carve his initials on a cabinet or table? Of course not.

MEDIEVAL SCHOLARSHIP

As we learned earlier, the spark of learning was kept alive in the monasteries, where young monks were taught to read and to make copies of old manuscripts. Beginning in the twelfth century new schools were set up in the cathedrals of the larger cities. These were often attended by boys who had no interest in a career in the Church. They wanted to learn to read, write, and perform mathematical calculations in order to keep records for the growing class of merchants.

Most scholars of this period were priests and monks who studied the writings of the early theologians. Over the centuries, as copies of handwritten manuscripts were copied and recopied, mistakes were inevitably made and then repeated. Inevitably, the scholars noticed inconsistencies and even contradictions among the various versions of a single text. What to do? They sought out the original Latin works that had been preserved in the monastic libraries. But then they discovered that even these volumes contained contradictions, although of a different sort. It seems that the Church Fathers often disagreed among themselves! Which one was right? It was all very confusing and unsettling.

Figure 2: The Spires of the Cathedral at Chartres, France

THE PAST COLLIDES WITH THE PRESENT

The study of the original writings of Christian theologians led to the reexamination of other ancient works that had little to do with religion. The Romans left behind a great wealth of literary materials, and scholars like Petrarch discovered in them a view of life that differed greatly from that of the Church. The Latin writers celebrated the resourcefulness of the individual and rejoiced in his potential to forge his own destiny. What a contrast to the Catholic portrayal of man as a miserable sinner, a helpless pawn whose life is determined by Divine Will!

In the twelfth century the writings of Aristotle, a brilliant Greek philosopher, became available in many parts of Europe. Among other things, Aristotle attempted to explain the existence of the universe in purely rational terms. What a shock this must have been for the priestly scholars who were trained to accept everything as a matter of faith! Aristotle's writings inspired many clerics to reexamine their own approach to knowledge and belief. Some, such as Peter Abelard and Thomas Aquinas, used the logic of the Greek to try to justify their religious faith. Their method of using logical arguments to prove the validity of religious doctrine and to reconcile contradictory viewpoints is known as scholasticism. It occupied the minds of many of the finest medieval theologians for a long time. As we will see, certain scholars later accused the scholasticists of becoming so blinded by logical theories that they lost sight of the essence of religious faith. (Can you see how this might happen?) The original Greek texts of the New Testament also became available in the twelfth century. And guess what! There were numerous contradictions between these and the Latin Vulgate (Saint Jerome's version of the Old Testament which had been the standard Bible of the Church since the fifth century). This discovery reinforced the scholars' determination to return to original sources for all matter of study.

THE FIRST UNIVERSITIES

Contrary to Petrarch's scathing words, the people of the Middle Ages did create a number of important things, including the university (although the concept of higher learning had its origins in ancient Greece). The university began as a gathering place for scholars and students who were anxious to share their love of knowledge. In time groups of teachers banded together to form a professional guild, known as a *universitas* (a Latin term meaning "an association of people"). They gave lectures to anyone who could afford their fees and they granted degrees, recognized throughout Europe, which served as licenses to teach. From these loose organizations emerged the first major universities in Bologna, Paris, and Oxford. By the thirteenth century many others had sprung up in the larger cities of Europe.

The university curriculum was based upon the works of classical (ancient Greek and Roman) authors, not the Church Fathers and the Bible. The students were eager to learn more about the nature of man rather than the relationship between man and God. Because they enrolled in the courses of the *Studia Humanitas* (studies of mankind) that had formed the core of a classical education (grammar, rhetoric, ethics, poetry, history, and philosophy), they came to be known as humanists.

University classes were taught in Latin, the language of the Church and therefore the language of scholarship. (Remember, for centuries the only literate people were the clerics.) For this reason a knowledge of Latin became the sign of an educated person. The students probably spouted it among the townspeople to flaunt their special status! Books were rare, so teachers would read aloud (these were the original "lectures") while students diligently took notes. They memorized the notes and recited them as perfectly as possible during examinations. Incidentally, in those days university students were younger than modern college students. A boy was eligible to attend a university at the age of twelve, and he might begin graduate studies in law, medicine or theology in his late teens.

THE SPREAD OF HUMANISM

Eventually, all scholars who studied human society came to be known as humanists. Their desire to learn from original sources inspired them to track down a wider range of ancient texts than had been previously available to learned men in western Europe. It seemed like everyone was singing the praises of the great thinkers of the ancient world. In the thirteenth century the Pope became so worried about the way the humanists were embracing Greek logic that he threatened to excommunicate (expel from the Church) any students at the University of Paris who were caught reading anything by Aristotle! But it was impossible to stem the tide.

In the fourteenth century Giovanni Aurispa brought two hundred Greek manuscripts from Constantinople to Italy, including the complete works of Plato, Aristotle's teacher. Plato had recorded the ideas of his own mentor, Socrates, in a long series of dialogues, but he also expressed original ideas about how people should be governed. In his opinion, the brightest and most highly educated men made the best rulers because they based their decisions upon rational analysis. Like many other thinkers of his time, Plato believed that since laws were made by people, they could be changed by people. The Church, on the other hand, had been preaching for centuries that the highest laws were made by God and were therefore permanent and unchangeable. Once again the rational thought of the past was bumping into the faith of the present. Plato had also pondered the meaning of reality, wondering whether something really existed or simply seemed to exist in the mind of an individual. Some scholars tried to reconcile the doctrines of Christianity with the abstract thinking of Plato, creating a new philosophy known as neo-Platonism. We'll hear more about this mystical view of the world later in our story.

For now, let's concentrate on the revolution of thinking that had begun. Armed with ideas gleaned from the ancients, the humanists joyfully embraced the image of man as a rational, self-sufficient individual who could determine for himself what was good or true. For them, the ideal man was the Roman citizen, who divided his time between enriching his scope of knowledge and contributing to the welfare of the government. (It's important to know that most Roman citizens had slaves to do their daily chores!) This exulted model from the past made contemporary society seem crude and misdirected. Furthermore, while the ancients had stressed balance and harmony, the present world seemed to thrive upon chaos and disorder.

Although the humanists sought ways in which people could live fuller, more meaningful lives, they continued to believe in the teachings of the Bible. Most scholars were devout Christians. What had changed was their attitude about the freedom of the individual to mold his own life. The emphasis was upon the "here and now," the natural and secular (non-religious) world, rather than the spiritual afterlife. Along with a new optimism about man's freedom of choice came the assumption that the more a person understood and enjoyed the beauty of life, the greater would be his appreciation of and belief in God. This link between a desire to understand the mysteries of the physical universe and a strong faith in God helped make the ideas of the humanists acceptable to many people. (Remember, nearly everyone in Europe was a Roman Catholic.)

THREE LITERARY GIANTS

Three extraordinary Italian scholars of the fourteenth century - Dante, Petrarch, and Boccaccio - produced the first great literary works that reflected the spirit of humanism. They wrote about secular issues as well as religious ones and dealt with a wide spectrum of human emotions. For them, love and greed were just as interesting as piety. (Perhaps more so!) Although they produced scholarly works in Latin, their most memorable books were written in the everyday language of their countrymen (the vernacular). Thanks to them, literature could be enjoyed by anyone who could read, scholar and merchant alike.

DANTE

Dante Alighiere (1265-1321) was educated in a cathedral school in Florence and later attended the University of Bologna. He became a brilliant classical scholar and a gifted poet. He met the inspiration of much of his writings when he was only nine - a lovely young girl known as Beatrice (she was eight). He saw her at a May Day festival. She was dressed in a crimson gown and to young Dante she looked like an angel. It was love at first sight, although they exchanged few words. The girl's identity is somewhat of a mystery, but many historians believe she was Bice, the daughter of a minor nobleman named Folco Portinari.

Dante thought about Beatrice constantly and wrote many poems about her. Yet, he never encountered her again until nine years later, when he met her as she was strolling with two other girls. Beatrice was dressed in white and seemed to the lovestruck Dante like the essence of purity. When she greeted him, he felt as though he had been struck by lightning! Shortly afterward, Beatrice heard some gossip linking Dante with another girl. She was so disturbed (not that she had a right to be) that she passed him on the street without speaking to him. He mourned for days and days! Beatrice later married another man (her marriage was arranged by her parents). She died at the age of twenty-five, but she remained the muse of the poet who loved her so passionately for the rest of his life.

Beatrice represented for Dante ideal and unattainable love. His poems about her were influenced by the medieval tradition of courtly love expressed by the troubadour poets of twelfth century France. Those early minstrels had composed verses about the love intrigues between wealthy nobles and attractive married (and thus unobtainable) women of the court. Thirty-one of Dante's poems about Beatrice are contained in his collection, THE NEW LIFE. His lyrical verses are interspersed with prose commentaries describing his great love. The title of the book refers to Dante's decision upon the death of Beatrice to devote the rest of his life to a new passion, philosophy. His beautiful love poems are still enjoyed for their melodic rhythm and unique blending of emotion and logic.

As a young man Dante was actively involved in Florentine politics, but when an opposition party gained power he was exiled from his own city. He made no effort to return, since he was sentenced to be burned

Figure 3: Statue of Dante at the church of Santa Croce, Florence

alive if caught in Florence! He spent the following years at the courts in several Italian cities, devoting much of his time to studying the works of such classical writers as Virgil, Cicero, Ovid, and Aristotle. He also pondered the views of theologians Saint Augustine and (Saint) Thomas Aquinas, and he carefully analyzed the Scriptures. These scholarly pursuits led to the creation of his masterpiece, a long narrative poem entitled THE DIVINE COMEDY, which he began in 1307. It ranks among the finest works of world literature, combining elements of medieval theology with the ideals of the humanists.

THE DIVINE COMEDY was written in *terza rima* (triple rhyme), a form Dante invented in which the first and third lines of a tercet (set of three lines) rhyme, while the middle line rhymes with the first and third lines of the next tercet. The language is the vernacular spoken in Tuscany (the region surrounding Florence). Written in the first person, the work describes the poet's imaginary journey through the world of the dead. It is divided into three sections: INFERNO (Hell), PURGATORIO (Purgatory), and PARADISO (Heaven). Dante firmly believed in the Christian concept of salvation (admittance into heaven as a reward for leading a moral and pious life). People who sinned against the Divine Law (rules expressed by the Church) would surely end up in a fiery hell, although if they repented for their errors they went to an intermediary place (purgatory) until, through the prayers of living friends and relatives, they had suitably atoned for their sins. Once purified (purged) they ascended into heaven. Remember these basic beliefs about getting into heaven. They had a tremendous influence upon the artists and writers of the Renaissance.

Given its religious theme, THE DIVINE COMEDY seems the typical work of a medieval Catholic. But it is also an allegory of mankind's search for a moral and meaningful life. And on yet another level, it is a satire of the society of fourteenth century Italy, filled with vivid (and often damning) portraits of well-known political leaders, poets, and philosophers of the time. We'll meet them soon.

Here's the plot. With the Roman poet Virgil as his guide, Dante leaves the "dark wood" of his middle age and passes through the gates of Hell, descending through the nine circles of the damned. Hell is described as a huge, funnel-shaped pit located directly beneath the holy city of Jerusalem. Its nine circles are a series of terraces, each one of lesser circumference than the one above. Each circle is designated for a specific sin, the lesser sins near the top and the more terrible ones at the bottom. Punishments correspond to the type of sins committed. As he and Virgil descend, Dante sees thieves struggling in a pit of snakes and demons, murderers perpetually drowning in a river of blood, and flatterers swimming in a canal of excrement! He observes fortune-tellers whose heads are reversed on their bodies so they have to walk backwards forever. (Why is this an appropriate punishment?) The worst sinners of all are the traitors, who are confined to a frozen lake. In the center of the lake, Judas, Brutus, and Cassius (history's three worst traitors) are eternally being crushed by the teeth of Lucifer (the devil).

The suffering souls Dante observes in Hell are in fact caricatures of contemporaries whom he personally knew or knew about. He clearly enjoyed assigning punishments to men he considered greedy or dishonest - particularly avaricious money-lenders and self-indulgent popes. He consigned the ancient authors to the first circle, known as the "State of Limbo" which was designated for the virtuous but unbaptized. (The writers had lived before Christianity became the state religion of Rome.) Their only punishment is to be deprived of the vision of God.

From the rim of Hell the two poets climb through a narrow passageway to the shore of the mountain island of Purgatory. They ascend seven terraces where the seven major vices are purged. For example, the eyes of the envious are sewn shut. At the top of the mountain is the "Terrestrial Paradise," which Adam and Eve had to leave because of their sins. (Their happy existence ended when Eve tempted Adam with a forbidden fruit, an apple.) Here Dante is joined by his beloved Beatrice, and together they ascend into the heavens to meet the souls of the

blessed at the outermost of ten concentric heavenly spheres. This is the abode of God, the angels and the saints.

Dante's journey through the afterlife can easily be interpreted as the common man's journey through this life. With the aid of his reason (represented by Virgil) a person can understand the evils of immoral behavior, take steps to deal with his own failings, and ultimately find happiness and fulfillment. Dante's masterful blending of the values of the pagan world of classical antiquity with those of Christianity make THE DIVINE COMEDY an important link between the Middle Ages and the Renaissance.

PETRARCH

Dante was the literary hero of the Italian poet we already met in the prologue of this book: Francesco Petrarca, known as Petrarch (1304-1374). He was born in Arezzo, Italy, but he spent his early years in Avignon, France. Petrarch studied law at the University of Bologna, where he also distinguished himself as a gifted classical scholar and a talented poet. (Sound like Dante?)

Petrarch's interest in the ancient world prompted him to search for original manuscripts tucked away in French and Italian monasteries, and he encouraged his friends to bring to him any that they found. His greatest discovery was a collection of letters written by Roman authors Cicero and Livy. He read these over and over again until he felt that he actually knew those thoughtful men who had lived over a thousand years earlier. In fact, he wrote letters back to them! In one, he thanked Livy for enabling him to forget the evils of the present and transporting him back to happier, better times. Once he pretended that Cicero visited him in France and wrote about their exchange of views! Petrarch built up an excellent classical library and made it available to other scholars. About forty-four surviving manuscripts of his personal collection have been identified.

Like most humanists, Petrarch considered ancient Rome to be the heart of western civilization, and he felt that its legacy of literature, philosophy, art, politics, and law had been ignored for too long. Of course, theologians had been reading Latin texts for centuries, and more recently scholasticists were applying Aristotle's logic to justify their own religious views. But Petrarch was among the first to propose that the culture of the classical world should be studied in its own right. He didn't view the Romans as the musty figures of a dead past but rather as fascinating men and women who came alive through their words in the ancient manuscripts. As we've learned, Petrarch had no problem communicating with them, and he believed they were equally approachable to others who were willing to make the effort. Like other humanists, he greatly admired the Roman concept of a virtuous citizen who felt a sense of responsibility to develop his talents as an individual and to use these talents to enrich the community in which he lived. He hoped that as scholars rediscovered the writings of the Romans, they would break through the darkness of their times and recapture the brilliance of antiquity.

Petrarch wrote many notes and letters (including the fictional epistles to his classical heroes) expressing his deepest feelings about friendship, love, and nature. His greatest work was THE BOOK OF SONGS - a collection of 366 poems inspired by his unrequited (unreturned) love for a young golden-haired woman he called Laura. He first saw Laura on April 6, 1327, in the Church of Santa Clara in Avignon, France. He immediately fell in love with her. (Does this remind you of Dante's obsession with Beatrice?) Her refusal to return his love inspired his greatest lyric poems. Petrarch compared Laura to Daphne, the lovely nymph in Greek mythology whose love was vainly sought by the god Apollo. (To escape his embrace, she turned into a laurel tree.) Little is known of Laura, but we do know that she died in the terrible plague of 1348. She expired twenty-one years to the day Petrarch first saw her in church.

Although he wrote his prose in Latin, Petrarch followed Dante's lead and composed his love poems in the vernacular of Tuscany. They represent a refinement of the lyric tradition of the troubadours, combining elegance and clarity with a sense of wistful melancholy. Most of the poems are sonnets. Petrarch did not invent the sonnet (it has fourteen lines with rhymes arranged according to a certain pattern), but his poems are so beautifully written that this form became the major genre of the poets writing in the fifteenth and sixteenth centuries.

Petrarch traveled widely and was popular in courts throughout Europe for his humanist ideas as well as his evocative poetry. In 1341 he was crowned poet laureate in Rome, the first to be so honored since ancient times. He spent the last six years of his life near Padua, Italy and died peacefully, surrounded by his Latin manuscripts. During his last months he wrote a letter about himself, addressed to later generations. It describes his major ambitions and ends with the words, "I strove to forget the present and join myself in spirit with the past." In so doing, he helped set the tone for the future.

BOCCACCIO

Giovanni Boccaccio (1313-75) was born in Florence and went to Naples as a young man to learn about the trading business from the wealthy Bardi family. While in

Naples he became friendly with a circle of humanists, who encouraged him to turn aside from the business career his father had intended for him in favor of scholarship. Like Dante and Petrarch, whom he greatly admired, Boccaccio was drawn to the richness of classical literature. He actually met Petrarch in 1530, and the two formed a friendship that endured until the older man's death. Boccaccio followed the lead of Dante and Petrarch in another way: he fell in love with a woman he could not marry. The object of his affections was Fiammetta (possibly the daughter of King Robert of Anjou). Like Beatrice and Laura, Fiammetta inspired his love poetry.

Boccaccio also composed pastoral allegories, heroic versions of myths, prose romances, novellas, a psychological novel (he invented this form), epic poems in rhyme, and numerous short lyrics. His best-known work is THE DECAMERON, a bawdy collection of 100 short tales about contemporary Italian life. In the introduction of the book we meet three young men and seven young women who have fled to the countryside to escape the plague that has invaded the cities. They decide to entertain each other with stories, which they share each hot afternoon. Every story has a different theme, and together they present a portrait of every level of the Florentine society of Boccaccio's day. The stories are written in prose in the Tuscan vernacular. (Boccaccio is considered the first great writer of prose in a modern language.) THE DECAMERON takes its name from the Greek word for ten, since the tales are told over a period of ten days. It was extremely popular among educated Italians (try to envision them sitting around a banquet table laughing about a colorful episode). Of course, the Pope found the book shocking and forbade any Catholic to read it.

Boccaccio devoted his later years to searching for ancient texts in Naples and at the Benedictine Abbey in Monte Cassino. He also found time to master the Greek language as well as classical history, literature, and mythology. He even produced a huge encyclopedia of ancient mythology, FAMILIES OF THE GODS. He wrote an affectionate biography of Dante, and in 1373 the Florentine government invited him to deliver a series of public readings of THE DIVINE COMEDY. In that same year he met Geoffrey Chaucer, the author of THE CANTERBURY TALES. Chaucer was the first English writer to compose literary works in the English vernacular, so the two men must have had much to discuss. Boccaccio died eighteen months after Petrarch. At the time of his death Florentine writer Franco Sacchetti remarked, "All poetry is now extinct."

THE ITALIAN LANGUAGE IS DEFINED

The heritage of the ancient past clearly molded the creative geniuses of Dante, Petrarch, and Boccaccio, but this legendary trio had to look within their souls to produce their extraordinary literary works. Their achievements had a profound effect upon those who lived after them. Not only did they launch a literary movement based upon the ideals of humanism, but they made the vernacular just as respectable as Latin for the written page. Before their time, there was no standard language in Italy (apart from the Latin of scholars and priests). Every region had its own distinct dialect. But THE DIVINE COMEDY, THE BOOK OF SONGS, and THE DECAMERON were so widely read that the Tuscan dialect became familiar throughout the Italian peninsula. By the fifteenth century it was spoken by every well educated Italian, and in time it would evolve into the language of modern Italy.

REVIEW QUESTIONS:

1. Describe the two parts of the Roman Empire. How were they similar? How were they different?

2. Which part of the empire lasted longer (western or eastern)?

3. What was the Catholic belief about the afterlife?

4. Why did medieval scholars first start looking for original manuscripts?

5. What is scholasticism?

6. How did humanism differ from medieval theology?

7. What are the three books of Dante's THE DIVINE COMEDY?

8. What are some of the interpretations of Dante's epic poem?

9. Why is Petrarch considered a humanist?

10. In what major way did Petrarch influence Boccaccio?

11. In what language were the major works of the "talented trio" of fourteenth century Italy written?

12. Who were the three ladies who inspired these poets?

FURTHERMORE:

1. Latin had evolved since the days of ancient Rome. The scholars of the Renaissance decided they wanted to write only in the "pure" Latin of Cicero (who lived in the first century BC). Their attempts to maintain Ciceronian Latin "froze" the language and prevented any further change in its structure. Eventually, only scholars and Catholic clergymen were fluent in Latin, so it became a "dead" language. Nonetheless, Latin is still taught in many schools today, partly because nearly one half of all English words are derived from that ancient tongue.

2. The humanists weren't the first to appreciate ancient times. The Frankish king Charlemagne was crowned in 800 as ruler of the Roman Empire in Europe. He used the Roman form of government, encouraged the growth of monasteries, and showed great interest in classical learning. Unfortunately, after he died his vast territory was split up and most of his ideals were (temporarily) forgotten.

3. The number three has a special significance in Dante's DIVINE COMEDY. Perhaps this is because a central concept of Christian theology is the trinity (Father, Son, and Holy Ghost). Dante's poem is divided into three sections, there are nine levels of Hell (a multiple of three), and numerous other examples of the poet's use of this religiously significant number. But it's important to know that three was also a magic number with the ancients - the Greeks had three graces (goddesses of beauty, personifying beauty, charm, and grace) and nine muses (goddesses associated with the arts, including music, lyric poetry, comedy, tragedy, and dance).

4. Dante was greatly influenced by Aristotle's ETHICS when he wrote THE DIVINE COMEDY. He once remarked that Aristotle was "the master of those who know."

5. When Petrarch was very old and dying, his friend Boccaccio advised him to take it easy and to stop writing. The older poet responded that he had to keep on, because his writing might be useful to "others far away, perhaps even those

who will be born a thousand years from now." No doubt his influence will live on until the twenty-fourth century, if not beyond!

6. In the sixteenth century Venetian poet Pietro Bembo would start a vogue for imitations of Petrarch. His PROSE OF THE VENACULAR set out proposals for a standardized language and style in Italy, using Petrarch and Boccaccio as his models.

PROJECTS:

1. In a much modified form, the ideals of the humanists survive in the study of the "humanities" in our modern universities. Find out specifically what is meant today by the humanities. What other types of courses are offered to university students?

2. Reread the description of Dante's vision of Hell and then make a diagram of it. It might be helpful to check out the information available in your library to obtain a more detailed idea of the various levels.

3. Obtain a copy of THE DIVINE COMEDY. Choose a passage and read it aloud to your class.

4. Petrarch was fascinated by the writings of Cicero and Livy. Select one of these two Roman writers and find out about his life and his works. Then write a short research report. Be sure to explain why Petrarch liked him so much.

5. Petrarch's sonnets about his love for Laura became the model for love poetry for centuries to come. Obtain a copy of his poems and read at least three of them.

6. Petrarch compared Laura to Daphne (and himself to Apollo). Find a book of Greek mythology and read the myth about Daphne and Apollo. Then explain how Apollo's infatuation with Daphne compares to Petrarch's love for Laura.

7. Boccaccio wrote THE DECAMERON at the time of the Black Death. Find out more about this deadly occurrence and write a short report.

8. Among the early admirers and imitators of Dante was Geoffrey Chaucer, who wrote THE CANTERBURY TALES. Obtain a copy of this book from your library. Read the introduction and then enjoy a few of the tales. Think about the ways in which Chaucer was influenced by Dante. Write a paragraph expressing your views.

9. Pretend that Beatrice, Laura and Fiammetta encounter one another in heaven. Imagine the stories they could share! Write a short skit based upon their conversations. It can be humorous!

CHAPTER II
ARTISTIC AWAKENINGS

The Catholic Church so dominated medieval society that the Middle Ages are known as the Age of Faith. The art and architecture of the period reflect this preoccupation with religious concerns. Magnificent stone cathedrals reach toward the heavens with their soaring spires and high arches, while elongated statues depict ethereal-looking saints and biblical figures. The emphasis is upon the majesty of God and the holy people associated with Christianity.

You might find medieval paintings rather primitive and unrealistic. It would be difficult to imagine actually speaking to the static, other-worldly figures or walking through the decorative landscapes that are strewn with symbolic objects. Even the size of the people varies in an unnatural way. The principal figures are quite large and centrally placed, while less important ones appear small and are sometimes even squeezed into a corner for lack of space.

Renaissance scholars snobbishly referred to the medieval style as Gothic - a word derived from the Goths, barbarians who helped bring about the fall of Rome. Times have certainly changed! Today Gothic buildings and figures are admired for their grace and majesty.

Figure 4: Gothic Statues Adorning the Cathedral at Chartres

BYZANTINE ARCHITECTURE AND ART

The Italian artists of the Middle Ages were influenced by the styles of the Byzantine Empire. This is partly because Italian merchants were able to observe first-hand the extraordinary buildings in Constantinople and then return home with enthusiastic accounts of what they had seen.

Sometimes Byzantine artists and architects came to Italy to design and decorate churches. The typical Byzantine church is very different from the Gothic cathedrals. First of all, it has a large central dome, a feature inherited from the ancient Romans. A bird's eye view shows the dome in the center of the four equal arms of a Greek cross. The magnificent church of Hagia Sophia (Holy Wisdom) in Constantinople (built in the sixth century) is considered the finest example of early Byzantine architecture. The octagonal church of San Vitale, which is of Byzantine design, was built in Ravenna, Italy, about the same time.

The interiors of Byzantine churches are decorated with mosaic pictures and designs. These are made from small pieces of colored stone or glass fitted and cemented together. As in the Gothic paintings, the fig-ures are stiff and stylized. (To stylize is to represent something according to a pattern rather than according to nature.) Madonnas (portraits of the Virgin Mary) lack natural-istic detail or any sense of movement, and because there is no natural setting all the figures possess a spiritual quality and seem to drift about, unencumbered by any earthly bonds. Byzantine paintings are equally un-realistic. Every figure faces forward and is set apart from the others (except, of course, Mary, who holds the baby Jesus). The back-ground is often decorated with patterns painted onto gold leaf.

And yet, the eastern figures are not to-tally lifeless. Since the Byzantine Empire was a storehouse of Greek culture, the local artists had ready access to the natural-look-ing classical paintings and statues. They in-corporated into their own pictures many of

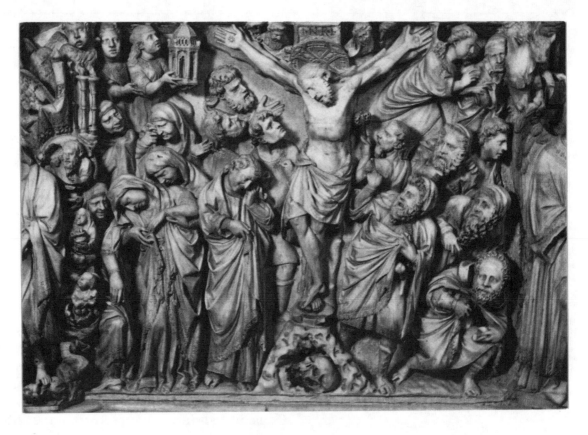

Figure 5: A Panel from Pisano's Pulpit at Siena

the features of the ancient works, such as the graceful folds of clothing, shadowing on the faces, and even, on occasion, foreshortening of an arm (distorting the arm to make it seem to be projecting forward). These attempts to introduce an element of realism make the Byzantine pictures more believable than most medieval paintings. They are a harbinger of things to come.

DRAMA CAPTURED IN STONE

An early glimmer of the humanist spirit appears in the works of Italian sculptor Niccolo Pisano (1220-84). Pisano was inspired by the realistic relief statues on the Roman sarcophagi (stone coffins) that had been brought by crusading knights to Pisa (Italy) from the Holy Land. (A relief statue is cut out of a stone background and appears to stand apart from it.) One sarcophagus had actually been incorporated into the facade of the Pisa Cathedral, while another became part of the tomb of a local noblewoman, the Countess Beatrice.

Pisano devoted most of his artistic career to carving the many-sided marble pulpits in Pisa's baptistery (a small building where group baptisms took place) and Siena's cathedral. He set new standards for decorating pulpits with action-filled relief panels. Like the stained-glass windows of Gothic cathedrals, the panels of the pulpits were originally intended to teach illiterate parishioners the stories of the Bible. But Pisano's figures are so lifelike that they can be appreciated for their artistic value alone. In each scene the sculptor has skillfully captured a moment in time, inviting us to sense the unfolding drama and to feel personally involved in the action. This close relationship between the viewer and a work of art had not existed for centuries.

The six panels of the hexagonal Pisa pulpit represent the life of Jesus. Although the figures are crowded together (more than one event is depicted on each panel), they are believable men and women, not drifting phantoms. The influence of the classical sculptures is evident in the folds of draped clothing, which clearly suggest the rounded forms of the human bodies beneath them. (Pisano had learned the same lesson as the Byzantines.) Above the panels are statues that symbolize Christian virtues. Pisano modeled the muscular figure of Fortitude on an ancient sculpture of the mythical hero Hercules that he had seen carved on the Roman sarcophagus at Pisa. Similarly, his Virgin Mary was inspired by the goddess Phaedra on that same tomb. By combining the symbolic images of the Christian tradition with the lifelike figures of classical art, and then adding a bit of drama, Pisano broke ground for a whole new style of sculpture.

Giovanni Pisano (1248-1314) was trained as a sculptor by his father, Niccolo. He carved sibyls (pagan prophets of antiquity) and Old Testament heroes in the facade of the cathedral of Siena. His figures seem agitated and frenzied, nearly bursting with passionate feelings. The figures he sculpted on the pulpit in the cathedral in Pistoia stand in untraditional (and natural) poses, making dramatic gestures, and his statues of the Madonna and Child radiate gentleness and love.

Giovanni had great talent and he knew it. Unlike his predecessors, who never dreamed of taking credit for their accomplishments, he carved on the pulpit of Pistoia the following words: "Giovanni carved it, who performed no empty work. The son of Niccolo and blessed with higher skill. Pisa gave him birth and endowed him with mastery greater than any before him." So much for humility!

FRESCOES

In the late thirteenth century many Italian painters began to work in a medium known as fresco. A fresco is a painting executed on wet plaster. (In Italian the word "fresco" refers to the wet, freshly plastered wall.) Actually, this was not a new technique - frescoes were painted in ancient Egypt and Crete - but the process had long been forgotten. Now, with the revival of interest in antiquity, frescoes became extremely popular once again.

The steps involved in painting a fresco were carefully described in the early fifteenth century by Tuscan painter, Cennino Cennini, in his BOOK ABOUT ART. Here's how it was done. First a coat of rough plaster *arriccio* was applied to a stone or brick wall. This would smooth the surface and act as a moisture barrier between the wall and the painting. The plaster was a mixture of lime, water, and fine sand (one part lime to three parts sand). When it was dry, the artist dipped a string in charcoal or wet paint, held one end, and snapped it against the wall. The strings made vertical and horizontal guidelines which would help him center the painting and align its various parts.

Next he made a preparatory drawing with a charcoal stick. After 1450 this step was replaced by the use of paper cartoons (stencil-like drawings): The artist drew the figures to be painted on a large sheet of paper and then pricked hundreds of tiny holes around the outlines of the figures. He then held the cartoon over the plaster and blew charcoal dust through the pinpricks to transfer the outlines onto the wet surface. Then he joined up the dotted lines. Once the preparatory drawing was on the wall, the artist took a brush dipped in water and sinopia (a red iron oxide pigment from Sinope on the Black Sea) and retraced the lines. When the sinopia was dry, he brushed off the underlying charcoal with a feather. Now he could begin the actual painting.

He added a second coat of finer plaster *(intonaco)* to a small patch called a *giornato* (an Italian word referring to the amount of work that could be completed in a single day). Then he rapidly retraced the outline of the drawing he had covered up with the fine plaster, using the cartoon or the remaining sinopia drawings as a guide. He began painting at the top of the fresco and worked down, so that any drips would fall on the *arriccio* and not on the *intonaco.*

The paint consisted of mineral colors thinned with water. As the plaster dried, carbon dioxide was absorbed from the air, converting the lime to calcium carbonate. This crystallized around the sand particles, binding them to the wall. When the paint was applied to the wet plaster, the carbonization process included the particles of pigment. This permanently fixed the colors and made them resistant to further action by water. Paint applied to dry plaster, however, would flake off. Fresco was an unforgiving medium: once the pigment was brushed onto the wet plaster it was absorbed immediately and could not easily be erased or altered. To correct a mistake the artist had to cover over a section and start anew. It was a race against time! This is why the artist worked on one small section at a time. If you look carefully at the frescoes you can actually see the lines of each separate *giornato.* The sense of urgency encouraged the artist to make quick strokes which added a sense of life and spontaneity not seen in other medieval paintings.

Of course, not all paintings were frescoes. The altarpiece was a wooden panel or folding set of panels that became an important part of the church interior in the thirteenth century. The Madonna and Child were often depicted on the main panel, painted quite large so that they could be seen by the entire congregation. To paint an altarpiece, an artist first covered the panel with a piece of linen to make a smooth surface and then coated it with *gesso* (fine plaster mixed with glue) as a ground for the underdrawing. Gold leaf (symbolizing purity) was then applied to the entire background, after which the figures were painted with a fine brush. The paint, called tempera, was made from the powdered pigments of ground mineral clays that were mixed ("tempered") with diluted egg yolk. It dried in a short period of time, since no one knew how to keep the egg yolk from hardening. Many of the late medieval altarpieces reflect the influence of Byzantine paintings and mosaics.

The Artists' Workshop

In fourteenth century Italy most paintings were produced by groups of artists associated with particular workshops. Each workshop was run by a master artist who obtained commissions for his group. The apprentices would grind minerals to make paint, clean palettes and brushes, and prepare wooden panels. Once these duties were seen to they were able to concentrate on learning the techniques of painting. After completing an apprenticeship, a young artist became an assistant. At this stage he could apply the outline sketch or cartoons of a fresco and paint in the background as well as some details of a work. The master, however, did the main parts of a painting, such as the faces of the major figures. Many assistants became specialists, some being very good at hands and feet, others at clothing, and others at natural backgrounds.

The artists belonged to professional guilds, which drew up contracts with their clients to indicate the theme of a painting as well as the number of people to be included and the specific colors to be used. Many of these contracts have survived, and they tell us much about how paintings were planned and executed in those early times.

Cimabue

Cenni di Pepa (1240-1302), known as Cimabue (meaning "bull-headed"), accomplished with a paintbrush what the Pisani had with a mallet and chisel. The narrative scenes in his cycle of frescoes in the Church of San Francesco at Assisi reflect his exceptional skill in creating a sense of drama. The crucifix that originally hung above the altar in the Florentine church of Santa Croce in Florence has been attributed to him. The lifeless, limp body of Christ fills you with a sense of pity and sorrow. Unfortunately, this work was badly damaged in the flood that ravaged the city of Florence in 1966.

According to legend, Cimabue once passed through a small village and noticed a shepherd boy sketching the head of a goat on a rock with a piece of slate. He was so impressed with the boy's talent that he offered to teach him to paint in his workshop. Not long afterward, the young apprentice painted a fly on the face of a figure Cimabue was drawing. The insect was so lifelike that the artist tried to brush it away! Who was this talented young fellow? His name was Ambrogiotto di Bondone (1267-1337), but he is known to us as Giotto.

Giotto Blazes A New Trail

Giotto admired the relief statues of the Pisani and wondered if he could paint figures that were as life-like and convincing. But creating the illusion of the third dimension (depth) is a difficult thing to do on a two dimensional surface (a painting has only length and width). Giotto solved the problem by adopting from Byzantine art the techniques of foreshortening and shading to create solid-looking figures. He also used lighting to suggest the roundness of a figure or object by illuminating one side and then painting the other side in a shadow. He further heightened the sense of realism by placing his people in natural settings in the Tuscan countryside.

After completing his apprenticeship, Giotto was commissioned to paint a series of frescoes about the life of Saint Francis on the walls of a new church built in the saint's honor in Assisi. He based most of his figures on the ordinary people he passed in the street, but he hired a local man to pose for the portrait of Francis. Because the eye and mouth are so expressive, he emphasized these features. He arranged his figures so that they seemed to be directly involved in the drama of the scene. One of his most celebrated works is his fresco of the death of Saint Francis in the church of Santa Croce in Florence. Anyone viewing this moving portrait of the dying man surrounded by a group of grieving monks cannot help but sense the

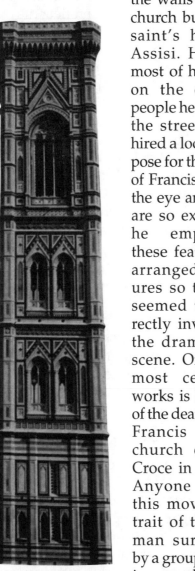

Figure 6: Giotto's Tower

brothers' sadness and loss. Find an illustration of the fresco in an art book and study the figures. Don't they seem real? Isn't the drama believable?

Giotto's major work was the series of frescoes painted on the walls of the Arena Chapel for the wealthy merchant, Enrico Scrovegni of Padua. Scrovegni hoped that by building and decorating the chapel he could atone for the sins of his father Reginaldo, a notorious moneylender. (Dante placed the elder Scrovegni in one of the circles of Hell!) The frescoes depict the lives of Mary and Jesus simply and poignantly. In the Lamentation, somber figures surround the body of Christ, their glances and gestures drawing our attention to Mary's sorrowful embrace of her dead son.

Pope Benedict XI wanted some paintings for the Basilica of Saint Peter in Rome, so he sent an envoy to find out what Giotto's work was like. When the man asked Giotto for a drawing he could take back to Rome, the artist took a brush and drew a circle on a piece of paper. Nothing more. The envoy was embarrassed to deliver this "drawing" to the Pope, but when Benedict saw the perfectly executed circle, he was impressed by Giotto's keen eye and absolute control of his paintbrush. By the way, the artist got the job.

Giotto traveled widely and found work in many Italian cities. He was also a shrewd businessman, who invested his profits in the weaving industry of his home town, Mugello (which lies on the outskirts of Florence). He dabbled in architecture, and as a result of this interest he was appointed the Director of Public Works in Florence. He designed the delicate and richly decorated bell tower (campanile) for the city's cathedral. It is known today as "Giotto's Tower". Although only the lowest portion was finished at the time of his death, he left behind a model so that it could be completed by several of his pupils.

Giotto was one of the first artists to become famous in his own lifetime. His friend Dante heralded him as the greatest living artist in the DIVINE COMEDY. Boccaccio later praised him for bringing the art of painting back to life after centuries of darkness, remarking in THE DECAMERON, "Giotto's art was of such excellence that there was nothing in nature that his paintbrush could not exactly reproduce, not simply to make a likeness, but to be the very thing itself. His work was so perfect that a man standing before it would often find his visual senses confused, taking for real what was only painted." Giotto died in 1337 and was buried in the Cathedral in Florence, a great honor bestowed only upon the most respected and beloved of citizens. Above his tomb is the epitaph, "I am the man who brought painting to life...whatever is found in nature may be found in my art."

Soon after Giotto's death, the terrible plague known as the Black Death arrived in Europe, transmitted by the fleas of infected rats. This was the plague that killed Petrarch's beloved Laura and drove the people in THE DECAMERON from the city. By 1353 over one third of the European population had died. This catastrophe set back the development of painting for nearly a century, as artists, worried that God might be punishing humanity for straying from medieval traditions, embraced the guidelines of Gothic art. They created lots of stiff ghostly-looking men and women. But in time, Giotto's lifelike figures and dramatic scenes would inspire new generations of artists to portray humanity in a more believable manner.

REVIEW QUESTIONS:

1. Describe a typical Gothic painting.

2. How did Byzantine art differ from Gothic art?

3. How do Niccolo Pisano's statues reflect the spirit of humanism?

4. Why was it unusual for Giovanni Pisano to sign his name to a work?

5. Why was a fresco considered a "permanent" painting?

6. What are *giornate?*

7. What is Cimabue's most famous surviving work of art?

8. In what way was Giotto influenced by the Pisani?

9. In what way was he influenced by Byzantine art?

10. What are three ways in which Giotto's works differ from traditional medieval paintings?

FURTHERMORE:

1. Giotto's contemporary was Duccio di Buoninsegna of Siena. Known as Duccio, he was active 1278-1319. Duccio combined the bold linear styles, splendid coloring, and intricate surface patterns of Byzantine art with a feeling of the human presence. Like Giotto, he placed emphasis on the shape of his figures. Duccio's great altarpiece in the Siena Cathedral, THE MAESTRA, focuses on Mary and the holy child. Giotto actually made a trip to Siena (it was a day's journey by horseback from Florence) and was very impressed by the painting. In later years Sienese painters would return the compliment by adopting the realism and naturalism of Giotto.

2. The paints of earth shades such as reds and browns came from clay high in iron. Sometimes the artists used costly minerals to create bright colors. The blue in Mary's robe in a fresco by Piero della Francesca is made from the highly prized stone, lapis lazuli.

3. Frescoes were vulnerable to dampness and freezing, so this method was seldom used in northern climates.

PROJECTS:

1. Find a good book about the history of art. Leaf through it until you find a typical medieval religious statue. Then find an illustration of the relief figures of one of the Pisani (father or son). What are the similarities between the two works of art? What are the differences? How does the medieval statue make you feel? How about the Pisano sculpture? Write two paragraphs expressing your observations.

2. Leaf through the art history book again until you find a typical medieval painting. Then turn to a painting by Giotto. Compare the two styles. Then write a paragraph or two explaining why Giotto's name is associated with humanism.

3. Using that same book, find an illustration of a statue of a robed figure made in ancient Greece or Rome. Then turn to an illustration of a robed Byzantine religious figure. Do you see any similarities? Make a list of what they are. Now turn to an illustration of one of Giotto's frescoes. Do any of the similarities on your list apply to it?

4. Giotto painted several scenes from the life of Saint Francis of Assisi. Who was the famous holy man? Find out about his life and write a few paragraphs describing what you've learned.

CHAPTER III
THE ITALIAN CITY-STATES

Now that we know something about the beginnings of Renaissance literature and art, let's take a look at Italian society. After the fall of Rome, most of the people of northern Italy lived in small villages. (This was also the case in other parts of western Europe.) However, certain cities on the Mediterranean coast took advantage of their strategic locations to carry on a very lucrative maritime trade with ports in the East, particularly Constantinople. The Italian merchants acquired luxury items, such as spices, silk, and jewelry, and shipped them home, where they were sold to other merchants at a good profit. Most of the items were then transported, along with locally produced wine and olive oil, by wagon through the Alps into France and Germany. There they were traded for northern products, like timber, metals, fish, and especially wool. The wool was brought back and sold to weaving establishments in Italy. They produced fine cloth that was soon in great demand among the wealthy classes of western Europe. In later years, Italian trading vessels packed with eastern wares began sailing through the strait of Gibraltar and directly up the Atlantic coast to the northern European port cities.

This flourishing trade brought prosperity to many Italian towns, as enterprising merchants opened up shops to sell the luxury goods of the East, while others employed local citizens to produce woolen cloth. Descendants of the upper class Romans of northern Italy lived near the towns in order to control the local trade and industry, but slowly the expanding middle class of tradesmen began to rival the nobility in wealth and political power. It was this emerging middle class that would eventually fund the great works of art associated with the Italian Renaissance.

The heritage of ancient Rome was visible in every corner of the Italian peninsula. The landscape was peppered with ancient ruins, and nearly every city and village had something - the remains of a temple, a statue, an aqueduct, or even a section of ancient pavement - to remind the local people of Italy's glorious past. These ruins fostered a sense of patriotism, and they helped spark the humanists' campaign to revive the values of the "good old days."

INDEPENDENCE AND RIVALRY

Although northern Italy was officially a part of the Holy Roman Empire (which also included much of modern Germany, Austria, and eastern France), many of its cities gradually obtained self-rule. An independent city and the territory surrounding it became known as a city-state. Like a small kingdom, it raised its own taxes, built its own defenses, and made its own laws. When the Emperor Frederick I threatened to bring northern Italy under tighter control in the twelfth century, sixteen of the city-states formed the Lombard League, which was backed and supported by the Pope. (He didn't want Frederick on his doorstep!) In 1176 the League defeated the Emperor's army, and when Emperor Frederick II renewed the struggle to control northern Italy in the following century, he was similarly rebuffed. This shows that the city-states could unite if they had to, although they went their separate ways again after Frederick II died.

A more significant result of this conflict

Figure 7: The Leaning Tower of Pisa

between the city-states and the Emperor, was the division of loyalties that arose among the northern Italians. Some supported the policies of the Emperor and felt that he should control the region, while others favored an Italian alliance led by the Pope. This resulted in the creation of two political factions: the *Ghibellines* (supporters of the Emperor) and the *Guelfs* (supporters of the Pope). These factions continued to exist long after the death of Frederick II and had an important effect upon the internal politics of the city of Florence, as we will see.

The Italian people were fiercely loyal to their city-states. A person didn't consider himself an Italian; he was a Florentine, a Venetian, or the citizen of some other city. This local pride was reflected in the competition that raged for centuries among the mini-kingdoms to construct the finest churches. Pisa built a vast religious complex in the late eleventh century that drew visitors from far and wide. (Unfortunately, the marble bell tower was built on an unstable foundation, and it has been leaning ever since!) The impressive cathedral of Siena was completed in 1264, and the foundations of Florence's greatly enlarged cathedral, Santa Maria del Fiore, were laid a few decades later. The spirit of rivalry thrived even within individual communities. An example of this was the race to build the tallest bell tower (campanile). Large numbers of them were constructed in the larger cities, often within view of each other. Some towers reached a height of 200 feet! In San Gimignano no fewer than seventy-six towers were built, of which thirteen survive to this day. In 1250 a law was enacted there limiting a campanile to ninety-six feet, but by that time the public interest had shifted to other matters.

Figure 8: The Towers of San Gimignano

THE MAJOR POWERS IN ITALY

In the early fifteenth century five major centers of power had emerged on the Italian peninsula: the city-states of Venice, Milan, and Florence; the Papal States; and the kingdom of Naples. Let's take a closer look at each of these.

VENICE

Pleasantly situated on the Adriatic Sea in northeastern Italy, Venice had been a prosperous trading center for centuries. The city was built upon 118 small islands in a lagoon (a body of shallow water separated from the sea by sandbanks). Four hundred bridges linked the islands, which were, in turn, crisscrossed by small canals. Given Venice's coastal location and lack of good farming land, it is not surprising that its earliest settlers made their living from the sea.

Venice was made a republic in the eighth century. Ruled by a *Doge* (Duke) and a Great Council made up of 200 wealthy merchants, it gradually became the most highly organized government west of the Byzantine Empire. (Half of the members of the Great Council came from twenty-seven families!) The Doge had little actual power and mainly performed ceremonial duties. He was elected for life (by the Great Council) from among the most noble Venetian families and had to be of a "respectable age" (often at least seventy). It was the Senate, elected from the membership of the Great Council, that made the laws, while the *Collegeo* (the cabinet) directed foreign policy. A small group called the Council of Ten was elected annually to handle emergencies, such as declaring war, as they arose. Competition to wear the black robes of political office was keen. Those wealthy Venetians who failed to enter the Great Council by the age of twenty-five were called *il trisi* (the sad ones).

Venetians were well aware that their prosperity depended upon their maritime trade. Beginning in 997, a lavish ceremony was celebrated annually on Ascension Day to acknowledge the city's gratitude to the sea. The state barge of the Doge, the Bucentaur, was decorated with gold and crimson cloth and towed into the Adriatic, followed by a procession of government leaders in gilded gondolas. When they reached the open sea, the Doge cast a golden ring into the waters, chanting, "Oh sea, we wed thee in sign of our true and everlasting dominion."

Although Venice was a republic, its citizens did not have a great deal of freedom. They were instructed by the Great Council to spy on their neighbors and report any suspicious behavior. The open mouths of the masks that were carved onto the facades of government buildings served as slots into which citizens could drop their messages about suspected criminals. (The slots were called the "mouths of truth.") There were no public trials. If the Council believed a person was guilty, he was strangled or left to slowly perish in a dungeon. Or he might be thrown in a special place in the lagoon where no fishing was allowed, or even buried upside down in the main piazza with his legs protruding above his grave! If an accusation was falsely made, the informer was simply fined.

The government carefully guarded the secrets of the city's main industry, glassmaking. Venetian merchants had learned how to make glass from their contacts in the East, and the Council was determined to keep the knowledge from spreading to other European cities. Any workman in the glass industry who attempted to leave Venice was accused of treason, hunted down, and killed!

Saint Mark's cathedral, dedicated to the patron saint of Venice, was built in the eleventh century. It is a

Figure 9: The Major Powers in Fifteenth Century Italy

fine example of Byzantine architecture, with its large central dome and design of a Greek cross as well as the splendid mosaics that entirely cover its interior. Saint Mark's was first used as a private chapel by the Doge. Every Venetian merchant who traveled to the East was required by law to bring back some object for the cathedral.

In the thirteenth century an army of Christian Crusaders were diverted from their journey to Jerusalem by a sly old Doge named Enrico Dandolo. He offered to transport the soldiers and horses across the Mediterranean at bargain prices - if they would first attack Venice's rival trading city, Zara (on the eastern coast of the Adriatic Sea). The Crusaders agreed, overran the city, and then were dazzled by the rich spoils, to which they greedily helped themselves. This made it easy for Dandolo to convince them to attack the even richer city of Constantinople. The treasure-seeking Crusaders assaulted that ancient capital with tremendous fury, destroying buildings, killing innocent inhabitants, and stealing whatever treasures they found. The four bronze horses presently over the entrance of Saint Mark's cathedral were among the booty taken from Constantinople. With this gruesome episode, the monopoly of trade in the eastern Mediterranean passed from Constantinople to Venice. Genoa, in northwestern Italy, was a major trading rival until Venice conquered it in 1380. In the fifteenth century Venice reached the height of its powers. Venetians now referred to their city as *Serenissima* (the most serene).

MILAN

The city of Milan was strategically sited on the Lombard plain along the main trade routes running from northern Italy through the Alpine passes into Germany. It was the capital of the western empire from 302 un-

til 402. Milan had been a center of trade in ancient times, and it regained this role as European commerce expanded in the eleventh century. It also grew famous for its manufacture of fine cloth and metal weapons.

Milan became a republic in the twelfth century, but beginning in the following century it was ruled by a series of despots. Gian Galeazzo Visconti (1351-1402) was a ruthless and ambitious tyrant, who achieved such clout on the European political scene that he was able to marry the daughter of King John II of France. (One of his sisters married a son of King Edward III of England.) To his credit, Visconti was also an early patron of the arts. (A patron is someone who pays an artist to produce a painting, sculpture or building.) The Milan Cathedral, the third largest church in Europe, was begun by his orders in 1385. Its huge roof is covered with 135 marble spires, each one bearing a religious statue. (The cathedral wasn't completed until Napoleon I oversaw its final stages in the early nineteenth century.) We'll learn more about the infamous Visconti family later in our story.

ROME AND THE PAPAL STATES

The Papal States consisted of a wide band of territories in central Italy, which were ruled by the Pope. The heart of this region was the city of Rome. Once the magnificent capital when the mighty Roman Empire encompassed the Mediterranean Sea, Rome shrank to a town of only a few thousand inhabitants in the early Middle Ages. Several popes tried to revive the city as a monument to their authority, but a long series of conflicts with the Holy Roman Emperors undermined their efforts, bringing bloodshed into its very streets. In 1309 things got so bad that the Pope was forced to flee to Avignon, France, leaving Rome to slide further into the abyss of squalor and despair.

The seat of the Papacy remained in Avignon for seventy years. This period is known as the Babylonian Captivity (a term derived from the time when the Jews were held captive in ancient Babylon). Freed from interference by the Pope, the Papal States were divided among the leading wealthy families and became independent kingdoms.

Pope Gregory XI returned to Rome in 1377, but France was not prepared to give up its control of the Papacy (all Popes ruling from Avignon had been French). What followed was the Great Schism, when there was not one but two popes - one in Avignon and one in Rome! Of course, this division of power (and confusion about who was in charge) further weakened the Papacy. The conflict finally ended with election in 1417 of Martin V as the single Pope - with a residence in Rome.

The city Martin ruled was a mess! Visitors to Rome sadly described the once proud capital as a shadow of its former self, no better than a provincial town. No major construction had taken place there for years, and the old, decaying structures were either abandoned or shoddily patched up. Cattle grazed in the ancient forum (once the center of Rome's imperial government) while pigs rooted for tidbits wherever they could. No wonder someone referred to the city as a "rubbish heap of history." It was a slum. The violence in the streets was so bad that an organization called the "Brotherhood of Prayer and Death" made rounds at dawn to collect the bodies of men slain the night before! Martin did all he could to restore order, but as we will soon see, it was his successor, Nicholas V, who would take the first steps to make the city fit for a newer, grander Papacy.

South of the Papal states were the king-doms of Naples and Sicily. This region, although large in area, was relatively primitive. There were no major cities, and most of the people were wheat farmers. Naples was controlled by the ruler of Anjou, France, while Sicily belonged to the Spanish kingdom of Aragon.

FLORENCE

Florence was the birthplace of the Italian Renaissance, and as such it deserves our very close study. The city was founded in 59 BC on the ruins of an earlier Etruscan settlement by the legendary Roman general and statesman, Julius Caesar. Florence lies along the Arno River at the foot of the Apennine Mountains in the gently rolling hills of Tuscany. During the Middle Ages, the city began to prosper as merchants began importing wool from England and silk from the East for local workers to refine, dye, and weave into fine cloth. This would be the city's main industry for centuries to follow.

Early in the thirteenth century, the first craft guilds (called *arti*) were established in Florence. These were associations of merchants, artisans, and professionals (such as doctors and lawyers), formed to protect the rights of their members. Eventually there were twenty-one guilds. Each one had its own rules to control the quality of its product or service. Only the most skillful could join. Given the importance of the cloth industry in the Florentine economy, among the most important guilds were the *Arte della Lana* (the wool merchants), *the Arte di Camimala* (the cloth merchants), and the *Arte di Por Santa Maria* (the silk merchants). Equally prestigious was the *Arte della Seta*, whose members wove and processed silk to create exquisite brocades, satins, and taffetas. Professional guilds included the *Arte del Cambio* (the bankers' guild) and the *Arte dei Medici, Speziali e Merciai* (the guild of doctors and apothecaries). Because of the materials they used, painters belonged to the same guild as the apothecaries. (Jars of colored pigment used for paint were to be found beside containers of herbs and other medicines in any apothecary shop.) Members of the major guilds looked down upon the minor ones, such as the guilds of butchers, vintners, tanners, and small-time tradesmen. In turn, these workers felt superior to the thousands of ordinary laborers - weavers, spinners, dyers, combers, carters, and others who did not belong to any guild at all. More than three-quarters of Florence's population fell into this last category.

By the end of the thirteenth century the guilds had gained control of the city government. As the merchants became the dominant class, the old families of the nobility lost much of their prestige and played a smaller role in Italian society than they had in earlier times. Some resourceful aristocrats used their talents to become businessmen, ambassadors to royal courts, or government officials.

The Florentine population was often torn apart by political factions. Remember the Guelfs and the Ghibellines? These two rival groups, which originally arose to support the interests of the Holy Roman Emperor (the Ghibellines) or the Pope (the Guelfs), continued to exist for generations. To advertise their allegiances, the Ghibellines wore white robes and white hats at political gatherings, and when they dined they cut their food sideways and drank out of goblets. The Guelfs, on the other hand, wore red robes and red hats, cut their food straight across, and drank wine out of cups! By the thirteenth century the Guelf party had recruited most of the merchant class of Florence and finally prevailed over the predominantly noble Ghibellines. (This is when Dante, a Ghibelline, was exiled from the city.) The Guelfs then divided into rival parties of Black and White Guelfs, each of which competed for power in Florentine politics. The Whites felt uneasy about the Pope's political power and also worried about the interest France was taking in the Italian peninsula. They soon resembled the old Ghibelline faction. And so the Florentines continued to argue among themselves over the same basic issues.

By the fourteenth century, the population of Florence had reached 100,000. The new stone and brick wall (with eleven gates) that was built in 1333 would contain the city and its citizens until the nineteenth century. Florence was now a republic whose political power extended throughout the surrounding region of Tuscany, encompassing six subject cities, including Pisa and Arezzo. The government was run by a city council (the *Signoria*). Every two months the names of guild members who were at least thirty years old were drawn from eight leather bags called *borse*. (The borse were always kept in the sacristy of the church of Santa Croce.) Men who were in debt were ineligible to serve on the council, as were those who had completed a recent term or who were closely related to men whose names had already been drawn.

The members of the council were known as *Priori*. There were never more than nine Priori, six of them representing the major guilds and three the minor ones. (Dante had been a Prior before his exile.) Like all northern Italians, the Florentines were extremely patriotic, and the council members took great pride in serving their government. For official functions, the Priori wore fine crimson coats with ermine lining, collars and cuffs. One of them was chosen to serve as *Gonfaloniere*, the standard bearer of the republic and custodian of the city's banner - a red lily on a white field.

(The name "Florence" was supposedly derived from the lilies that grew along the banks of the Arno River.) The Gonfaloniere had gold stars embroidered on his coat to indicate his special status.

The Priori served short (two-month) terms in order to reduce the chances of corruption or favoritism. (This is strange reasoning, given the fact that the entire system catered to the interests of the "favored few.") In times of crisis, a public assembly *(parlamento)* was summoned, consisting of all male citizens over the age of fourteen. This assembly elected a small group to handle the crisis. The rest of the time the Priori dealt with local issues that arose. They received rather modest salaries, but during their terms of office they resided in the luxurious *Palazzo della Signoria.* There they were attended by a large staff of green-liveried servants, who met their every need and prepared excellent meals. Every evening they were entertained by a "buffoon" who told funny stories and sang comical songs.

The Florentine government was far from democratic. It excluded the aristocracy (the *Grandi* or "big men") as well as ordinary craftsmen and laborers (the *Popolo Minuto* or "little men"). In fact, most members of the old nobility had so little power that it became standard government procedure to ennoble a man who was making a nuisance of himself, thereby taking away his right to vote! The wealthy merchants made up a class known as the *Popolo Grasso* (fat men). They ran the show. The lowest class consisted of the unskilled workers. The only way they could show their dissatisfaction was by rioting, which they often did.

The prosperity that the cloth industry brought to Florence made the merchants receptive to the humanist ideal of carving out one's own destiny, financial or otherwise. So important was commercial success in Florence that to be rich was considered honorable, to be poor disgraced. A silk merchant named Gregorio Data stated it well: "A Florentine who is not a merchant, who has not traveled through the world, seeing foreign nations and peoples and then returned to Florence with some wealth, is a man who enjoys no esteem whatsoever."

The wealthy merchants often commissioned artists to paint walls or altarpieces in their local churches. One reason they did this was to atone for making a business profit. (This was considered sinful in the eyes of the Church. Remember how Giotto was commissioned to paint the frescoes in Padua by Enrico Scrovegni, who hoped to make up for his father's gains as a money-lender?) In later years businessmen often kept a "conscience account" in which funds were set aside specifically for contributing to works of charity, just as their modern counterparts

Figure 10: The Palazzo della Signoria

do. Of course, the merchants also savored their new status as benefactors. Like the citizens of ancient Rome, they were contributing to the well-being of their community.

In 1348 three galleys brought the Bubonic Plague to Genoa from the East. As we learned in the last chapter, the plague, known as the Black Death, rapidly spread throughout Europe. It killed over half of Florence's population. As death ravaged the cities of northern Italy, trade came to a near standstill, and the prices of all products dropped dramatically. Those Italian merchants who survived the disease responded to the economic crisis in inventive ways. When the wool prices plummeted, many of them began importing more silk, while others turned to leather, furniture, and metalwork. Meanwhile, the low grain prices prompted Italian farmers to channel their efforts into the production of wine, olive oil, and cheese. These products have remained major factors in Italy's prosperity up to the present time.

EVERYDAY LIFE IN FLORENCE

At the dawn of the Renaissance Florence was a bustling city whose narrow, twisting streets were lined with several-storied buildings of plastered brick. Stores and workshops were located on the ground floor of many of the structures, while the upper levels contained apartments. These were cramped quarters, and in most cases the kitchen became a bedroom at night, when woven straw mats were placed on the floor. There were no closets, so wooden chests were filled with clothing and packed with bay leaves to keep away the fleas, lice, and bedbugs that seemed to be everywhere. The few windows had no glass (this was much too expensive) but were covered with oiled cloth. At night, a wick in a dish of olive oil provided the only light. Since there

was no system of plumbing and sanitation, garbage and human waste were routinely dumped out of windows into the streets, creating an unhealthy (and foul-smelling!) environment.

Scattered among the crowded apartment buildings were the large houses of the successful merchants. The typical dwelling had an enclosed courtyard and a private well, which was a great luxury in those days when most families fetched water from a public fountain. Although it had many rooms, there were no hallways or connecting corridors. To get to his bedroom, a guest might have to pass through several other rooms. This was less of a problem than you might think, since in early times people had less concern for privacy than we do nowadays. Some homes had a primitive toilet - a board with several holes suspended over a diverted stream flowing through a narrow space between buildings. Most people, however, made do with a chamber pot, which, as we've learned, was emptied into the street.

The *Piazza della Signoria* (Square of the Signoria) was the civic heart of Florence, the setting for political rallies and festivities. It was dominated by the large *Palazzo della Signoria* with its tall bell tower. The Palazzo's bell sounded the alarm of an approaching army (calling all men to the city walls and gates) or summoned citizens to the square for a public assembly. Even today the building, now called the *Palazzo Vecchio* (Old Palace), continues to function as Florence's town hall. Along one side of the square was a colonnade, or loggia. In later years it would house beautiful statues inspired by those of antiquity.

Sometimes riotous activities took place in the square. On one occasion a man was nearly eaten alive (he was badly bitten) by Florentines who were maddened by his political speech! Another time wild boars and lions were released for citizens to shoot. There are even accounts of wild buffalos being stampeded across the cobblestones - just for fun! The square was also the site of public executions (another crowd-pleaser).

Florence had a number of churches, including the Gothic churches of *Santa Maria Novella* and *Santa Croce.* But the spiritual center of Florence was the cathedral of *Santa Maria del Fiore.* We'll learn more about this marvelous building in the next chapter.

STYLES OF DRESS

Clothing styles of fourteenth and early fifteenth century Italy were very strange by modern standards. The basic attire of a merchant or craftsman was a loose fitting, long-sleeved shirt and long wool stockings, which were fastened with ties to the shirt. Late in the fifteenth century, the stockings came up to the waist - in fact, they were similar to our modern tights. Over his long shirt an older man, or someone of an important social status, would wear a lucco - an ankle-length gown of black or dark purple cloth with long wide sleeves, a hood, and buttons (a recent invention) down the front. A well-off younger man would wear a shorter sleeveless tunic rather than a lucco, with a belt knotted at the waist. Footwear generally consisted of sheepskin or chamois boots. In the late fourteenth century, fashionable men wore very pointed shoes

Figure 11: A Very Pointed Toe

called poulaines. Sometimes the toes were stuffed with rags to exaggerate their length, which sometimes measured six inches or more. Eventually, the points went out of style and round toes were in. But then, in the 1460's, pointed shoes became all the rage again. This time the toes got so long they had to be chained and fastened at the knees!

Most men had their hair cut about shoulder length, and they used curling tongs to make it turn under. They wore a wide variety of hats, the most popular style being the *mazzocchino* (a woolen cloth rolled into a crown with the free end drooping over the shoulder). Some young dandies wore a round felt hat called a *cupolina tondo* (little round dome). Italian men of the humbler classes - laborers and peasants - wore shirts and trousers made from coarse woolen cloth. Not so concerned with the latest fashion, they were probably more comfortable than their wealthier neighbors.

The typical Italian merchant's wife was renowned for her elegant and sumptuous clothes, which were primarily intended to show off her husband's commercial success. Her undergarment was a chemise, a long version of a man's shirt which fell to her ankles. Over this she wore a simple, flowing dress with a tight bodice and a high neckline. Next came a brightly colored silk or brocade overdress heavily embroidered with flowers, fruits and scrolls, gold thread, pearls, or other jewels. On her feet she wore soft leather slippers. The wardrobe of a merchant's wife might cost more than the house she lived in! The women of the lower classes made their dresses from plain woolen cloth, which they sometimes embroidered. Since the fashion demanded a pale skin and fair hair, wealthy Florentine women, who tended to be dark haired and olive skinned, dyed their hair (or wore a wig of white or yellow silk) and bleached or powdered their skin. They wore many

Figure 12: A Young Florentine

There were no dry cleaners in those days. A housewife (or her servants) boiled the linens and scrubbed the wools with homemade lye soap. Grease spots were rubbed with fuller's earth (an absorbent, claylike substance moistened with lye). Silks were gently washed in heated water. When brocades, gold or silver tissues were badly worn, they were burned to recover the valuable metals.

Although bathing soap was invented in England in the fourteenth century, it did not become an important household item in Europe for a long time. The well-to-do took a bath every few weeks (less often in the winter), and the rest of the time they relied heavily on perfume to cover up any foul body odors. Many people carried perfumed handkerchiefs or wore small perfume bottles as pendants on necklaces.

NORTHERN ITALIAN CUISINE

Italian households did not dine on pizza and spaghetti with tomato sauce (tomatoes grew only in America until European explorers brought some back with them in the sixteenth century), but they enjoyed a number of dishes that are commonly served in today's Italian restaurants. Pasta was a basic part of most meals. Pasta noodles supposedly originated in the Tuscan city of Siena, green lasagna (pasta made with spinach juice) came from Bologna, and ravioli (filled pasta shells) was first served in Genoa. (Some historians believe that the concept of noodles was originally brought back from China by the Italian explorer Marco Polo.) Favorite sauces of the fourteenth century included *pesto* (ground pine nuts, basil, garlic and olive oil) and *panna* (which had a butter and cream base). Then as now, a popular soup was *minestrone* (vegetables and pasta cooked in a chicken broth). And everyone, even children, drank the local wine. It was diluted with water.

kinds of elaborate head dresses, such as the high, cone-shaped hennin, which rose three to four feet high and was draped with a veil.

Compared to modern times, the people of the fifteenth century had few articles of clothing. Even the wealthy owned only a few outfits. Children wore clothing made from the cast-offs of the adults. They never knew the luxury of jeans and sweatshirts but were condemned to wear uncomfortable miniature versions of their parents' costumes. A well-to-do family would often distribute fashionable clothing to all of their servants so that the entire household would favorably impress a visitor.

Two meals a day were served: dinner at about 10 o'clock in the morning and supper (a lighter meal) at 5 PM. (Everyone had a very light breakfast when they first arose.) As you might expect, the wealthy merchants enjoyed more exotic fare than the average family. They feasted upon such delicacies as guinea fowl, spiced veal, pork jelly, thrushes, pike, eel, trout, peacock, and turtle dove. Meat that was not fresh was strongly flavored with spices (pepper, cinnamon, cloves, nutmeg, saffron, which was extremely expensive, or ginger) imported from the East. The main purpose of the spices was to cover up the unpleasant taste of the rancid meat. There were no refrigerators in those days, so the meat was preserved with salt. After a while it had an awful taste, and this is when the spices came in handy! A favorite dessert of the wealthy was rice cooked in the milk of almonds served with sugar and honey. While the diners feasted on these delicacies, they were often entertained by a group of musicians.

Italians were eating with forks long before this useful utensil had been accepted in other parts of Europe. (The fork was a welcome improvement over eating with one's fingers.) When napkins were introduced in Florence in the fourteenth century, diners had to be advised not to spit into them or use them to blow their noses! Other dining etiquette of the time included rules against scratching oneself at the table (even the wealthy were afflicted with lice and fleas), cleaning the ears with one's fingers, or putting feet on the table. Imagine how terrible table manners must have been before these rules were made!

Of course, ordinary laborers ate more simply. The staple of their diet was bread (made from wheat, barley, or rye). This was often mixed with water and cabbage and cooked as a stew. Meat was very expensive and was only served on special occasions.

THE REPUBLIC DEFIES TYRANNY

In the early fifteenth century (1402) the huge army of Gian Galleazo Visconti, Duke of Milan, advanced menacingly towards Florence. Visconti, who considered himself the heir of Julius Caesar, intended to bring all of northern Italy under his rule. Already he had subjugated the cities of Verona, Padua, Vianza, Siena, Pisa, and Perugia. Florence, the only remaining obstacle to his ambitions, seemed isolated and extremely vulnerable. But its citizens were determined not to be beaten by the ruthless tyrant. They reinforced the city walls, armed themselves, and hoped for the best. Luck was on their side, and Visconti suddenly died. Florence had been spared, and soon afterwards Siena, Pisa, Perugia, and Bologna declared their independence of Milan.

The fact that they had stood so firmly in the face of tyranny filled the Florentines with tremendous pride. Remembering their classical heritage, they compared themselves to the early Romans, who defended their republic against all enemies. The glories of the ancient past took on a new meaning. Leonardo Bruni, a humanist scholar, wrote an ambitious twelve-volume work, THE HISTORY OF THE FLORENTINE PEOPLE (the first major historical work of the Renaissance). Like Petrarch, Bruni felt a great kinship with the people of earlier times, and he once remarked, "I have the feeling that the days of Cicero and Demosthenes (a Greek orator) are much closer to me than the sixty years just past".

ADVANCES IN EDUCATION

The revival of Greek learning in the West began when scholar Manuel Chrysoloras was invited to Florence from Constantinople in 1395. A few years later (after the incident with Milan) Pietro Paolo Vergerio of Padua wrote a treatise on education, proposing a return to the classical balance of body and spirit in a program that stressed athletics as well as scholarship. He believed that the goal of education was to bring out the best in every individual and to prepare children for a competitive life in the world of business.

Vittorino da Feltre was invited by Duke Gianfrancesco Gonzaga of Mantua in 1423 to establish a school based on classical principles for his son and those of his principal courtiers. Classes met in the Duke's splen-

Figure 13: Statue of a Wealthy Merchant

did villa, *La Giocosa* (the Joyful House), whose walls were painted with bright pictures of children at play. Vittorino said that learning should be fun (a novel concept in those times), and he was the first to use games to teach mathematics and movable letters to teach spelling. His students were not punished for working slowly (as they were in the traditional schools) but were simply required to finish their assignments while others played. Vittorino introduced his students to classical literature by reading aloud many of the myths and legends. Later, the students read the ancient works on their own, carefully analyzing them and discussing the key ideas. In addition to academic subjects, the school offered courses in swimming, horseback riding, and wrestling, as well as lessons in good manners.

In later years, the number of students at *La Giocosa* grew to about seventy, many of whom boarded at the school. A few girls attended, and poor boys of intellectual ability attended for free (they were among the first scholarship holders). The curriculum of the Joyful House might seem familiar today, but it was considered quite revolutionary in the fifteenth century Italy.

THE CITIES UNITE

As we have learned, the rivalry among the Italian city-states was often intense. Sometimes the squabbles evolved into wars. Because the citizens themselves were reluctant to leave their businesses and join in the fighting, the governments began to hire professional soldiers. Soon most of the major city-states had armies of mercenary (hired) soldiers who were led by captains called *condottieri*. (The name "condottieri" comes from the contracts - *condotte* - that the captains signed to fight for a particular city for a certain length of time.) Sometimes the *condottieri* found themselves fighting against the very city that had paid them the previous month!

In 1454 a treaty known as the Peace of Lodi was signed by the five major powers of Italy - Venice, Milan, Florence, the Papal Lands, and Naples. The Italians were spurred to take this measure by the conquest of Constantinople by the Ottoman Turks. (They worried, and rightly so, that the Turks might continue to gobble up parts of Europe.) But they also saw the commercial benefits of peace within Italy. According to the treaty's terms, each power was to recognize and respect the boundaries of the others. Should there be an attack by outsiders, the powers would unite for their mutual protection. Most important, they would stop squabbling with one another. The Peace of Lodi established a period of stability and prosperity in Italy that made it possible for all kinds of good things to happen.

REVIEW QUESTIONS:

1. What was the major industry in northern Italy?

2. What were the five major powers in Italy?

3. Who was the Doge and what were his duties?

4. What was the Babylonian Captivity?

5. Describe the Florentine craft guilds.

6. What was the Signoria?

7. How democratic was Florentine government?

8. Why did wealthy merchants often commission artists to paint the walls of churches?

9. What was a lucco?

10. What was the staple food of most middle class meals?

11. What event caused the Florentines to compare themselves to the Romans?

12. Describe the curriculum of the Joyful House.

FURTHERMORE:

1. The core of Venetian naval power was its large fortress (the Arsenal) which contained shipyards and factories. This was the largest industrial complex of the Renaissance. (It was enclosed by two miles of fortifications.) It employed thousands of workers who used methods later seen in the modern assembly line. An early example of mass production, the Arsenal had ready made parts, such as oars, masts, and sails, and could build a complete galley in a very short time. Replacement parts were kept in ports all over the known world. The Venetian state leased the galleys to individual merchants, making a handsome profit.

2. Even today Florence has a city council, which functions similarly to its fourteenth century model. (It meets, of course, in the Palazzo Vecchio, formerly the Palazzo della Signoria.) But the modern city has some problems never imagined in earlier times. Although its population numbers only 372,000, a relatively small number for a major city, Florence is invaded annually by nearly three million tourists who spend at least one night, and this doesn't account for day trippers! This means that there are seven tourists (overnight) per inhabitant!

3. Slaves were common in fifteenth century Florence. A well-to-do household had at least one. An owner had total power over his slaves, who were treated as chattel and classified in inventories with domestic animals! Luckily, the children of slaves automatically became free

citizens. Most slaves of fifteenth century Florence were Tartars captured in the region of the Black Sea. The government officially allowed the ownership of slaves provided they were not Christians!

4. Many processes were involved in changing the raw wool into cloth. Each was performed by a specialist. Spinners turned the wool to yard, dyers dyed it, weavers made it into cloth, fullers stepped the loose weave and pounded it firm, shearmen raised the nap, cropped it, straightened and pressed the finished cloth.

5. Silk was first produced in China about 4,500 years ago. The silk threads come from the cocoon made by a silkworm for protection as it grows into a moth. To make silk fabric, the delicate threads of the cocoons are unwound and then twisted together into longer threads. These are woven on a loom to produce a beautiful and durable cloth. It takes over 2,500 cocoons to produce just twenty ounces of thread, which explains why silk is so expensive. For 2,000 years the process of making silk was a closely guarded secret.

6. In the fifteenth century King Ferrante of Naples put down an insurrection of his barons. What followed was a reign of terror, when Ferrante put to death each of his opponents, embalmed their bodies, and kept them on public view as a warning to others!

7. To raise money to pay for shipping cargoes, Italian merchants sold shares in each venture to divide the costs and risks among several people. These joint stock companies were the forerunners of modern companies that sell stock to shareholders.

PROJECTS:

1. Each of the guilds of Florence had a special emblem painted on a shield. Consult the books in your classroom or library and find out what they were. Then, using poster board, draw five or six of them with colored markers. Be sure to label each one.

2. Draw a map of Italy, indicating the five major powers of the fourteenth and fifteenth centuries.

3. Draw a picture of a typical merchant and his wife of fifteenth century Florence.

4. Find out more about the condottieri. Who were some of the most famous captains? Write a short report.

5. The next time you go to an Italian restaurant closely study the menu. Which dishes might have been served during the early Renaissance (fourteenth and fifteenth centuries). Which ones couldn't possibly have been? Write a short summary of your findings.

6. Consult a book about Florence. Find a photograph of the Piazza della Signoria and read the descriptions that accompany it. What is the main function of the famous square in modern times?

7. San Marino is an Italian city-state that has remained independent to the present day. Find out more about this interesting place and write a short report.

CHAPTER IV
THE ERA OF THE MEDICI

Florentine art and architecture reached their pinnacle in the fifteenth century when one family, the Medici, controlled the local government. During these rich years, the innovations of Giotto and the Pisani and the visions of the humanists were enthusiastically embraced by new generations of artists and philosophers. Supported by the wealthy merchant class, an unusually talented group of men created some of the greatest works of the early Italian Renaissance.

ARRIVAL OF THE MEDICI

The Medici first settled in Florence in the thirteenth century as cloth merchants. Their name suggests that their ancestors were pharmacists. *Medici* means "preparers of medicine." In later years, their enemies would mockingly refer to the clusters of red balls on the family crest as "those pills." The Medici were always active in local politics, several members being appointed to the prestigious position of Gonfaloniere. There were also a few who were known as troublemakers. (Their names frequently appeared on lists of those sent into exile or involved in lawsuits.) But it was in banking that the family made its mark.

THE ITALIAN BANKERS

Florence could never have had a thriving trade industry without solid financial backing. The Italians had long been considered the best bankers in Europe. They were always present at the major trading centers in France and Germany to exchange one currency for another, making a good profit in the process. In fact, the word "bank" comes from the *banco* (bench) the money changers sat upon. They also issued bills of exchange - letters written by bankers in one country instructing those in another to make payments in the local currency to the bearers of the bills. It was even an Italian - a Franciscan monk named Fra Luca Pacioli - who created the double entry system of accounting to record the assets and liabilities of a company.

Several Italian families, such as the Bardi and the Peruzzi of Florence, used the money they had amassed in the cloth industry to create their own large banking houses. They handled such huge sums that kings and emperors often came to them when they needed funds to pay their armies, to build new palaces, or simply to cover bribes. This made the families even wealthier and tremendously influential. Often, the banking houses had branches in more than one city. The major financial street in modern London is Lombard Street, which was named after the Italian moneylenders from Lombardy who settled there in the thirteenth century.

Florence soon became the banking center of Europe. The city's currency, the gold florin, was first minted in 1252. It contained exactly 3.5 grams of gold, and this amount remained unchanged until 1533, making the florin the most stable currency of its day. One side of the coin was stamped with the city's Latin name, *Florentia,* and a portrait of John the Baptist, the city's patron saint; on the obverse side appeared the lily, the symbol of Florence. In time, the florin became the international currency of western Europe, overtaking the Venetian ducat. In

1420 there were 2,000,000 florins in circulation (and seventy-two bankers in the city of Florence).

THE ESTABLISHMENT OF THE MEDICI BANK

Giovanni di Bicci de Medici (1360-1429) used his wife's dowry to found a bank. By investing in trading companies (in which he demanded a controlling interest) and obtaining a temporary monopoly of the finances of the Pope (a truly major client), Giovanni made his bank the biggest in Florence. His personal wealth of 80,000 florins could have paid the annual salaries of 2,000 laborers in the cloth industry. To ease his conscience for being a "sinful banker" (remember how the Church condemned making a profit through business?), Giovanni spent much of his wealth on the construction of churches, the support of art, and contributions to charity. These activities helped to conceal his genuine love of money behind the facade of philanthropy and concern for the public good. We will soon see how his descendants followed his lead in patronizing the arts to glorify the family image. Giovanni served several terms in the Signoria, and in 1421 he was chosen Gonfaloniere.

COSIMO DE MEDICI

Cosimo de Medici (1389-1464), the son of Giovanni, was a financial genius. He helped his father make the Medici bank one of the most profitable businesses in Europe. Thanks to his efforts, the bank had branches in sixteen major cities. When Cosimo was nearly forty Giovanni died, leaving his son his immense financial wealth and political clout. Soon afterwards, Cosimo challenged the power of the ruling family of Florence, the Abrizzi. They temporarily stopped him

in his tracks by arranging for his arrest (he was accused of fraud). Cosimo was held in a cramped cell in the bell tower of the Palazzo della Signoria. But the Abrizzi hadn't recognized the extent of Medici influence. In reward for his generosity in the past, one of the conspirators set Cosimo free, and he fled the city. He was warmly welcomed everywhere - the Venetians even staged his triumphal entrance into their city. Meanwhile, the Florentine economy began to flounder, so Cosimo was summoned home. Now it was the Abrizzi who were sent into exile, while Cosimo set about consolidating his control of the city. In time he would become in fact, if not in name, the unchallenged ruler of Florence.

As a young man Cosimo had studied the writings of the ancients, and he had been impressed by the Greek ideal of moderation in one's life. ("Nothing in excess" was a well-known Greek motto.) He applied this principle to his business dealings, always proceeding in a prudent and cautious manner. He occasionally took risks, but only when the odds for success were extremely good. He was a practical man who enjoyed solving problems by skillful negotiation. Cosimo once remarked, "You may pursue the infinite, but I pursue the finite; you may set your ladder against the vaulted heavens, but I set mine firmly on the ground."

Determined not to flaunt his great wealth, Cosimo took great care to appear as an ordinary citizen, drinking local wine, dressing modestly, and riding a mule rather than a horse. He was publicly genial and approachable, greeting hundreds of fellow citizens by name. He was also an uncanny judge of character.

Unlike his father, Cosimo had political ambitions that went beyond the role of Gonfaloniere. By using his family funds to bribe citizens to vote into power the men he favored, he managed to govern Florence for thirty years without ever receiving an official title. The Medici bank furnished or denied loans to the Florentine government according to how Cosimo felt about the current political situation. Most people willingly supported his views, reasoning that what was good for the Medici bank was good for Florence.

Cosimo commissioned the highly esteemed architect, Michelozzo, to design a town palace (*palazzo*) to serve as his family residence. It was built at the corner of Via Largo, the widest street in Florence at that time. Cosimo chose a simple, austere design and an unimposing outer surface of rusticated (unfinished) stone. Its four three-story wings formed a square around a courtyard. The building included business offices and storerooms on the ground floor. Despite the practical reasons for the palazzo's large dimensions, Cosimo's critics were quick to complain that he had built a palace that would "throw even the Colosseum at Rome into the shade." However, it became the model for all noble Florentine houses built after it in the fifteenth century.

In 1439 Cosimo arranged for Florence to host the ecumenical council, which had been working vainly for years to reconcile the Roman Catholic and Eastern Orthodox Churches. The Pope, the Patriarch of Constantinople, and the Holy Roman Emperor were his personal guests at the newly completed palazzo. Cosimo saw to it that these celebrities were lavishly entertained with spectacular processions and festive banquets. It seemed as though Florence had become the most important place on earth, which, of course, was one of the banker's primary goals.

Cosimo used his diplomatic skills to end the long feud between Florence and Milan with the signing of the Peace of Cavriana 1441. Nine years later, he financed Francesco Sforza, an ambitious condottiere,

in his successful effort to overthrow the Visconti dynasty that had ruled Milan for generations. Medici loans kept Sforza's new government afloat and made the former soldier a strong and grateful ally. The bank even served as a buffer against invasion. When Venice and the kingdom of Naples joined forces against Florence, Cosimo recalled loans he had previously made to them and paralyzed their military operations! He later played an important role in the creation of the Italian League, formed by the five major powers of Italy after the Peace of Lodi.

Despite his efforts to seem like "one of the people," Cosimo was, in fact, the first of the "merchant princes" of Florence. He presided over a court that included the most celebrated Italian artists and scholars of the day. Believing that artists were people of extraordinary talent, who should be treated like celestial spirits, not beasts of burden, he paid them well for their efforts. In fact, he became the most generous and discriminating art patron Florence had ever known. He had a lot to do with the changing image of the artist from manual laborer to creative genius.

Cosimo was well versed in Latin, and he adored books and manuscripts. He encouraged his friends to take an interest in learning by allowing them to borrow from his vast library. He loaned money to impoverished students and even founded the Platonic Academy, which became a center for the discussion of humanist ideas. Marsilio Ficino was the leading member of the Academy. His edition of the works of Plato (the first complete translation of Plato into Latin) made the Greek philosopher's ideas readily available to western scholars. Ficino believed that classical philosophy and the Christian religion were in harmony with one other, and he played a major part in bringing the pagan themes of the ancient world into Christian art. We'll learn more about this in the next chapter. Cosimo spent 40,000 florins renovating the monastery of San Marco, including a library to house classical texts. He reserved a monk's cell for himself there so he might rest, read, meditate, and be reminded of the simpler aspects of life. He also oversaw the construction the church of San Lorenzo, which would later house his library.

In 1464 Cosimo died peacefully in extreme old age while listening to a reading of Ficino's translation of Plato. For several weeks before his death he often sat alone in a chair with his eyes closed. When asked why he did this, he responded, "to get used to the dark." He was posthumously given the title *Pater Patriae* (Father of the Nation) by his native city. This prestigious title had been awarded in the past to the mightiest emperor of Rome, Augustus. It was inscribed on Cosimo's tombstone in the crypt at San Lorenzo.

A Stellar Trio

Good things often come in threes. Fifteenth century Florence produced a trio of artistic geniuses - Donatello, Brunelleschi, and Masaccio. They were the brightest stars of the Medici court. Like the Pisani and Giotto, they were inspired by the masters of antiquity. Their extraordinary works mark the beginning of the Italian Renaissance. (The Pisani and Giotto are considered forerunners of the age.)

Donatello

Donatello (Donato di Bette Bardi, 1386-1466) was a gifted sculptor. Like Giotto, he sketched the people of Florence as they went about their daily activities, and he used a live model whenever he sculpted. So committed was he to creating realistic

works of art that he was once heard to exclaim to a statue he was sculpting, "Speak then! Why will you not speak?" Indeed, many of his figures appear to be frozen in a dramatic moment in time, and this theatrical element helps them to "come alive" for anyone who views them.

Donatello's marble statue of Saint Mark stands in the classical pose of *contrapposto* (a relaxed position in which his weight is placed on one foot and his opposing shoulder is raised). Imagine yourself waiting for something in a long line of people. Wouldn't you be standing in this position, rather than with your weight equally distributed on

Figure l4: Donatello's Statue of Saint George

both feet? The ancient sculptors often used the contrapposto pose to make their statues appear natural, but the technique had been forgotten for centuries until Donatello rediscovered it. He also copied the way the ancients carved the folds of the drapery to suggest the movement of the body beneath. Find a picture of this statue in an art book, and study its natural appearance.

The young sculptor established his reputation with his marble statue of Saint George (the legendary dragon slayer). This work, which originally stood in the niche of a guild building, was the first Renaissance statue to stand unsupported against a wall (unlike the traditional relief statues). One look at Saint George reveals a great deal about his personality and state of mind. His slightly twisted body and the intense expression on his face suggest strength and supreme confidence. He is watchful and alert, ready to spring into action whenever the dragon shows its ugly face.

Donatello's greatest work was DAVID, a bronze statue of the biblical hero commissioned by the city of Florence and completed in 1430. Bronze was a popular medium in ancient times, but medieval statues were usually carved in stone or wood. Once again, Donatello had "rediscovered" an earlier technique. David stands in the casual contrapposto position, gazing down on the head of the slain Goliath. He embodies youthful grace and dignity; his nudity (a symbol of his vulnerability) is emphasized by the hat and greaves (leg armor) he wears. Donatello's DAVID was the first life-size bronze free-standing statue since antiquity (and also the first nude).

The statue became a symbol of Florentine liberty. (The winged helmet worn by Goliath was a symbol of Milan's Visconti family. Remember how Florence had stood tall against Milan?) It was originally placed in the palace courtyard of Cosimo de Medici, mounted

Figure 15: Donatello's Statue of David

on a base engraved with an inscription extolling Florentine heroism and virtue.

According to legend, Cosimo was so impressed by Donatello's talents that he gave him a stylish new wardrobe. However, the sculptor was too embarrassed to wear such fine clothes, and so he returned them. (Fifty years later, artists would dress like courtiers, as we will see. But the time had not yet come.) This is not to say that Donatello did not take tremendous pride in his work. He once furiously broke a head that he had sculpted because the merchant who ordered it offered him too low a price!

In 1445 he began his huge bronze equestrian statue of the renowned condottiere Erasmo da Narni - nicknamed Il Gattemelata ("the Slick Cat"). It was modeled after the sole surviving ancient Roman equestrian statue, that of Emperor Marcus Aurelius. (The Roman statue had escaped destruction by anti-pagan zealots in the late years of the Empire because it was wrongly believed to represent Christian Emperor Constantine!) This time Donatello "reinvented" the ancient technique

Figure 16: Mary Magdelen

of portraying a great general on horseback. The "Slick Cat" sits proudly in the saddle, a model of commanding energy.

The late works of Donatello reflect more violent emotions than his earlier statues. A good example is his wooden sculpture of Mary Magdelen, who was reputed to be a sinful woman. According to tradition, Mary

Magdelen used her ill-gotten fortune to help Christ and became his only female friend. After he was crucified, she took refuge in a cave in France where, for thirty years, she atoned for her earlier sins. While artists traditionally depicted her as young and beautiful, Donatello's figure is an emaciated, vacant-eyed old woman dressed in animal skins - a vivid portrayal of the ravages of aging and the horrible effects caused by years of self-denial.

Donatello's statues were famous in his own time, and generations of sculptors would take their cues from his innovations before setting out to give form to their own artistic visions. When he died in 1466, the artist's body was placed in a tomb near that of Cosimo de Medici in the Florentine church of San Lorenzo.

BRUNELLESCHI

Filippo Brunelleschi (1377-1446) is known as an architect, but he was originally trained as a goldsmith and sculptor. In 1401 he entered a competition sponsored by the Guild of Cloth Importers *(the Arte di Calimala)* to design a set of doors of the Florence Baptistery. (The Baptistery was situated near the Cathedral and, as its name implies, was used for baptism.) The seven greatest sculptors of the day were pitted against one another. They were asked to create a bronze relief sculpture depicting the biblical story of the sacrifice of Isaac. The finalists were Brunelleschi and Lorenzo Ghiberti, and after much debate the committee in charge chose the more traditionally arranged figures of Ghiberti by a narrow margin.

Ghiberti would spend the next twenty-five years creating beautiful bronze panels for the doors illustrating many episodes from the Old Testament. When at last they were completed, Ghiberti was immediately

Figure 17: A panel of the Gates of Paradise

commissioned by the guild to produce a second set. These ten panels, each one depicting several different episodes from the Bible, became the sculptor's masterpiece. Ghiberti included a portrait of himself in the frieze of prophets and sibyls surrounding the panels. (Look at the figure above. He's the balding fellow with the arched eyebrows.) When the panels were revealed to the public, the acclaim was unprecedented. The figures are so realistic and emotionally inspiring that the artist Michelangelo later remarked that the doors could grace the gates to Paradise. (They've been known as the Gates of Paradise ever since.) Ghiberti had good reason to be proud of his accomplishments, and he decided to write an autobiography (entitled *COMMENTARI*). He was the first artist to write a book about himself. However, he stretched the truth

somewhat when he wrote, "Few things of importance have been done in our land where I have not had a hand in the design or the direction." He was even more arrogant than Giovanni Pisano!

But let's return to Brunelleschi. He was so disappointed by his failure to win the competition that he gave up sculpture completely and turned to architecture. This seems like an abrupt change of direction, but, as we'll soon see, artists of this period often tried their skills at more than one discipline. Brunelleschi's decision turned out to be a good thing, too, since he became the greatest architect of the early Italian Renaissance.

About this time, he became friendly with the young Donatello, and the two decided to travel together to Rome. There the budding architect analyzed and measured the ancient ruins and drew sketches of them, while Donatello carefully studied the statues. Brunelleschi was impressed by the simple, balanced lines of the Roman buildings: their rounded arches, straight columns and domed roofs seemed to blend perfectly together to form a symmetrical unit. The two young artists became so enraptured with the ancient works that they decided to base all their future creative enterprises on those of antiquity. They were soon referring to themselves as "the heirs of Rome," although other artists, noting the collection of ancient coins and gems they had amassed, dismissed them as "treasure seekers."

In 1418 the Guild of Wool Merchants in Florence announced a competition to design a dome for the Cathedral of Santa Maria del Fiore (known today as the Duomo). This Gothic building had been started in 1294 but was not completed. The original architect (Arnolfo di Cambio) had been instructed to design a church "so magnificent in size and beauty as to surpass anything built by the Greeks and Romans." Arnolfo obliged by building the world's largest Catholic church. (Today it is surpassed only by Saint Peter's in Rome, Saint Paul's in London, and the Cathedral in Milan.) Unfortunately, Arnolfo died before figuring out how to cover the enormous octagonal opening, which required a domed roof larger than any built before.

Brunelleschi thought about the domed structures he had seen in Rome, particularly the Pantheon. Then he consulted the ten books on architecture written by Roman engineer Pollio Vitruvius (the only treatise on architecture that had survived from the ancient world). Pouring over these volumes of the past and pondering the sketches he had made in Rome, he slowly came up with a revolutionary design for the dome.

The huge size was the greatest challenge. Normally a builder would use a temporary wooden framework shaped like a hemisphere to support the construction of the dome until the mortar had hardened. However, the base of the cathedral's dome was more than 136 feet in diameter, and no trees could be found to span so wide a space. Even if the wood was available, the framework would have collapsed under its own weight. Someone suggested that the space beneath the proposed dome be filled with earth containing random handfuls of coins to support the construction. When the dome was completed, the children of Florence could dash in, dig for the coins, and take away the earth at the same time!

Brunelleschi had a better idea. He designed a double dome with a strong inner shell that would support most of the weight and a light outer one. He would build the inner dome one layer of bricks at a time, the weight of each new layer supported by the one previously constructed. Each row would be

Figure 18: The Pantheon in Rome

Figure 19: Brunelleschi's Dome and Giotto's Tower

stepped slightly inward, creating a herring-bone pattern, so as the construction proceeded the structure would gradually taper toward the center. For added strength, a masonry of eight massive self-supporting stone ribs would be built. With this plan, no wooden framework or scaffolding would be needed inside the dome.

Between this inner shell and the outer one would be a complex web of smaller ribs and connecting horizontal buttresses that would tie the principal ribs together. A stairway between the shells would be used instead of scaffolding for the workers. (It is still possible to walk there.) Crowning the top there would be a lantern (a small structure admitting light into the interior). The dome would be elegant in its simplicity, majestic in its size.

Brunelleschi nearly did not get the job because he refused to show anyone his plans before he started work. He explained that if the other architects saw his model, they would steal his ideas. When the guild committee members remained adamant in their demands to see his design, he challenged them to stand an egg on its end. No one could, so Brunelleschi banged the egg on the table and stood it on its cracked top. When the committee complained that anyone could do that, the architect replied, "Yes, and you would say the same thing if I told you how to build the dome!" They allowed him to go ahead, but his old rival, Lorenzo Ghiberti, was appointed to help him (and keep an eye on him). Furious and insulted, Brunelleschi protested so loudly about Ghiberti's inexperience in architectural design that the committee reluctantly gave in and let him work alone. This must have really embarrassed the arrogant Ghiberti!

Work began on the dome in 1421. Brunelleschi gathered such a vast supply of bricks, marble tiles, timbers, and stones that it seemed like he was building a dome over the entire city. As the project progressed, he ingeniously solved the smaller problems that arose. He invented a hoisting machine with pulleys so that the masons wouldn't have to carry up their materials. He de-

Figure 20: the Pazzi Chapel at Santa Croce

It took sixteen years to build the dome. Actually, it was completed after Brunelleschi's death by a younger architect, Michelozzo (the same man who designed Cosimo's palazza). Rising over 300 above the ground and vaulting a wider space than had ever been spanned before, the dome was an amazing achievement - a triumph of human genius and ingenuity. Although linked to medieval design in its use of ribs, its simplicity and symmetry recalled the best of the classical past. The Duomo became a model for all future domed buildings, and even today it is the focal point of Florence's skyline.

When plans for the dome were still on the drawing board, Brunelleschi began work on the *Osperdale degli Innocenti* (Foundling Hospital) in Florence. Find a picture of it in an art book. Brunelleschi loved the geometric designs involved in classical architecture - the circles and squares, hemispheres and cubes that combine to create a unified whole. He was particularly drawn to the form of the rounded arch, which he incorporated into a colonnade (a series of wide arches separated by slender columns) for the facade of the Hospital. With mathematical precision the height of each column equals the width of the bay between columns and also its depth from column to wall. As a result, each bay is really a cube of space. By combining the classical columns, arches, and pilasters (column-like structures attached to the wall) and stressing their geometric lines Brunelleschi de-

signed guttering to drain off rain water and small openings to provide light and reduce wind force. He installed mini-restaurants in the work area so that the laborers didn't have to descend for their meals. He even inserted hooks to hold up scaffolding for future cleaning or repairs. And he consistently praised the efforts of the hardworking men. People who stopped by to observe the construction were astonished to see that the structure was indeed taking shape with no visible scaffolding or supporting framework.

fined the new Renaissance style of architecture.

He managed to find time to work on several other buildings, including the Florentine churches of Santa Maria degli Angeli, San Lorenzo, and Santo Spirito as well as the elegant Pazzi Chapel in Santa Croce. Each new building was a refinement of his geometric style. Every column, arch and pilaster was designed in direct proportion to the other elements, the many integral features forming a harmonious unit. Times were certainly changing. The pointed arches and soaring vaults of the medieval Gothic churches that reached towards the heavens were gradually being replaced by structures that seemed to hug the earth. Renaissance architecture reflects, in stone and bricks, spirit of humanism.

Around 1420 Brunelleschi painted two panels to demonstrate his theory of linear perspective. (Linear perspective refers to creating a sense of depth or receding distance on a flat surface by the use of imaginary lines). His ideas were probably derived from his careful studies of architectural design. According to his theory, all parallel lines in the foreground of a painting should converge at a single vanishing point on the horizon. (Imagine yourself standing on a huge lawn that has just been mowed. Look at the far end of the lawn. Don't the lines made by the lawnmower seem to come together in the distance?) Brunelleschi pointed out that close-up figures should appear larger than distant ones. (This seems obvious to us now, but back then most artists continued to follow the medieval formula of basing the size of a subject on his importance.) Brunelleschi's theory of perspective certainly makes sense, and it would strongly influence the painters who lived after him.

As we learned earlier, Cosimo de Medici had great respect for the talented artists he patronized, referring to them as "celestial spirits." Brunelleschi agreed with that judgment, adding that painting, sculpture, and architecture were not mechanical arts (like carpentry) but were liberal ones (like mathematics and poetry). A picture, statue, or building was as much a product of the mind as of the hand; the true artist was not a mere craftsman but a man of learning and imagination.

By his achievements and by his words, Brunelleschi set the groundwork for a whole new definition of architecture and art. Sadly, he never saw the completion of any of his major structures. Like an omen from the Olympian gods, a lightning bolt struck (but did not damage) his uncompleted dome just a few months before he died.

MASACCIO

The third in the trio of great artists was Masaccio (Tommaso di Giovanni di Simone Guidi, 1401-1428). He was nicknamed *Masaccio* ("Slovenly Tom") because he was so involved in his artistic endeavors that he paid little attention to his personal appearance. A friend of Donatello and Brunelleschi, he is considered the greatest Italian painter of the early Italian Renaissance.

Masaccio greatly admired the works of Giotto and set out to emulate them. He studied human anatomy so that his figures would be lifelike. He experimented with the interplay of light and darkness, painting shadows so as to give definition to the forms they fell across. This technique is known as *chiaroscuro*, from the Italian words *chiaro* (bright) and *oscuro* (dark). It produces the illusion of roundness and weight in an object or figure. In many of Masaccio's works the light comes from a single source or direction. In addition, his broad, quick brush strokes suggest motion and drama.

Masaccio became the first artist to use Brunelleschi's principles of linear perspective in a major painting when he produced his fresco of the Holy Trinity in the church of Santa Maria Novella in Florence. He created the illusion of a chapel receding into the wall on which it is painted, and he reinforced the effect by placing the figures on a shelf that seems to project forward. The picture is composed in such a way that our attention is drawn toward the focal point of the work, a pyramidal group composed of the Virgin and Saint John at the bases and God the Father and the crucified Christ at the apex. Massacio's fresco marks the beginning of a new method of arrangement of figures based upon geometric forms. We'll see this again and again.

His greatest works are the frescoes he painted in the chapel of the Brancacci family in the church of Santa Maria del Carmine, Florence. The scene of THE EXPULSION OF ADAM AND EVE is an intense psychological drama. The naked forms of the grief-stricken couple are molded in light and shadow, which gives them form and substance as they tearfully stride out of Paradise. Another fresco, entitled THE TRIBUTE MONEY, depicts the Apostles gathered in a circle around Christ as they are confronted by a tax collector. Again, light and shadow give each figure a solid appearance. Christ's instruction to Peter to pay the tax collector is told through solemn gestures and expressions. According to the Bible, when the tax man came to collect tribute, Christ told Peter he could find the money in the mouth of a fish in the nearby Sea of Galilee. Peter cast for the fish, found the coin, and paid the man. In the fresco, Peter appears in the distance to the left, finding the coin. (It has been proposed that this picture symbolizes the Florentines' despair at having to pay an extra tax to support the fight against Milan.) By arranging the figures of this simple scene in a semicircle around Christ, the artist adapted the circle Brunelleschi employed in architecture. Masaccio amazed his contemporaries with the dramatic and lifelike quality of his paintings. By the late fifteenth century, the Brancacci Chapel became a major point of pilgrimage for nearly every Italian artist. Sadly, Masaccio died at the age of twenty-seven. Imagine the great art he would have left to us had he lived longer.

So there we have the incredibly talented trio of Donatello, Brunelleschi, and Masaccio - sculptor, architect, and painter - who broke the boundaries of convention, merging their own innovative techniques with traditions of the past. Thanks to them, art was rapidly evolving from the medieval style of humanized faith into a lifelike representation of mankind. The Italian Renaissance was in full swing!

THE TREATISES OF ALBERTI

In 1435 humanist and architect Leon Battista Alberti wrote a treatise explaining Brunelleschi's theories about perspective in a book entitled ON PAINTING. The Italian translation was dedicated to Brunelleschi himself, the original having been written in Latin. Alberti considered art a branch of science, and his book explains how the artist should employ principles of mathematics and geometry to depict the physical world.

Alberti's ten volumes on architecture (ON THE ART OF BUILDING) represent the first major treatise on that subject since the one by the Roman Vitruvius, on which it was loosely modeled. Alberti defined architecture as a noble science and the architect as a well educated man of genius who applies his talents masterfully. Like Brunelleschi, he lauded the simplicity and symmetry of classical design, which, he believed, reflect the order and balance of the natural world.

Alberti's writings played a central role in spreading the new theories of art and architecture. Conversations between artists now centered upon vanishing points, lines, and angles, and the subjects of their works were described in terms of squares and cubes. Some people really got carried away and emphasized perspective over content - in many of these, arch after arch recede into the vanishing point in the distance. Paolo

Figure 21: Santa Maria Novella, Florence

Uccello (1397-1475) became so enamored with the new techniques that one night his wife found him muttering again and again, "What a wonderful thing is perspective!"

Alberti exhibited his prowess in architecture with the design of buildings in Florence, Rimini, and Mantua. His black and white marble main facade of the church of Santa Maria Novella is a fine example of geometric design and classical proportions. It fits into a perfect square, and a second square within the large square, encompass-

ing the upper story and pediment, has an area exactly half that of the main section.

In addition to his work in art and architecture, Alberti wrote about sculpture, moral philosophy, marriage, horses, agriculture, the ruins of Rome, secret codes, applied mathematics, law, music, and the Tuscan dialect, among other things. He was also a poet, a social commentator, and an adviser in half a dozen princely courts in Italy. He even wrote and passed off as genuine a comedy attributed to a Roman playwright. And he was a gymnast who could leap over a man's head with his feet tied together! Alberti exemplified his own belief that "men can do all things" and is a shining example of a new ideal of his age, the multi-talented "Renaissance man."

FLORENCE IN THE MID-FIFTEENTH CENTURY

By the middle of the fifteenth century, Florence had become one of the largest cities in Europe. Brunelleschi's dome hailed the city's renown as a center of art and culture. In fact, "Dome-sickness" was the term used to describe the sadness (home-sickness) that afflicted Florentines when they traveled to other places. Donatello's statue of the lion, Marzocco, guarded the papal apartment of the Convent of Santa Maria. Holding a shield emblazoned with the Florentine emblem, the *fleur de lis* (lily), Marzocco was yet another symbol of the city's strength and independence. His name is derived from *Martocus* (little Mars); the Roman god of war

(Mars) was the patron deity of ancient Florence.

It was a boom period. Trade and business had never been better, and rich merchants were becoming richer. They sent their sons to schools to master mathematics for business careers and to learn about antiquity so that they could converse knowledgeably in social settings. (This was the mark of gentility.) They built huge city homes (palazzos) and country estates (villas) in the classical style, filling them with collections of ancient coins, vases, and statues. They competed among themselves to hire the best artists to beautify the churches, their private chapels, and their own imposing domiciles.

The ideals of the early humanists had grown into a whole new way of looking at life. What had begun as a scholarly interest in ancient literature had evolved into a cult of antiquity. Florence, proud of its independent spirit and its active community of artists and thinkers, hailed itself as the "new Athens." (Athens was the heart of ancient Greece. Like the Athenians, the Florentines placed a high value on human ingenuity.) Academies, modeled on Cosimo's Platonic Academy, sprang up among elite communities throughout northern and central Italy. Pomponio Leto founded the Roman Academy, whose members met regularly for dinner to discuss classical topics. They addressed each other by Roman nicknames such as Marcus and Julius and they even wore togas!

Wealthy merchants in the major cities often presided over festive Roman-inspired banquets. The entertainment was just as important as the food. Each new course was introduced by a fanfare of trumpets followed by music suggestive of the type of food about to be served. Boar or venison were announced by the horns of hunters, fish was introduced by songs about water, while wine called for lyrics about Bacchus

Figure 22: Marzocco

(the Roman god of the vine). In between courses, the diners enjoyed classical poetry and dance. When it was time for desert, dwarfs, jugglers, or musicians were often carried into the hall in giant pastries, suddenly bursting out of them to the delight of all. As in ancient Rome, the banquets could go on for hours. The cook for the d'Este Court at Ferrara wrote that while the guests dipped their hands in perfumed water, singers and musicians provided background entertainment for the seventeenth course!

LORENZO THE MAGNIFICENT

Cosimo de Medidi was succeeded by his son, Piero "the Gouty," who was physically frail and soon died. Piero was succeeded by his son, Lorenzo (1449-1492). He was educated at the Platonic Academy and the recently established University of Florence. As a lad, Lorenzo had learned much about politics from Cosimo, with whom he often played long games of chess. He later visited the ruins of ancient Rome with Alberti and marveled at the city's rich heritage. Lorenzo enjoyed talking with the artists who frequented the Medici palazzo and took an active interest in their theories. He learned to play several musical instruments (music was one of his passions) and composed poetry. In short, he was a gifted, well-educated young man, admirably equipped to follow in the footsteps of his legendary grandfather. Later generations would know him as *Il Magnifico* ("The Magnificent"). Not that he looked the part. Lorenzo was rather unattractive, having a swarthy complexion, heavy features, a long, pointy noise, and a harsh, high-pitched voice. However, he was so charming that people soon forgot about his ungainly physical appearance.

He was only twenty when he suddenly found himself the head of the Medici dynasty and in charge of the fate of Florence. Although the city was still technically a republic, Lorenzo would rule the government "from behind the scenes," just as Cosimo had once done. He was a skillful diplomat, and he made it a major goal to maintain peaceful relations with the other major city-states of Italy.

Peace didn't come right away, however. Not long after he took over the reins of power, Lorenzo's life was threatened by a conspiracy led by the powerful Pazzi family (banking rivals of the Medici) and supported by the wealthy Pitti family and even

by Pope Sixtus IV. (The Pope was angered by a clash between his business interests and the policies of the Medici bank.) Lorenzo and his brother, Giuliano, were attacked beneath Brunelleschi's dome as a priest was conducting Mass. Giuliano was stabbed to death, and Lorenzo narrowly escaped by hiding behind the bronze doors of the Sacristy.

As news of the attack spread throughout the city, the Florentines rallied in support of the Medici. Within hours most of the conspirators were hanging from the windows of the Palazzo della Signoria. A grateful Lorenzo commissioned the young artist Botticelli (more about him later) to depict their dangling bodies in a painting, and he had wax portraits of his dead brother placed at every street corner in Florence. Those conspirators who escaped were relentlessly hunted down. One was dragged home from Constantinople, and Lorenzo took personal satisfaction in sketching his execution. After the Pazzi Conspiracy, Lorenzo was always accompanied by ten armed bodyguards, one holding a drawn sword.

Jacopo de Pazzi, the patriarch of the Pazzi family, had opposed the conspiracy at first but was won over by the Pope. After Giuliano was murdered, Jacopo escaped to the village of Castagno, but the villagers recognized him and brought him back to Florence. There he was tortured, stripped naked, and hanged from the Palazzo della Signoria. He was later buried in Santa Croce, but he didn't rest in peace. A group of Florentines, blaming the recent heavy rains on his evil spirit, dug up the body and threw it into a ditch in an apple orchard. And this wasn't the end of it. The body was later removed and dragged through the streets of Florence by a mob shouting, "Make way for the great knight!" They propped up the rotting carcass against the Palazzo Pazzi, where the decomposing head was used as a door knocker! Eventually, the remains of poor Jacopo were thrown into the Arno River.

Among the first conspirators executed were an Archbishop and a young (teen-aged) cardinal. The cardinal's uncle was none other than the Pope. Now Sixtus really had something to be angry about. Seeking vengeance for his murdered nephew, he allied himself with King Ferdinand of Naples and began assembling an army of mercenaries to attack Florence. At this point Lorenzo set off, alone and unarmed, on a secret journey to Naples. He used his skills of diplomacy to charm Ferdinand, enticing him with a generous offer of gold florins if he (the King) would switch allegiances. This venture took great courage: Ferdinand had previously murdered more than one important guest! Fortunately, he accepted the bribe and pulled out, forcing Sixtus to abandon his plans. A triumphant Lorenzo was toasted as a great hero by the greatly relieved citizens of Florence.

Like his grandfather, Lorenzo never held public office, but his advice and opinions were sought in every major government decision. Knowing that Florence could not compete with stronger powers on the battlefield, he maintained peace by forming alliances, lending money, and making gifts (actually, they were bribes). He masterminded extensive financial deals with many of the leaders of Europe. In medieval times monarchs had focused their energies on war; for them military victory meant glory and survival. But the men who ruled northern Italy in the fifteenth century knew that the key to success lay in skillful negotiation, and Lorenzo was a master at it.

Lorenzo did not share his grandfather's interest in business, however, and because of his neglect the bank came close to collapsing on more than one occasion. (Lorenzo used public money to cover his losses.) He preferred the challenge of politics, and the profits he might have reinvested in the family business were spent on

Figure 23: The Medici Villa at Poggio a Caino

his highly refined life style. Lorenzo loved to spend time at his several country estates. The extensive gardens of the villa at Caraggi were laid out geometrically and planted with cypress and myrtle, the trees of antiquity. (The new theories of art even affected gardening!) Often he would stroll about the grounds, reading the descriptions by Roman poets Horace and Catallus of the Roman countryside. Every year on November 7 he held a banquet at the villa in honor of Plato's birth. Caraggi became the gathering spot of a brilliant circle of poets, artists, and musicians.

Lorenzo started a school for sculptors in the garden of the Medici Palace in Florence. He employed a former pupil of Donatello to act as instructor and loaned him numerous paintings, antique busts and statues, which were set up in a studio and around the grounds. Like Cosimo, he continued to support the local churches and monasteries, but he concentrated his wealth on a private collection of ancient vases, cameos, bronze statuettes, jewels, and lavishly illustrated classical manuscripts. His vast collection of books became the first public library in Europe. (It was freely available to all.) But although he enjoyed learning about the ancient world, it was Dante and Boccaccio who inspired Lorenzo to compose lyrical verses about the countryside in the Tuscan vernacular.

BOTTICELLI

Among the artists Lorenzo supported was Alessandro di Mariano dei Filipepi (1445-1510). He is known by his nickname, *Botticelli* (little barrels), a reference, perhaps, to his forebears who were coopers (barrelmakers). Young Botticelli was apprenticed to a goldsmith, in whose workshop he developed a taste for the precise, incised line that would later characterize his art. In the

1460's he studied painting under the guidance of well-established artists Fra Filippo Lippi and Andrea del Verrocchio. These masters taught him how to paint solid looking figures and to contrast light and dark to create the illusion of roundness and depth. And yet, from the beginning Botticelli's figures were so much more graceful than those of his teachers. His emphasis upon line rather than physical substance endowed them with an ethereal, almost spiritual quality. Although he understood the importance of perspective, he never made it a crucial part of his works. As a result, the men and women in his paintings often seem to be drifting, in a most refined and elegant manner, through empty space. His unique style has been described as "pure visual poetry."

In the 1470's Botticelli was the darling of Lorenzo's brilliant circle. He painted THE ADORATION OF THE MAGI as a sort of homage to the Medici family. It depicts Cosimo and Lorenzo as the Wise Men kneeling before the infant Jesus. They are dressed in the styles of their own age. This peculiar custom of placing wealthy patrons in contemporary attire among the traditional figures in biblical scenes became quite common during the Renaissance. The artist even included himself in the painting among the Magi. (You can see him in the right foreground, wearing a yellow robe and gazing right at you.) The Medici family had long promoted the family's connection with the Magi, whom they considered their patron saints. They sponsored a religious fraternity devoted to the Eastern sages, and on Epiphany family members processed through Florence in the role of the ancient kings. This probably inspired Botticelli's painting.

The fascination with Greek deities among the people of Lorenzo's court is reflected in Botticelli's mythological paintings. The two most celebrated of these are *LA PRIMAVERA* (SPRING) and THE BIRTH OF VENUS. The first is an imaginative and dreamlike interpretation of the ancient legends associated with springtime. Nature is represented by the Roman goddess of spring (Flora), while the three graces (goddesses associated with poetry, music, and drama) symbolize the arts. This painting hung for years at the Medici villa at Castello. THE BIRTH OF VENUS depicts the goddess of love and beauty arising from an enormous seashell. Like *LA PRIMAVERA*, it is filled with symbols designed to appeal to the sophisticated men of Lorenzo's court. For the humanists, the birth of the goddess symbolized the rebirth of ancient forms of art.

Botticelli also painted a number of religious works, and in 1481 he created a series of evocative and poetic drawings to illustrate an edition of Dante's DIVINE COMEDY. Then, suddenly, he had nothing to do with the Medici. He painted no more blissful, elegant figures. Instead, his works took on a disturbing tone. The cause of this big change was a man named Savonarola.

SAVONAROLA

Before we meet this infamous man, let's return to the story of Lorenzo de Medici. Since he was not inclined to devote much time to the family business, the Medici bank began a long downward spiral. One by one, the branches in London, Bruges, and Milan had to be closed. In 1490 a number of factors (the most important one was an attack upon Italian traders by the Ottoman Turks) caused the Florentine economy to sag, and the local merchants unfairly blamed Lorenzo. They claimed that he spent too much time on his court and not enough on business. Suddenly, "Il Magnifico" was vulnerable.

This is when Girolamo Savonarola arrived on the scene. He was an Italian friar from the city-state of Ferrara who became a fiery religious reformer. He had been invited in 1489 by a well-meaning Lorenzo to live at the recently rebuilt monastery of San Marco, but he was so shocked by the worldliness of Florence that he turned against the Medici family. A spell-binding preacher, Savanarola packed 10,000 people each Sunday into the Duomo to hear his tirades against greed and materialism and his demands that Lorenzo account for his sinful ways. His sermons were so moving that his followers became known as the *Piagnoni* (the Weepers). Among them was a worried and mournful Botticelli. No wonder his last paintings are so serious and religious in tone. The friar condemned parties, gambling, swearing, horse-racing, and anything else that he considered a corruption of Christian values. He urged the Florentine people to abandon all earthly pleasures, warning that if they did not heed his words a terrible crisis would befall the city.

Lorenzo died at Careggi in 1492 at the age of forty-three. That seems like a young age for a vigorous man to pass away, and it shouldn't have happened. All he had was an attack of gout, a slight fever, and a stomach infection - nothing life threatening. But his doctors "did him in" by forcing him to swallow a mixture of ground up pearls and precious stones, which was supposed to cure his ills! (We'll find out more about such barbaric medical practices later in our story.) As Lorenzo lay dying, he turned his face to the wall to avoid the continuous reproaches of Savararola. He had called the friar to issue the last rites, but Savonarola refused unless he "restored the liberty of the Florentines." What an attack upon the man who had devoted his life to his home city! When "Il Magnifico" died, Pope Innocent VIII remarked, "The peace of Italy is at an end."

The Pope certainly knew what he was talking about, because soon afterwards King Charles VIII of France attacked Florence, fulfilling Savonarola's awful prophecy of calamity. When Lorenzo's son surrendered the city to him, the furious Florentines ordered all the Medici out of town. Young Piero de Medici fled to Rome with his brothers, Giuliano and Giovanni (the future Pope Leo X, who was disguised as a friar). As Charles marched south from Florence to conquer other parts of Italy, Savonarola (who had wiled his way into the king's favor) held the terrified citizens in the palm of his hand, filling the vacuum of power by becoming the city's new ruler.

For four years the friar and his bands of armed disciples controlled Florence. He issued decrees calling for continual fasting and demanding the removal of all art treasures from the churches. He appointed squads ("Blessed Bands") of children, who spied on their parents and patrolled the streets, rebuking over-dressed women and denouncing gambling. In a huge "Bonfire of the Vanities" in the Piazza della Signoria, Savonarola's followers burned all the non-religious paintings they could find, as well as fancy clothing and ornaments, wigs and false beards, mirrors, pots of rouge, musical instruments, and classical books. Of course, there were some who opposed all this. Gangs of young dissenters, the *Arrabbiati* (the Angry) once snuck into the cathedral and filled the friar's pulpit with cow dung!

Savonarola believed that he could make Florence so holy that its example of piety would spread to the rest of Italy. Pope Alexander VI became alarmed by his excesses and excommunicated him for his fanatical behavior, but Savonarola ignored the papal bulls (written orders) and denounced the pontiff as an agent of Satan! He went on to criticize the immorality of the Pope (he had good reason to do so, as we will see), and predicted the ultimate punishment of the Catholic Church for the sinful acts of its leaders.

After four years, the Florentines grew weary of the friar's narrow-minded views and puritanical teachings. When the Pope placed the city under an interdict in an effort to shackle Savonarola (no church services could take place), a mob dragged the friar from his headquarters at San Marco. He was tried and condemned by a local court. On May 23, 1498 he was hanged for heresy in the Piazza della Signoria, near the site of his famous Bonfire of the Vanities. His body was then burned.

Early in the sixteenth century the Medici returned to Florence. But things would never be the same as before. They established a dynasty of dukes, who no longer made any effort to hide the fact that they ruled the city. The old spirit of optimism and experimentation that had nurtured Florence's golden age was gone, and the torch of creativity was passed on to Rome.

REVIEW QUESTIONS:

1. Why were banks so important to the cloth merchants?

2. How did Cosimo differ from his father?

3. How is humanism reflected in the statues of Donatello?

4. What was the major technique that allowed Brunelleschi to construct the dome?

5. What is linear perspective?

6. How was Masaccio influenced by Donatello and Brunelleschi?

7. List three adjectives that describe the wealthy merchants of fifteenth century Florence.

8. How did Lorenzo deal with the men involved in the Pazzi conspiracy?

9. Why was Lorenzo called "the Magnificent." (Give your own opinion.)

10. How did Botticelli's paintings differ from the other Renaissance works we have studied?

11. What was Savonarola's Bonfire of the Vanities?

12. How was the rule of the returning Medici different than that of Cosimo and Lorenzo?

FURTHERMORE:

1. The insignia of the Medici family was a cluster of red balls on a gold background. Its origins are a mystery. Some scholars believe that if the early Medici were pharmacists (as their name implies) the balls must represent pills. Others say that the circles are in fact benzants, coins from Byzantium (the same as appeared on the coat of arms of the Guild of Moneychangers to which the Medici belonged). But there is also the legend that the family was descended from Averardo, a brave knight who fought for Charlemagne. He had passed through Tuscany on his way to Rome and near Florence had come upon a savage giant, the terror of the poor peasants of the region. Averardo fought and killed the monster. During the fight

Figure 24: The Medici Insignia

his shield received several massive blows from the giant's mace. Charlemagne had rewarded Averardo's bravery by allowing him to commemorate his victory by representing the dents on his coat-of-arms by red balls (*palle*) on a field of gold.

2. The wonderful frescoes of the Brancacci Chapel have narrowly escaped destruction. In 1680 the Marchese Francesco Ferroni tried to take over the patronage of the chapel and ordered his men to "get rid of these ridiculous men in their cassocks and old-fashioned outfits." Grand Duchess Vittoria della Rovera prevented their removal. Then in 1771 a fire burned down most of the church, but fortunately the chapel survived.

3. Muzio Sforza of Milan won the name *sforza* (force) for his brave deeds. He later drowned while helping a page cross a stream just before a battle. His son, Francesco, carried on his military tradition and became one of the greatest of the condottieri. He married Bianca Maria Visconti, daughter of the last Visconti duke, and made himself Duke of Milan. (We've learned recently that he was supported by Cosimo de Medici.) His wife was as brave as he was. While he was away fighting a campaign, she led a band of soldiers to attack a rebellious town rather than send for her husband's help. With her at his side, Francesco ruled Milan for sixteen years.

Their son, Galeazzo Maria Sforza (1444-76), was taught by the finest humanists to be a perfect Renaissance prince. He learned to sing in French, to write in Latin, to read Greek, to play the organ and the clavichord, to dance, and to deliver lengthy classical speeches before the court. In 1466 he succeeded his father, and to everyone's surprise he told all humanists at court to leave, returned his Latin books to the library, and set about leading a life of debauchery. Three of his own courtiers murdered him a decade later. Francesco's second son, Ludovico (called *Il Moro* because of his swarthy complexion), had a magnificent Renaissance court, where he patronized some of the greatest artists of the time. What a family!

4. Carnival was a festival celebrated by all classes of society in the towns and cities of Italy. Everyone put on masks and pretended to be someone else, and the crowds filled the streets to dance, drink, sing, and eat "carnivorously" (hence the term "carnival"). In the time of Lorenzo the Magnificent the Florentine Carnival was noted for its extravagant spectacles, parades, and processions. Lorenzo even wrote music for some of the events.

PROJECTS:

1. Write an essay comparing Cosimo de Medici to Augustus of ancient Rome.

2. Two Medici women became queens of France. Catherine married Henry II, and was mother of three French kings. Marie married Henry IV, and was mother of Louis XIII. Two Medici men became popes: Leo X and Clement VII. Choose one of these famous family members and write a report.

3. The Platonic Academy was inspired by Plato's Academy, which was established in Athens in the fourth century BC. Find out more about this early gathering spot for scholars. Then do some research on the Platonic Academy. Think about what you've learned. Now write a short report, comparing the two academies.

4. Donatello perfected the bronze casting technique. Find out the various steps in-

volved in casting a statue in bronze. Then make a poster or graphic design to illustrate them.

5. Verrochio was a master sculptor in his own right. One of his greatest works was his bronze statue of David. Consult an art book and find an illustration of the statue. Then write a paragraph or two comparing it to Donatello's DAVID.

6. The Medici family was engaged in Florentine politics for a long time. Consult a book about them. Then, on a piece of poster board, draw their family tree.

7. Find a book containing a large illustration of Botticelli's *LA PRIMAVERA*. Read the commentary. You might want to check other sources as well. Then, using the illustration, identify the figures in the painting and explain what they symbolize.

8. Botticelli wasn't the only artist to depict the Medici in a religious painting. In 1459 Benozzo Gozzoli began the frescoes of the chapel in the Medici palazzo in Florence. Lorenzo and Cosimo are among the figures (Lorenzo appearing as the youngest of the three Magi). Gozzoli also included a self-portrait and signed his work by means of the inscription on his cap. Look in the art books available to you and find the two paintings of the Medici depicted as Magi. (Botticelli's ADORATION OF THE MAGI and Gozzoli's PROCESSION OF THE MAGI). Study the two paintings. What are the differences and similarities? Write a short report discussing your findings.

9. Paolo Ucello loved perspective. Find out more about this Italian painter and write a short report. (Be sure to include xeroxed copies of some of his works as illustrations.)

CHAPTER V
THE HIGH RENAISSANCE

In the mid-sixteenth century, Italian painter and architect Giorgio Vasari wrote a monumental book, entitled THE LIVES OF THE MOST IMMINENT ITALIAN ARCHITECTS, PAINTERS AND SCULPTORS. Modeled upon ancient Greek and Roman biographies of famous men, Vasari's LIVES was carefully researched and included his own critical judgments. This was the first major work to concentrate exclusively on the history of art, and, despite a number of inaccuracies, it became the standard reference on the Italian Renaissance for the next two centuries.

The whole concept of the *renaissance* (rebirth) of art was invented by Vasari. He divided the evolution of this rebirth into three stages corresponding to the childhood, youth, and maturity of a human being. Vasari believed that art was reborn in Italy in the late thirteenth century, when the Pisani and Giotto broke away from the Middle Ages and ushered in the "good modern manner." (He wrote, "...painters owe a debt to Giotto...the same debt they owe to nature." Can you explain what that means?) The works of Donatello, Brunelleschi, and Masaccio represented the youth of the revival of western art, and the great artists of the sixteenth century brought it to its maturity, its "Golden Age." At last, Vasari marveled, the works of Leonardo da Vinci, Michelangelo, Raphael, and Titian reached a state of perfection that exceeded the models of classical antiquity.

Vasari's Golden Age of Italian art is known to modern scholars as the High Renaissance. It was during this exciting period that the innovations of the earlier masters we have been studying found their fullest expression. While admiring the harmony, grace, and balance of ancient art, the artists of the High Renaissance went far beyond copying the works of the past. What began as an attempt to represent the physical world as realistically as possible evolved into a belief that nature could, and even should, be improved upon by the imagination and talents of the artist. The paintings and statues of the High Renaissance depict handsome, idealized men and women who embody the elegance and refinement of the age. While the figures of Masaccio tend to be standing or sitting quietly, those of the new generation of artists move freely, often straining every muscle. By this time, competence in such techniques as linear perspective and chiaroscuro was taken for granted. Art had certainly come a long way since the Middle Ages, when its main function was to tell a biblical story. Now it was not the end (purpose) but the means (method) that counted, and a fine painting was valued simply for what it was, not what it meant. Strangely enough, some of the greatest works of western civilization were created in Italy during a time when the cities were being torn apart by a long series of wars, epidemics, and religious crises, as well as the usual political squabbles. We'll learn about these disruptive events in a later chapter.

LEONARDO DA VINCI

Vasari began his section on the Golden Age in THE LIVES with Leonardo da Vinci (1452-1519), describing him as a divinely endowed genius who ranks among the angels. Leonardo was born near the small hamlet of Vinci, east of Florence. He had little formal education and spent much of his childhood frolicking in the wooded hillsides of Tuscany. At the age of seventeen he began an apprenticeship in the workshop of painter Andrea del Verrocchio, one of the bright stars of Lorenzo's court.

Verocchio was a goldsmith, engineer, and sculptor as well as a painter. He instructed Leonardo to carefully observe the tiniest details of nature and to include them in his paintings. However, it was Giotto and Masaccio who inspired the young apprentice to paint lifelike figures. According to legend, Verrocchio once asked Leonardo to add an angel to a painting he was working on (THE BAPTISM OF CHRIST). Leonardo obliged and created a figure that was so realistic and emotionally appealing that Verrocchio decided to give up painting and concentrate on sculpture for the rest of his career! (Does this remind you of Brunelleschi?)

In 1472 Leonardo became a master painter in the Guild of Saint Luke. (Saint Luke was the patron saint of painters.) He experimented with new techniques to create the illusion of the third dimension (depth or perspective) and discovered that he could make objects appear to recede into the distance simply by diminishing the degree of detail and the intensity of color. In many of his paintings, objects in the distance appear in shades of blue. He dabbled with chiaroscuro and tried softening the edges of the images in a painting so that the colors and tones gradually shifted from light to dark without clear cut demarcations. This technique, known as *sfumato*, made the figures seem to emerge from the background. He observed that shadows come in colors; artists traditionally painted all shadows grey, but Leonardo painted a shadow on snow blue, one in the grass dark green, and general cases simply painted the shadow a darker shade than the object itself. These various techniques helped Leonardo to create scenes that were so believable that Vasari claimed he had "endowed his figures with motion and breath."

Unlike the earlier artists we have studied, Leonardo usually used oil paints. The idea of mixing powdered pigments with oil to make paint was not new: artists in ancient Greece, Rome and Byzantium used vegetable oils to dilute their paints, but the concept had been forgotten until Flemish artists began mixing the powders with linseed oil. The old tempera pigments were gradually abandoned by most Italian artists after 1470, when Antonello da Messina brought the new medium of oils to Venice. A major advantage of oil paint is that it dries more slowly than tempera, giving the artist more time to work on small details. (Remember how quickly the egg yolk in tempera dried?) Colors could be blended right on the panel, and this produced a continuous scale of hues that included rich, velvety dark shades never seen in a fresco. Oils enabled the artist to create a wide range of visual sensations - the glitter of gold, the sheen of silk or satin, the deep pile of fur, the sparkle of jewels, the softness of velvet, the delicacy of lace, and even the wrinkles and blemishes of the human face. Different thicknesses, varying from a thin, translucent film (known as a glaze) to the thickest material (called impasto) could be applied to make objects appear to stand out or recede into the background.

THE ADORATION OF THE MAGI (this was certainly a popular theme) was Leonardo's first large group painting. Although this unfinished panel contains only the underdrawing (like a cartoon), it shows us that, from the beginning, Leonardo applied principles of mathematics and geometry to the planning of his works. The figures in this painting are arranged among deep shadows in a pyramid shape so that our eyes are drawn to the principal subject, the Holy Child. The figures in the "Christmas scene" were traditionally painted in profile, with Mary and the Child on one side of the picture and the kings on the other. Leonardo's subjects look directly at you, making them more interesting and the drama of the moment more compelling. Leonardo frequently left his paintings unfinished, as he did with this one. He had an extremely curious mind, as we will soon see, and he often dropped one project when a new challenge appeared. Of those paintings he completed only twelve have survived.

At the age of thirty, Leonardo went to Milan to work for Ludovico (*Il Moro*) Sforza. Ludovico was descended from Francesco Sforza, the condottiere who had seized power from the Visconti. (Lorenzo de Medici, as you will recall, helped Francesco gain power in Milan.) Because Ludovico's authority depended upon his army, Leonardo recommended himself for a position in his court by drawing plans for collapsible bridges, machines for draining trenches, siege equipment, armored cars, and multi-barreled guns (ancestors of the modern machine gun). As an afterthought, he briefly described his peacetime activities - architecture, sculpting, and painting! He got the job and spent seventeen years in Milan. Much of his time was devoted to designing costumes, scenery, and revolving stages for court plays. However, he did paint a portrait of Ludovico's young mistress (LADY WITH AN ERMINE) and the famous MADONNA OF THE ROCKS, both of which are excellent examples of his use of sfumato.

In 1495 he began his masterpiece, THE LAST SUPPER - a fresco decorating the wall of the refectory (dining hall) of the monastery of Santa Maria delle Grazie. With a masterful blending of light and shadow, he dramatized the twelve disciples' reaction to Christ's startling announcement, at a Passover feast, that one of them would betray him. Each man responds in a different way. Judas, the culprit, guiltily leans away into the shadows. Leonardo often used gesture to reflect inner feelings, having noted that "painted figures ought to be done in such a way that those who see them will be able to easily recognize from their attitudes the thoughts of their minds." His mathematical approach to design is reflected in the way the disciples are arranged in neat divisions of two groups of six, each group subdivided in half. In earlier paintings of this subject, the disciples simply sat in a long line behind the table, with Christ in the center. Leonardo's groupings are much more natural. (Think about it. At a large family dinner, do we all sit in a row behind the table and stare straight ahead? Of course not! Each person interacts with the relatives seated nearby.)

Leonardo worked long hours on THE LAST SUPPER, often forgetting to eat. He frequently walked the streets of Milan, looking for faces upon which to model the disciples. Some days he did no painting at all. The prior of the monastery complained that he would come in, stare at the fresco for two hours, make six brush strokes and leave. Reacting to this criticism, Leonardo remarked that he was having difficulty visualizing the face of Judas, but if the prior was in a great hurry, his own (the prior's) face would do very well!

He was always experimenting with materials. Wishing to work more slowly on the fresco than wet plaster and tempera would allow, he applied a solution of tempera mixed with oil to dry plaster. The results were disastrous. Almost immediately the paint started to peel. Today, after repeated attempts at restoration, THE LAST SUPPER survives only as a magnificent ruin.

While in Milan Leonardo designed a bronze equestrian statue of Ludovico's father, Francesco. (Do you remember who made the first Renaissance equestrian statue?) This was to be the largest bronze statue ever made, but after six years he had produced only a huge clay model of the horse. When the French invaded Milan (more about this in a later chapter), the many tons of bronze that had been put aside for the statue were snatched away by the government and used to make guns. Adding insult to injury, French archers used the clay model for target practice and totally destroyed it!

Returning to Florence after the French invasion, Leonardo began work on his portrait of *MONA LISA* (MY LADY LISA). This is probably the most famous painting in the world today. According to Vasari, Lisa (del Giacondo) was the wife of a Florentine nobleman. Leonardo wanted to avoid the melancholic look so often seen in the portraits of his day, so he hired musicians and buffoons to entertain Lisa and make her smile. (Actually, perhaps from shyness, she only offered the mysterious half smile that has made her so famous.) He painted more of her torso than was customary in portraits (a painting usually included only the face and upper chest), and he arranged her folded hands in such a way that, once again, he had formed a pyramid drawing our attention to the focal point, her face. Leonardo's mastery of sfumato and chiaroscuro make Lisa appear to be moving out of the darkness. This painting was a personal favorite of the artist. He kept it with him wherever he lived, and it was at his bedside when he died. Today it is displayed in the Louvre Museum in Paris. As you you enter the room, the lady seems to follow you with her eyes, quietly laughing to herself.

Leonardo wanted to understand everything he could about the natural world so that his art would be as "real" as possible. He was constantly asking himself questions. Why were sea shells found in the mountains? How were the locks in Flanders designed? What causes cracks in walls? What is the origin of clouds and wind? How does a body function? By studying the smallest structural details of an object, he believed that he could learn how it functioned. He was fascinated by the flight of birds. Although he was a vegetarian, he often went to the town market to buy live birds. He set them loose in a closed room and studied their movements. When he was done, he set them free.

He dissected over thirty corpses to better understand human anatomy (until Pope Leo X barred him from the mortuary in Rome). Once, having discovered a centenarian (a hundred-year-old man) in a hospital in Florence, he patiently awaited the old man's demise so that he could examine his ancient veins. Leonardo made detailed drawings showing the make-up of bones, tendons, and muscles, and he accurately explained their functions. He considered the human body to be the ultimate machine, and he used it as a model for many mechanical devices. For example, he analyzed the tendons of the hand to design a keyboard and the upper larynx to make a musical recorder. He was fascinated by deformities as much as by beauty. He once got a band of peasants drunk so he could sketch their glassy-eyed facial expressions!

Leonardo recorded most of his observations in a series of 116 notebooks, which he planned to be the basis of an encyclopedic work about nature. Over 7,000 pages of the voluminous books still exist. (Two notebooks were discovered as recently as 1965.) They are written in a peculiar right-to-left script, which must be read using a mirror. Scattered among the descriptions are sketches and preliminary drawings of many of his paintings as well as mathematical puzzles, the detailed studies of bones, muscles, and wings we have just learned about, and drawings of such inventions as diving helmets, musical instruments, a life jacket, a parachute, and the lock gates for a canal. There are also designs of all sorts of machines: a military tank, a human powered flying machine, ball-bearing mechanisms, steam cannons, machine guns, a mechanical digger, steam engines, a car powered by springs, and cranes.

Many of Leonardo's machines would never have worked in practice, but his ideas were far more advanced and imaginative than those of his contemporaries. Some of his projects had great potential: his flying machine was a prototype for our modern hang glider. He also proposed that the sun does not move, a radical view in those days when leading scientists (and the Church) insisted that the sun revolves around the earth. Few people took this idea seriously. Later in the century, Copernicus would come to the same conclusion and stir up a great deal of controversy. But that time had not yet come. Because Leonardo routinely performed experiments to find out why things happened, he is regarded by many as the founder of modern science. He proudly signed one collection of his writings, "Leonardo, disciple of experiment."

This artistic and scientific genius spent his last years working at the French court of Francis I, arranging fireworks displays and designing clever devices for pageants and parades. He made a mechanical lion for the king that took a few steps forward and then opened its breast to reveal a mass of white lilies, the symbol of France. It is a sad commentary that the finest mind of his age was reduced to making gadgets for bored courtiers. Leonardo's talents were appreciated by only a handful of his contemporar-

ies, and when he died, his notebooks lay forgotten in an attic. It was not until Vasari's book appeared fifty years later that he was acknowledged as one of the greatest men who ever lived.

THE RESTORATION OF PAPAL AUTHORITY

Do you remember the Great Schism of the Church when there were two popes - one in Rome and one in Avignon, France? After the Papacy was restored in Rome in 1417, Pope Martin V took the first steps toward strengthening the authority and dignity of the Catholic Church. By the end of his term he had wrestled control of the Papal States from the local nobility and begun the clean-up of the city of Rome. Two decades later, a group of rebellious barons drove Martin's successor, Pope Eugene IV, from Rome. (He fled down the Tiber River in a rowboat, disguised as a monk.) The Pope found refuge in the Florence of Cosimo de Medici, and that city became his headquarters for nine years.

Eugene was mightily impressed by the ideas and accomplishments of the humanists he encountered in Florence, and when he finally returned to Rome, he invited Donatello and several others to accompany him. He also employed Flavio Biondo, a historian and archaeologist, as papal secretary. Biondi catalogued the surviving monuments of ancient Rome in three encyclopedic volumes, and, using relics, inscriptions, and early chronicles, he wrote lively descriptions of the manners and customs of Imperial Rome. His works encouraged the development of chorography (the study of local history from surviving remains). After Biondo's efforts, generations of excavators engaged by succeeding popes would unearth all sorts of fascinating ancient ruins and artifacts.

In 1447 a humanist scholar named Tommaso Parentucelli was elected Pope Nicholas V. He was a highly motivated and energetic little man who loved books. As an impoverished monk he had gone into debt collecting the works of classical writers. He once advised Cosimo de Medici on texts to obtain for his expanding library. Nicholas was convinced that the values and ideals of the ancients could pump fresh life into Christianity, so he hired dozens of scholars to copy classical texts, while his agents scoured Europe in pursuit of rare volumes. His collection of 9,000 books and manuscripts (all bound in red velvet with silver clasps) formed the nucleus of the Vatican Library. It would become the greatest library in the western world.

Nicholas was the first pope to envision a revival of the grandeur of ancient Rome. He set in motion a major restoration of the decaying city, ordering the streets to be repaired and the worst slums to be demolished. He consulted Alberti for the reconstruction of the city's crumbling bridges and aqueducts, and he had the foundations laid for a new papal palace on Vatican Hill. Nicholas held a jubilee in Rome in 1450 to attract pilgrims to visit the city. (Their offerings would enrich his building fund.) Over 100,000 people came, and so many crowded on to the main bridge across the Tiber River that it collapsed! Unfortunately, much of the revival of Rome led to the progressive destruction of the ancient ruins, as temples and other structures were looted for their stone. Workmen removed over 2,000 wagonloads of marble from the famous Colosseum in a single year. They also quarried the fine stone from the Circus Maxiums, the Forum, the Arch of Titus, and the Temple of Venus.

During the rule of Nicholas, the Ottoman Turks overthrew Constantinople (in 1453), an act the Pope considered to be as much a blow to scholarship as to religion. As it turned out he was wrong, since scholars fleeing from the Byzantine capital would dramatically enrich the humanist movement in the West.

Sixtus IV came to power in 1471. Another scholarly theologian, he donated over 1,000 Greek and Latin manuscripts to the Vatican Library (which he opened to all interested scholars). He improved everyday life in Rome by constructing many more new roads and bridges, and by having the ancient pipes and aqueducts cleaned and restored to a functioning state, thus providing an abundant supply of cold, clear water. He built the Sistine Chapel, which he named after himself. Its proportions are the same as those of Solomon's Temple described in the Book of Kings in the Bible. Sixtus also established the Sistine choir, which would help to make Rome a center of sacred music.

Not all of the Pope's activities were admirable, however. He placed many of his relatives in high positions of the Church. (He made five nephews and one grandnephew cardinals.) The practice of basing appointments upon family connections is known as nepotism. It is never a popular practice, since the appointees are not necessarily qualified for the position. This was certainly true with the Pope's nephews, and his appointments led to a great deal of opposition among the other clergy, as well as among the ordinary parishioners. Sixtus even made his uneducated twenty-year-old servant the Bishop of Parma. He was the Pope who supported the Pazzi Conspiracy against Lorenzo the Magnificent, basically because it was in the best business interest of his family.

In 1492 Pope Calixtus III followed Sixtus' example and promoted his ambitious and self-serving nephew, Rodrigo Borgia (a Spaniard), to a high position in the Church.

Borgia later became Pope Alexander VI by bribing the cardinals to vote for him. He then spent much of his time promoting the interests of his family (he had several illegitimate children). He married his daughter, Lucrezia, to three of Italy's rulers, (One at a time!), and supported the efforts of his son, Cesare, to carve out a kingdom of his own among the Papal States. We'll learn more about Alexander's famous offspring later in our story.

JULIUS II AND LEO X GLORIFY ROME

By the dawn of the sixteenth century, the population of Rome had expanded to 100,000. Julius II, a nephew of Sixtus IV, became Pope in 1503. (Yet another example of nepotism!) He was a clever politician and a fine soldier, who personally led his armies into battle to protect the Papal States from invaders and to restore the Papacy's temporal (political) power. (His military campaigns earned him the nickname, "the warrior pope.") Believe it or not, he was sixty when he first wore the papal mantle. Julius allegedly vowed not to shave until he managed to rid Italy of all usurpers. His portraits reveal that he always had a long beard.

In 1508 Julius began an ambitious plan to beautify Rome as a means of glorifying his own image. He convinced wealthy citizens to build impressive palaces, churches, and public buildings by promising them tremendous tax concessions. When portions of the city were excavated to make room for new structures, a large number of ancient Roman artifacts were unearthed. These were gathered to form the papal collection of antique sculpture, to which Julius added the now famous APOLLO BELVEDERE and THE LAOCOÖN statues. The APOLLO, a Roman copy of a Greek statue of the Olympian god, was made in the fourth century and discovered in his family vineyard when Julius was still a cardinal. THE LAOCOÖN, a Greek statue of a Trojan priest and his sons struggling with two snakes, was made in the first century BC. It was discovered in 1506 in another vineyard near the ancient Baths of Trajan in Rome. These two highly realistic ancient statues strongly influenced the artists who came to Rome to view them.

Julius chose architect Donato Bramante to direct his vast building program. Trained as a painter, Bramante had turned to architecture at the Milanese court of Ludovico Sforza. He was there at the same time as Leonardo and shared his interest in geometric patterns. From the beginning, Bramante's buildings reflect his enchantment with the harmonious proportions of

Figure 25: The Tempietto

classical design. His first major work in Rome was the *Tempietto* (little temple), a small domed structure built on the spot where Saint Peter was crucified. It was the first Renaissance building to imitate the form of a circular ancient temple, and it became a prototype for sixteenth century church design.

Bramante's first commission for Julius was a series of classically inspired courtyards and galleries connecting the old Belvedere Palace of Pope Innocent VIII with the buildings of the Vatican Palace. He designed a wide spiral staircase within the tower that serves as an entrance to the papal palace. It could be ridden up on horseback in case of emergency. Because Bramante used marble from the local ancient ruins, he came to be known by many as "Ruinante!"

All this building activity inspired Julius to replace the old church of Saint Peter, which now seemed too dilapidated and old-fashioned for the times. The church had originally been constructed in 325 by Roman Emperor Constantine on the site of the alleged grave of Saint Peter. Bramante was commissioned to design the new church. The foundation stone was laid in 1506.

Bramante's design was based upon a Greek cross. (Because the four arms of the Greek cross were of equal length, architects considered it an ideal form.) A major dome was to be built over the center, with minor domes and bell towers at the ends of the four arms. (If this reminds you of the Byzantine churches, you have an excellent memory!) Unfortunately, the death of Julius in 1513 and that of Bramante the following year prevented the work from progressing much beyond the planning stage. But it was a start. The rebuilding of Saint Peter's would occupy ten architects for a period of 120 years. When completed, it would be the largest church in the Christian world.

Pope Leo X was the second son of Lorenzo the Magnificent. He was educated by humanist scholars and made a cardinal when he was eighteen. (It was Leo who escaped from Florence with his brothers, when the city was attacked by the French.) He was a bull-necked, pop-eyed, red-faced, fat man. But although he lacked the charm of Julius and Alexander, he was quite sophisticated in his tastes, as you might expect from Lorenzo's offspring. When he became Pope at the age of thirty-seven, Leo allegedly told a friend, "Let us enjoy the Papacy." His goal was to duplicate the glittering court of his father in the Vatican Palace, but on a far grander scale.

Leo patronized a wide circle of artists, scholars, and musicians, and he continued Julius' pet project - the construction of Saint Peter's. He spent so much on building new structures and tearing down old medieval ones in Rome that he nearly emptied the papal treasury. Fortunately, unlike his predecessors, he tried to preserve the ancient ruins. Leo loved to read, and he accumulated great numbers of books and manuscripts, which he added to the Vatican Library. He also set up a Greek school and expanded the university in Rome until it had more than 100 teachers. The most significant event of Leo's papacy was Martin Luther's attack on the Roman Catholic Church. We'll learn more about this in Chapter IX.

MICHELANGELO

Let's return to Julius II. Some people remember him only as the patron of Michelangelo Buonarroti (1475-1564), a Florentine sculptor, painter, poet, and architect. Vasari described Michelangelo as the genius "who surpasses them all" (even Leonardo). Many modern art critics also view him as the supreme Renaissance artist. He was fascinated by the beauty and strength of the human body, which he believed to reflect the nobility of the human spirit. His art is not just an imitation of nature but an idealized, deeply personal vision of mankind.

Michelangelo was apprenticed to the highly respected painter, Domenico Ghirlandaio, and he later attended the art school established by Lorenzo de Medici. There he studied ancient sculptures under the guidance of the aged Bertaldo di Giovanni (Donatello's former pupil). The young artist was a perfectionist, and he often denigrated the work of Pietro Torrigiano, a fellow student in Lorenzo's school. On one occasion, Pietro become so enraged by the constant criticism that he broke his tormentor's nose!

Michelangelo's father, a wealthy man, had at first opposed his becoming an artist. Although the works of painters and sculptors were greatly admired in the fifteenth century, no member of the upper classes wanted his son to enter the trade. Fortunately, Lorenzo stepped in and convinced the elder Buonarroti to give his son a chance. In the years that followed, the status of the artist in society would dramatically improve.

There is a legend about Lorenzo coming upon Michelangelo in the villa garden as he was carving a statue. He asked what it was and was told it was "an old faun." (A faun is a Roman mythological figure that is half man and half goat.) Lorenzo then remarked that it didn't look old because its teeth were too good. Without thinking twice, the young sculptor knocked out one of the faun's front teeth with his chisel! Lorenzo was as amused by this irreverent act as he was impressed by the quality of the statue, so he invited the lad to move into his villa as a member of his household. Thus, at the age of only fourteen, Michelangelo found himself at the center of the Italian art world. He remained there for four years, polishing his artistic skills while mingling with some of the leading poets, artists, and philosophers of the day.

When Lorenzo died Michelangelo returned home, only to be unsettled by the teachings of Savonarola and worried about the friar's prophecy of impending doom. Unlike the humanists, who celebrated the power and potential of mankind, Michelangelo viewed man as a lonely and unhappy creature, the victim of circumstances beyond his control. This pessimistic attitude was a product of the artist's introspective temperament. Unlike the sociable and outgoing Leonardo da Vinci, Michelangelo was a brooding fellow, never content to rely upon others because he believed that he could do everything better himself. Often he did not complete a project because it was too ambitious and he was unwilling to ask for help.

While living in Florence, he found a way to study human anatomy. He made a deal with the prior of the local monastery of Santo Spirito, agreeing to carve a wooden crucifix for the church if he could dissect corpses in the abbey's cloisters. The knowledge of the muscles, bones, and organs of the body he obtained from these dissections would help him to create extremely realistic figures. He later traveled to Venice and then to Bologna, where he spent a year as the guest of a nobleman. His host introduced him to the works of Dante, Petrarch, and Boccaccio, and even encouraged him to write poetry.

In 1498 Michelangelo was commissioned by a cardinal in Rome to carve THE PIETA, a sculpture of the Virgin Mary cradling the dead body of her son, Christ, after it was taken down from the cross. Look at an illustration of this statue. The life-like figures show how much the sculptor had learned about human anatomy. The limpness of Christ's body is emphasized by the gentle folds of his mother's drapery. The pyramid shape of the two figures draws our attention to the apex - the face of Mary. (Leonardo, of course, had accomplished the same thing with a paintbrush.) Can you sense the tenderness and sadness in her youthful face? Unlike other artists, Michelangelo believed that the Virgin should appear as a young mother. When criticized about this, he replied that Mary's purity had protected her from the effects of aging. Besides, he remembered his own mother, who had died young. Mary raises her left hand. Does this express her resignation or her questioning of her son's terrible fate?

THE PIETA is the only work Michelangelo ever signed. According to legend, he once overheard a nobleman remark that such a young sculptor could never have created such a marvelous piece of art. That night he carved his name on the stone to prove that he had! During this early period Michelangelo also carved a larger-than-life statue of Bacchus, the Roman god of wine. The drunken face and swaying pose of the young god create a sensation worlds apart from the grief expressed in THE PIETA.

One of Michelangelo's major challenges came from the directors of the Duomo in Florence. In 1501 they commissioned him to carve a monumental statue of the biblical hero, David. The dimensions of the statue were dictated by a massive, but shallow, block of pure white marble quarried in 1466. A figure of a giant had been chiseled out of the block by a second-rate sculptor, botched, and then abandoned. Imagine how difficult it must have been to carve something original out of someone else's figure. If he succeeded, Michelangelo's statue would be fourteen feet high, the largest free-standing marble statue since classical times.

He took on the project enthusiastically, and when he finished, Vasari proclaimed that he had "worked a miracle in restoring to life something that had been left for dead." DAVID stands defiantly with his sling over his shoulder, determined to defeat the formidable giant, Goliath. He appears calm (standing in contrapposto position), yet his muscles ripple and his veins pulse with tension. The statue is a hymn to Michelangelo's vision of the beauty, grace, and controlled strength of a great hero. It was such a hit in Florence that it was installed in front of the Palazzo della Signoria, where it represented the fiercely independent spirit of Florence. Vasari's final comment on the statue was succinct: "Anyone who has seen Michelangelo's DAVID has no need to see anything else by any other sculptor, living or dead."

Figure 26: Michelangelo's David

In 1505 Julius II asked Michelangelo to paint the ceiling of the Sistine Chapel with a pictorial cycle of biblical history, from the creation of Adam to the coming of Moses. It would be the artist's greatest achievement. Working alone, he spent four and a half years painting a huge tableau of his own design. Vasari wrote that he labored in great discomfort, "having to work with his face looking upwards, which impaired his sight so badly that he could not read or look at drawings save with his head turned backwards."

The ceiling posed an enormous challenge. To cover its vast expanse, he laid out an imposing, powerful structure of imaginary architecture and then filled its sections with 340 figures in nine scenes from Genesis and twelve from the New Testament. Gigantic likenesses of Old Testament prophets and ancient sibyls (female seers) sit upon thrones around the edges and between the scenes. They are included because they had prophesied the birth of Christ. Scholars believe that the prophet Moses is a portrait of Julius. The focal point of the tableau is the CREATION OF ADAM, in which the contact of fingers symbolizes God's gift of life to the reclining figure of the first man. Michelangelo constantly complained as he worked on the ceiling that he was a sculptor, not a painter. So be it. The figures of the vast fresco are so solid-looking and realistic that they seem to have been carved out of paint.

The major work of his later years was THE LAST JUDGMENT on the altar wall of the Sistine Chapel. Julius had suggested that Michelangelo decorate the wall after completing the ceiling, but nothing more came of it. One of his successors, Paul III, commissioned the artist to take on the task. It was another huge area (covering 1,800 square feet), the largest ever tackled for a single work without any kind of subdivid-ing framework (as was the case on the ceiling). Once again, Michelangelo took on the challenge, and when the fresco was unveiled in 1541 the Pope fell to his knees in awe.

Michelangelo had created a swirling motion of activity around the central figure of Christ. In the lower left the dead are torn from their graves and carried by wingless angels toward the center to be judged by Christ. The righteous continue upward to join the ranks of the blessed in heaven, while the contorted bodies of the damned are hurled below, their faces filled with anguish and despair as they contemplate the horrible fate that awaits them in hell. Several pathetic sinners are knocked out of Charon's boat with the angry blow of an oar. (In Greek mythology Charon was the ferryman who transported the spirits of the dead across the River Styx.) Once again we have an interesting mingling of pagan and Christian traditions. Christ himself is depicted as young and vigorous, resembling the classical god Apollo, half rising from his seat to separate the just from the fallen. He is flanked by the Virgin Mary and the martyred saints. Michelangelo's self-portrait can be seen in the skin held by Saint Bartholomew (who was flayed alive).

This fearsome vision of the Final Judgment provoked instant controversy. Much of the criticism was focused upon the nudity of the vast majority of the figures. (This was considered unsuitable for a religious subject.) While the work was still in progress one critic had complained that the figures were "better suited to the baths and taverns than among the heavenly chorus." Michelangelo responded by painting the face of the critic on his figure of the donkey-eared Midas, the mythical Greek king who appears as the judge in hell! Others objected that Christ was beardless and seemed too young. The next Pope, Paul IV, urged

Michelangelo to "tidy up" the fresco, to which the artist replied that the Pope should first tidy up the world and the painting would follow suit! Shortly before Michelangelo's death, a second-rate painter named Daniele da Volterra would be commissioned to provide draperies for the principal nudes. (This earned him the nickname *Braghettone* - "breeches maker"). Even more clothing was painted on in later centuries. These attempts to add respectability harmed much of Michelangelo's painting and made recent attempts to restore it difficult.

While working on THE LAST JUDGMENT, Michelangelo had time to sculpt a bust of BRUTUS, the leader of a conspiracy that killed Julius Caesar. (Brutus, you may recall, was one of the three villains of history whom Dante assigned to the jaws of Satan.) Michelangelo's portrait of the perfidious traitor (Caesar had treated him like a son) was inspired by the imperial busts of ancient Rome. Many consider BRUTUS to be an idealized portrait of Lorenzino de Medici, who killed his cousin, the Duke Alessandro, in 1537, attracting all the anti-Medici sympathizers of Florence to his side. Like many of Michelangelo's other statues, this one was left unfinished. (Another sculptor, Tiberio Calcagni, later carved the drapery and finished the neck and chin.)

In 1535 Michelangelo was appointed chief painter, sculptor, and architect of the Vatican Palace. He devoted his final years to the construction of Saint Peter's Cathedral. Bramante had designed a dome that was considered too massive and heavy. Michelangelo studied Brunelleschi's dome in Florence and then designed a taller, more pointed version. Like Brunelleschi's dome, his would have a double shell. The ribbed inner shell would be made of wood and the outer shell would consist of wood and lead. The structure would rise 435 feet.

Michelangelo died in 1564 at the age of eighty-eight before the dome was built. It was completed in 1590 by architect Giacomo della Porta, who carefully followed Michelangelo's sketches. The artist's body was buried in the church of Santa Croce in Florence. Duke Cosimo de Medici I donated marble for a monument, which was designed by Vasari and sculpted by Battista Lorenzi. Beneath a bust of Michelangelo are three statues, representing Painting, Sculpture, and Architecture. They sit eternally mourning the loss of the great man.

Figure 27: Michelangelo's Bust of Brutus

Figure 28: The Dome of Saint Peter's

RAPHAEL

Raffaello Sanzio (1483-1520) was perhaps the best loved artist of the High Renaissance. Raphael (he is known by the Anglicized version of his name) was a native of Urbino. He was apprenticed in the workshop of the well-respected painter Perugino and was later invited to the court of the Duke of Urbino, where his father was the court painter. His refined and affable manner made him the very model of a Renaissance courtier.

In 1504 Raphael settled in Florence. This was the time when Michelangelo and Leonardo were setting new standards in the world of art. He carefully studied the works of these masters and incorporated many of their techniques into his own style. But there is a unique poetic quality to his paintings, as can be seen in the numerous gentle, sweet-faced Madonnas he created during this period. (Isn't it interesting how an artist's personality is often reflected in the portraits he paints?)

In 1508 Julius II commissioned Raphael to paint the walls of a suite of chambers in the Vatican Palace. The Pope had in mind a series of frescoes that would reflect the religious and philosophical ideals of the High Renaissance. On the walls of the first room, the Stanza della Segnatura, Raphael painted large frescoes celebrating the four aspects of human accomplishment: theology (DISPUTATION OVER THE SACRAMENT), philosophy (SCHOOL OF ATHENS), the arts (PARNASUS), and law (CARDINAL VIRTUES and GIVING OF THE LAW). Each wall in the room has an arch to support the curved ceiling. Raphael ingeniously incorporated this architectural feature into his pictures. The frescoes combine elements of classical culture and Christian theology, reflecting once again the humanist belief that there can be a harmonious relationship between the two in the search for truth and beauty.

The painting entitled SCHOOL OF ATHENS established Raphael's reputation. An allegory of secular (non-religious) learning, it portrays Plato and Aristotle surrounded by other famous Greek philosophers as they debate with one another. Plato gestures upwards towards the heavens as the ultimate source of understanding, while Aristotle stretches out his hand, palm down, to indicate the importance of gathering practical knowledge by observing the natural world. Looking on approvingly from two niches in the walls are statues of the Greek deities, Apollo and Athena. Many of the elegant figures attending the philosophers are portraits of Raphael's contemporaries, including Leonardo da Vinci (who poses as Aristotle), Bramante, and Michelangelo. He even included himself.

The frescoes of the stanze were painted when Michelangelo was just starting work on the ceiling of the Sistine Chapel. Raphael met the older artist at this time, but the gruff Michelangelo disliked the young man immensely and accused him of stealing his ideas. We know that Raphael was influenced by Michelangelo's earlier works, but the main model for his figures was the Apollo Belvedere in the Vatican Museum. Although Vasari claimed that he sneaked into the chapel at night with architect Bramante, it is most probable that Raphael first viewed the figures on the ceiling in August, 1511, when the scaffolding was temporarily removed to celebrate the feast of the Assumption of the Virgin. So Michelangelo's attacks were unfounded.

Upon the death of Bramante, Pope Leo X placed Raphael in charge of the construction of the new Saint Peter's. (As we know, Michelangelo later took over this command.) There were even rumors that the young artist would be appointed a cardinal. But suddenly he died on Good Friday, 1520, his thirty-seventh birthday. What a terrible loss to the world of art. At Raphael's request he was buried in the Pantheon. His last painting, TRANSFIGURATION, unfinished at the time, was displayed over his coffin. Cardinal Bembo wrote the following epitaph:

> This is Raphael's tomb, while he lived
> he made Mother Nature
> Fear to be vanquished by him and, as he
> died, to die too.

THE HIGH RENAISSANCE IN VENICE

Unlike the other Italian cities, Venice was a colonial power whose vast maritime empire stretched eastwards to the island of Cyprus. Its many ports gave Venetian merchants ready access to the points at which spices, silks and dyes from Asia reached the Mediterranean Sea, particularly Alexandria,

Egypt. By the dawn of the sixteenth century, Venice also owned a sizable territory on the Italian mainland, which was known as *Terraferma*. The wealthy men who ran the Venetian republic never allowed a single family to seize control, as had happened in Florence and Milan. Since there was no court, the artists sought the patronage of the government itself. The leaders of the republic gladly obliged and supported any works that reflected the city's majesty and affluence.

For centuries Venetian artists had painted on wooden panels made of poplar, oak, or silver fir, but after 1450 a new material - canvas - became the preferred painting surface. This heavy cloth had been used for many years for temporary festival decorations and theatrical scenery. It gradually became popular for other large scale paintings because it could be rolled up and transported easily. Canvas has the added advantage of resisting the ravages of moisture better than wooden panels, and this in itself made it very popular in the damp city of Venice. (Relatively few Venetian artists considered painting a fresco, since this process requires a dry environment.) As we learned earlier, oil paint was brought to Venice in 1470. Canvas proved to be the ideal surface for this type of paint.

Making use of the new materials, Venetian artists soon won great renown for their oil paintings. Unlike the painters we have been studying, who were noted for their skillful application of the rules of perspective and their realistic (although idealized) rendering of the human body, the Venetians became famous for their bold use of color. Giovanni Bellini (1430-1516) was the first Venetian artist to master the use of oils. He was trained by his father, Jacopo, a fine painter in his own right, and produced a number of vivid portraits and richly glowing altarpieces. Giovanni had a knack for

transforming the mundane routines of everyday life into special, meditative moments. He broke from the tradition of Byzantine art (until now most Venetians were directly influenced by the nearby Byzantines) by placing his figures in natural positions and surrounding them with realistic landscapes. But it is the warmth of his colors and the intricacy of detail achieved by the slow-drying oil paints that make his works memorable. Bellini was appointed the official painter of the Venetian republic in 1483 and is credited with establishing Venice as an artistic center on a level with Florence and Rome.

In 1527 Rome was sacked by a Spanish army. (We'll find out why in the next chapter.) This vicious attack caused Roman artists and scholars to flee to other cities. Doge Andrea Gritti enticed many of them to come to Venice. The contributions of these exiles would help to make Venice a dynamic cultural center celebrated not only for its oil paintings but for its architecture, music, and craftsmanship.

TITIAN

Tiziano Vecellio (1488-1576), known as Titian, was the dominant painter of the Venetian Renaissance. He was a prolific artist - an extraordinary 400 of his paintings have survived. Born in the southern Alps, Titian went to Venice as a young man to study painting and worked there throughout most of his long life. (He lived to be ninety.) In the early years, he studied with Giovanni Bellini, who allegedly remarked that the boy drew his figures so fast that he would "never succeed as a painter." It was another artist, Giorgione, who taught him a bold brush technique and how to apply a glaze to make a painting appear bright and shimmery. Titian so totally mastered the techniques of Giorgione that modern authorities are unsure whether certain works of the period were a collaboration of the two artists or were done by one or the other - and if so, which one!

In 1516 Titian became the official painter of the Venetian Republic, but this did not prevent him from accepting commissions from other Italian cities. In 1518 he completed the large altarpiece painting, THE ASSUMPTION OF THE VIRGIN. By applying thick layers of individual brushstrokes in pure colors, chiefly red, white, yellow, and black, he created the illusion of well-rounded figures whose skin seems to glow with incandescent light. In painting MADONNA WITH SAINTS, Titian disregarded the traditional rules of composition, placing Mary and the child to the side of the main focus. Compared to the classical works we have studied, this one appears lopsided and unbalanced, but Titian relied upon his mastery of color and brushstroke to bring everything together.

Pietro Aretino was a writer and courtier who arrived in Venice in 1527. He became Titian's friend and publicity agent. Aretino distributed pamphlets about the artist's talent and arranged for his introduction to Holy Roman Emperor Charles V, who commissioned Titian to paint his portrait. The full-length figure he produced exudes such elegance that Charles immediately appointed him court painter and even knighted him. According to legend, the Emperor once did the artist the honor of picking up a brush he had dropped. The image of a powerful ruler humbling himself before a painter indicates how greatly the prestige of the artist had grown since the fourteenth century. Titian and Charles developed a close relationship that lasted for years, and the Emperor's portrait made full-length paintings fashionable throughout Europe.

Widely sought after by kings, princes, and popes, Titian was one of the few painters of his time to acquire a fortune through his art. He was a rapid worker, which explains why he completed so many paintings. Although he was well known for his religious, mythological, and historical paintings, his fame rests upon his portraits. He had a talent for penetrating the personality of the sitter and conveying it with dignity and vitality. His paintings have a sensual quality about them because of his ability to depict so convincingly the textures of velvet, fur, flesh, jewels, and metal.

When he visited Rome in 1543 to paint a portrait of Pope Paul III, Titian met Michelangelo. The older artist complemented him on his "lively manner" of painting, but he added that it was "a pity good design was not taught in Venice." And yet, design, in the sense Michelangelo used the word, became less important to Titian as he relied more upon the effects of color and brushstroke to create an emotional impact. In his later masterpiece, CHRIST CROWNED WITH THORNS, the figures emerge from the semidarkness and shimmer with light that seems to radiate from within. Vasari, who visited the artist in his Venetian workshop in 1566, remarked that Titian "walks in step with nature: hence each one of his figures is alive and in motion, with flesh that quivers."

PALLADIO

Architectural design in the later years of the sixteenth century was dominated by Andrea di Pietro della Gondola, known as Palladio. Trained as a stonemason, he became the protegé of humanist scholar and amateur architect, Count Giangiorgio Trissino of Viscenza. Trissino taught him Latin and encouraged his interest in ancient art and architecture. He nicknamed him Palladio after the mythological patron god-

Figure 29: Palladian window

dess of the arts, Pallas Athena. (Some historians claim he was named after the fourth-century Roman writer Palladius. Take your pick!)

The two men traveled together to Rome on three occasions. Each time Palladio studied and carefully sketched many of the ancient ruins. He published his drawings in a guidebook on the antiquities of classical Rome. But what he really wanted to do was design his own buildings, and he soon got his chance.

Like Vasari, he incorporated many of the features of the ancient structures, such as columns, pilasters, and loggias (colonnades) into his designs of churches, civic buildings, villas, and palazzos. The use of symmetrical wings projecting from the sides of a central structure were to become hallmarks of his style. He introduced the temple front (tall pillars topped by a triangular pediment) to the design of villas and palazzos. The pediment was often decorated with the family's coat of arms. He also created the Palladian window: an arched window consisting of three panels, the middle one higher than the other two.

His most famous domestic dwelling, the Villa Rotunda near Vicenza, is a model of classical symmetry. Viewed from above it is a perfect square, with four smaller squares (porches coming off of each side. The villa is crowned with a dome, clearly inspired by the Pantheon in Rome. (Compare the picture below to figure 18.) Palladio's use of a central dome on a villa was a bold innovation, but it was so well received that it led to a long tradition of domed country homes. His elegant private palaces and

Figure 30: The Villa Rotonda

majestic public buildings made Venice's Grand Canal the most beautiful thorough-fare in Europe.

Palladio devoted more than twenty years to the preparation of his famous trea-tise, FOUR BOOKS OF ARCHITECTURE. This massive work explains the principles of Vitruvius and Alberti in a manner that is easy to understand. It is filled with plans, elevations, and decorative schemes for his own buildings, a clever marketing strategy that helped to promote his designs through-out Europe. Palladio created the first inter-national style of architecture since the Gothic structures of the Middle Ages. It is known today as neo-classicism ("new clas-sicism"). President (and architect) Thomas Jefferson owned a copy of his treatise and consulted it frequently when he designed his own Virginia home, *Monticello* (an Ital-ian word meaning "little mountain" and referring to the spot upon which he built his neo-classical dwelling.)

FROM HARMONY TO DISTORTION

The artists of the High Renaissance cer-tainly scaled the heights of excellence. How could the generations that came after them hope to compete with such masterpieces? What was there left to accomplish? The re-sponse of many was to adopt a completely different approach to art. These artists are known as Mannerists. The term "Manner-ism" comes from the Italian word *maniera* (style). During the sixteenth century maniera referred to playfulness in art. The object was to be inventive, not as a means of depicting nature, but as an end in itself.

The Mannerists often exaggerated fea-tures of Renaissance art, just for fun. For example, where Michelangelo had drawn and sculpted many nudes in twisted or con-torted positions to express their inner an-guish, the new generation of artists filled biblical scenes with hordes of energetic muscle-bound athletes! Some artists filled their paintings with obscure symbolism (were they teasing the intellectual art lov-ers?), while others sought to draw attention to their works by totally disregarding the balance and symmetry of classical works and filling their canvases with bizarre and unnatural objects. One critic remarked that Mannerists seemed to find beauty in things that were deformed and sought to please by giving displeasure.

THE MADONNA WITH THE LONG NECK by Parmigianino (begun in 1532) is an excellent example of Mannerism. Find a picture of it. The figures have strangely elongated bodies. The Virgin has the long graceful neck of a swan, which contrasts with her massive legs. Her odd physique resembles the metal jug which is (inexpli-cably) being carried by a young man. A prophet appears in the distance, but he is so radically reduced in size that he looks like an elf at the Madonna's feet! And rather than distribute the figures in an orderly and balanced manner, Parmigianino has crammed a group of angels into one small corner of the painting.

Benvenuto Cellini (1500-71) was a Florentine goldsmith and sculptor. His AU-TOBIOGRAPHY (inspired by Vasari's LIVES) gives us a fascinating account of the life of an artist in the later sixteenth century. This is not to say that Cellini was typical. He was a scoundrel, who traveled from court to court seeking his fortune and es-caping punishment for his petty crimes. But in the process he created some beautiful objects - jewelry, seals, and metalwork - for nobles, popes, and sovereigns.

One of the few pieces of Cellini to sur-vive until our times is an elaborate gold and enamel saltcellar on an ebony base, which he presented to Francis I of France in 1543. It is a typically Mannerist piece of art, a "tour de force" of inventiveness and caprice. Two nude figures, representing the earth and the sea, recline in rather awkward positions. The earth figure resembles Aphrodite, the Greek goddess of love and beauty, while the other figure appears to be Poseidon, Greek god of the sea. She sits beside a disproportionately small Greek temple, which holds the pepper, while he carries an under-sized but finely wrought ship, which contains the salt. Can you imagine such an elaborate "salt and pepper set" gracing our modern tables? Cellini wrote in his book that when he was carrying the gold for the saltcellar to his workshop he was attacked by four thieves, all of whom he defeated single-handedly. (He was also somewhat of a braggart!)

In 1545 Cellini was accused of embezzling precious metals and gemstones. So he fled from France back to Florence, where he persuaded Duke Cosimo I (de Medici) to commission a bronze statue of PERSEUS AND MEDUSA. The attractive Greek hero Perseus stands triumphantly atop the gruesome bleeding trunk of the monster Medusa, holding her severed head in his hand. His eyes are averted, since a glance at her eyes will turn him to stone. Today you can see the statue in the loggia beside the Piazza della Signoria in Florence. Although Cellini's Perseus was closer to nature than the art of most Mannerists, Michelangelo dismissed the artist as "a maker of snuff-box ornaments!"

The greatest painter of the late sixteenth century was Venetian artist Jacopo Robusti, known as Tintoretto (1518-1594). His nickname means "little dyer," a reference to his father's trade as a dyer *(tintore)*. (Italian artists, you may have noticed, loved nicknames!) He was a pupil of Titian, from whom he learned much about the use of

Figure 31: Cellini's Perseus & Medusa

color, brushstroke, and the effects of chiaroscuro. Tintoretto often made wax and clay models and set them in a box with a candle in order to experiment with different lighting effects. He covered his vast canvases with dramatic scenes. Unlike the classical paintings, his seem disorderly and confusing - so much is happening at once. In THE FINDING OF ST MARK'S REMAINS, the intensity of the action is increased by the abrupt contrast of light and darkness. There is an unnatural sense of perspective as well, objects in the distance appearing strangely close. A contorted figure rolls back his eyes as the demon that had possessed him escapes from his mouth like a wisp of smoke.

How eccentric this work seems when compared with one of the balanced and refined paintings of Raphael or Leonardo!

Although Mannerism began in Italy, it eventually spread throughout much of the rest of Europe. Many art historians consider this movement to be the beginning of modern art. What do you think?

REVIEW QUESTIONS:

1. According to Vasari, what were the three stages of the rebirth of art?

2. What was the advantage of oil paint over tempera?

3. Describe, in detail, Leonardo's MONA LISA.

4. What was so special about Pope Nicholas V?

5. What were some of the original statues in the papal collection of antique sculpture?

6. Who was Bramante?

7. In what ways did Pope Leo X reflect the interests of his father, Lorenzo the Magnificent?

8. What did Michelangelo consider himself? (A painter or a sculptor or both?)

9. Describe Michelangelo's PIETA.

10. What did Michelangelo's statue of DAVID symbolize?

11. What is the connection between Brunelleschi's dome in Florence and Michelangelo's dome in Rome?

12. What are the main characteristics of the paintings of Titian?

13. Describe Palladio's style of architecture.

14. What is Mannerism?

15. Describe Cellini's saltcellar.

FURTHERMORE:

1. Leonardo da Vinci was inspired by the many volumed work by Roman architect Vitruvius to draw the ideal male figure, known as Vitruvian Man, in his notebook. Vitruvius believed the circle and square to be perfect shapes, and described how the body of a human being could fit perfectly within those shapes. Leonardo drew a man in a spread eagled position (arms up legs apart) to show that he fit into perfect circle. Then, in the same drawing, he showed him with his feet together and arms outstretched, fitting easily into a perfect square. This view of measuring the world in terms of man is an ancient one (a Greek philosopher once wrote, "Man is the measure of all things) and was central to humanist philosophy.

2. As a young art student, Michelangelo once was given the head of a statue to copy. He did such a good job that when he returned the copy to the owner in place of the original (having buried it for a time in a vineyard to make it seem older), the man didn't notice any difference. The truth only came out when Michelangelo was overheard telling a friend about what he had done. Later, when he was living in Lorenzo's villa, Michelangelo's statue of a sleeping Cupid was successfully sold by a dealer as a genuine work of antiquity. It was later purchased by Isabella d'Este, the famed art patroness of the court of Mantua.

3. Today Saint Peter's is protected by the Swiss Guards. Their costumes were designed by Michelangelo and Raphael. They are Swiss because they are recruited among Swiss Catholics. Vatican City is an independent country, the smallest in the world.

4. Intellectually gifted men, who in modern times might turn to science or math, were drawn during the Renaissance to art and architecture. They were intrigued by the complex harmonies that could be achieved by following the strict rules of linear perspective.

5. When he began to sculpt Michelangelo envisioned the presence of a statue within the stone that needed to be set free. So, in a manner of speaking, he considered himself a liberator rather than a creator. Some of his late statues of bound slaves seem as if they are indeed struggling to free themselves from their stone prisons.

6. Vasari was proud of the fact that he could paint very quickly. When he bragged to Michelangelo about how he had completed the Great Hall in the Chancellor's Palace in Rome in 100 days, the great artist sniffed, "That's obvious."

PROJECTS:

1. Why do you suppose Leonardo wrote his notebooks in reverse? Try some mirror writing, just for fun. Then write a paragraph expressing your opinions about why Leonardo wrote in this unusual way.

2. Read the sonnets of Michelangelo.

3. Make a timeline of the eighty-eight years of Michelangelo's life, noting major political events as well as his own artistic accomplishments.

4. The tools of the sculptor have changed very little since early times. They consist of hammers and pointed chisels. Find out how these tools are used to turn a block of stone into a figure. Make a poster to illustrate the process.

5. Think about the personalities and interests of Leonardo, Michelangelo, and Raphael. Then write a short skit about them. Pretend that they are middle schoolers living in today's world. Have them argue about something, such as who will do the decorations for school play. This can be a comedy or a serious drama.

6. Leonardo once wrote, "Impatience, the mother of stupidity, praises brevity." What does this mean? How does the quote relate to the lifetime accomplishments of Leonardo? Can you think of an example from your daily experiences to which the quote aptly applies?

7. Leonardo once described the eye as the window of the soul. What did he mean by that? Write a paragraph explaining your views. Give examples.

8. El Greco (Domenikos Theotokopoulos) of Crete visited Venice and was drawn to the paintings of Tintoretto. He later

Figure 32: The Zuccaro Window

settled in Toledo, Spain, and produced paintings even more startling and unorthodox than those of the Venetian painter. Find out more about him.

9. Figure 32 is a drawing of the window of the Palazzo Zuccari in Rome, designed by Mannerist architect Federico Zuccari. It looks a lot like a medieval gargoyle. What a contrast to the Palladian windows designed at the same time! Use your imagination and design three original windows (or doors) in the Mannerist style.

10. Obtain a copy of Cellini's AUTOBIOGRAPHY and read several chapters.

11. Aristotle wrote that artists should "paint people better than they are." Choose three Renaissance artists and explain how they followed the Greek philosopher's advice.

CHAPTER VI
THE RENAISSANCE MAN AND WOMAN

So far we have learned a great deal about the people of Florence, Rome, and Venice, but there were also many smaller city-states in northern Italy that contributed to the flowering of the Renaissance. The greatest of these was Urbino, a small duchy in the mountains of central Italy. It was the birthplace of Bramante and Raphael.

In 1444 Federico da Montefeltro became Urbino's new Duke when his elder brother died. He had been trained as a condottiere, and when he inherited Urbino he absorbed the surrounding mountain towns and made his duchy three times larger than it had been. Federico was an able ruler, who divided his time between Urbino and the sites of his military ventures. As a condottiere he fought in the service of such powerful men as the dukes of Milan, the kings of Naples, several popes (including Sixtus), and Lorenzo de Medici. When he was home, he made a great effort to keep in touch with his subjects. He often went to the market, entering shops to exchange pleasantries and doffing his cap to everyone he met. This led to the common expression, to be "as busy as Federico's bonnet."

Federico had been educated by Vittorino da Feltre (remember the "Joyful House?"), and he developed a lifelong love of books. He knew Greek and Latin well, and he enjoyed discussing topics as diverse as Julius Caesar's campaigns, Aristotle's philosophy, Livy's histories, and the writings of Saint Augustine. He hired five scholars to read aloud at dinner. One of his major goals, he once said, was to learn something new every day. Federico created the finest library since ancient times, which he prized above all his other possessions. He kept forty scribes busy for fourteen years copying manuscripts for his large collection. (The ducal library was later added to the Vatican Library.)

Federico used the wealth he earned as a mercenary to build an elegant palace, which he filled with beautiful statues and paintings. He attended Mass daily in his private chapel, but to show his love of the classics he had another chapel dedicated to the Greek muses built beside it. A true humanist, he saw no conflict between the ideals of the ancients and those of Christianity. In his study there were twenty-eight portraits of famous men, including the Greek poet Homer and the Roman playwright Seneca as well as Saint Thomas Aquinas and King Solomon.

The Duke's second wife was Battista Sforza, a member of the ruling dynasty in Milan. She married when she was only thirteen. Battista spoke Greek and Latin, was a patroness of the arts, and even governed Urbino when her husband was away. Together Federico and Battista presided over a glittering court that attracted humanists and artists from all over Europe. The 500 members of the court included 200 servants, four teachers, an astrologer, five "readers aloud at meals," forty transcribers of books, two organists, the keeper of the bloodhounds, and a man who tended the Duke's pet camel-leopard. Elisabetta Gonzaga grew up in the court of Mantua and married the son of Federico and Battista. She brought to Urbino her own circle of scholars, artists, and musicians, making the court the most celebrated in Italy.

THE COURTIER

Baldassare Castiglione was a diplomat who spent much of his time in the courts of Milan, Mantua, the Vatican and Urbino. He was inspired by the elegant men and women of Federico's court to write a book, THE COURTIER, which set fourth the standards of gentlemanly conduct. Written as a series of after-dinner discussions among the courtiers and ladies of Urbino, it became the arbiter of taste for western society. Much of what are considered "good manners" in today's world date back to Castiglione's code of behavior.

And what was the ideal courtier? According to Castiglione, he was "well rounded," skillful in many diverse activities. For example, he could play various musical instruments, recite and compose poetry, and dance with grace and elegance. He had a solid knowledge of classics, an understanding of art and sculpture, and the ability to speak several languages, including, of course, Greek and Latin. His conversation was witty and refined. (It was considered a cardinal sin to be boring!) He could perform admirably in several sports, particularly wrestling, riding, tennis, and running.

Just as art should conceal the work that goes into its creation, the courtier should be modest and make his achievements seem effortless. Every act should be performed with *sprezzatura* - an unforced ease of accomplishment - and he should discuss his interests knowledgeably without making others feel uncomfortable. In other words, he should do well in everything without seeming to try hard. This quality of effortless superiority would be considered the mark of the gentleman for centuries to come. In fact the word *virtuoso* entered the Italian language in the sixteenth century to describe a towering personality who made an art of his every act.

Castiglione was clearly influenced by the ancient ideal of the responsible citizen with a finely tuned mind and body. To this he added a dash of medieval chivalry: a courtier was encouraged to fall in love with an attractive (and married, thus ineligible) lady of the court. He could reveal his feelings only from a distance, writing love poems and notes praising her beauty.

THE COURTIER was translated in several languages and became a bestseller throughout much of Europe. As a handbook of proper behavior, it helped to civilize society. However, the book is not without its faults. For example, the courtier is advised never to cheapen himself by mingling with members of the lower classes. Let's not forget that the sophisticated culture of the Italian Renaissance involved only the "upper crust," a small fraction of society, and Castiglione's elitist views can offend modern readers. Furthermore, by emphasizing outward appearances Castiglione actually encouraged the people of the court to indulge in all sorts of evil schemes and ruthless murders while hiding behind the mask of impeccable manners.

HIGH FASHION IN THE SIXTEENTH CENTURY

We learned earlier about the elegant fashions of the wealthy classes in fifteenth century Italy. By the High Renaissance these had become extremely extravagant and flashy. The courts and major cities of sixteenth century Europe were, in fact, centers of display and ostentation, where the rich tried to outshine one another in their eye-catching finery.

Since medieval times, there had existed a set of official regulations, known as the "sumptuary laws," that specified the types of dress considered appropriate for every social rank. These were originally intended to protect the local weaving industry by limiting the importation of expensive foreign cloth, but they also helped to maintain the social structure. Only the wealthiest members of society were allowed to wear the finest materials. For example, royalty could wear the fur of the ermine, but nobles wore fox. Squirrel or rabbit were acceptable furs for the middle class. The lower classes had to settle for coarsely woven wool, which, of course, was all they could afford anyway. Certain cities limited the number of silk and velvet garments that could be owned by a single person, and in Florence women of the humbler classes were forbidden to make buttons from any material but wood.

Some laws regulated certain styles of dress for reasons of practicality. Remember those long pointed toes that became popular in the fourteenth century? In 1464 an English statute banned any cobbler or leatherworker from making the toe of a courtier's shoe more than two inches long. As a result, the squared-off toe became the rage at the end of the century. Other ordinances in Milan and Venice regulated the low necklines and long trailing skirts among the ladies. However, few people observed these rules. Excess was the norm in high society. Rich French women wore elaborate headdresses that were so high that entrances to rooms and buildings had to be altered for them! Everywhere in Europe those who could afford it were were determined to flaunt their leisured status by wearing the most highly impractical and exorbitantly expensive clothing available.

The typical courtier of the sixteenth century strode about like a proud peacock, thanks to the efforts of his personal fashion designer. His detachable puffed sleeves billowed from a short, fitted doublet of satin or velvet and then tapered at the wrist. A stiff fluted collar (called a ruff) graced his neck. His tight, wool stockings glistened with silver threads. A startling effect could be achieved by wearing stockings of different colors or patterns. Over the doublet he wore a jerkin, usually trimmed with fur and belted at the waist. To complete his costume, the courtier wore a velvet cap with a feather stuck through its brim, scented leather gloves, golden necklaces, and a sword with an ornate hilt.

A new fashion, known as slashing, had become popular in Germany in the late fifteenth century and then spread throughout Europe. The outer material of a courtier's doublet, sleeve, or hose was cut (slashed), and the contrasting fabrics beneath were pulled through the openings. This produced a very colorful effect. At first the slashings were small, intricate patterns, but in the late sixteenth century they became long, vertical lines. Slashing marks were even imitated with engravings on metal armor.

Slashing originated on the battlefield of Grandson in 1476 when German mercenaries became intrigued by the way the Swiss troops made undergarments from the tattered banners and tents of their enemies - these protruded colorfully through the holes of their own ragged clothing. The popularity of slashing might have begun as a reaction to the sumptuary law forbidding the lower classes to wear clothing of more than one color, but the new look was soon associated with the well-dressed courtier.

In later years, the multi-colored effect of men's clothing was enhanced by a new technique called "bombasting." Garments were thickly stuffed with dyed cotton wool or similar padding. Then the material was slashed and the padding as pulled through. This created a puffier look. Courtiers began to wear short padded breeches that puffed out above the cuffs at mid-thigh. The Spanish ones were called "pumpkin breeches." (Seriously!)

Figure 33: A Courtier of the Sixteenth Century

The long flowing gowns of the ladies of the court billowed gracefully when they walked. Many of them had long trains, like those of a modern wedding gown. Elaborate head-dresses were made from starched and folded linen, a style originating in northern Europe. Some ladies wore a hennin - a high, cone-shaped headdress with a long scarf attached to the peak. This dated from medieval times. Many new styles of headgear evolved among the courts of the south, the most extreme being the French creations we've already learned about. When a high forehead became fash-ionable, the women plucked their eyebrows and shaved their hairlines to achieve "the look." Another bizarre fad was clogs - wooden shoes with four-inch heels. These were extremely awkward footwear, although they proved quite useful for keeping long hemlines above the mud of city streets. Eventually, they became so high that a lady had to be supported by her maids when she walked!

Spanish women of the sixteenth century started a new style by wearing rigid corsets made of iron or bone to make their waists

Figure 34: That Hourglass Figure

seem tiny. Their skirts fit over conical metal frames called farthingales, which further accentuated the narrow appearance of their waists. No wonder these women appear so stiff and somber in their portraits! Before long, all European aristocrats were wearing these terribly uncomfortable contraptions in the hopes of having the perfect hourglass figure. A well-dressed woman also carried a fan, a handkerchief, and a pair of scented gloves.

The brocades and velvets of the apparel of both men and women were often covered with pearls, gold embroidery, and precious stones. Imagine the weight of their clothing, and how hot it must have been in summer! Eager to compete with the courtiers, the wealthy merchants and their wives spent fabulous sums on their own extravagant attire.

THE ROLE OF WOMEN

You might think that well-off Renaissance women lived a charmed life, enjoying the poetry written in their honor by admiring courtiers or planning the new season's wardrobe. But even at the highest levels of society, women were not the equals of men. Not even close! In fact, those who smiled the sweetest and spoke the least were the most highly regarded by the court. The same was true among the lower classes, where women were expected to do as they were told by their fathers or husbands. It was a man's world, no doubt about that.

So what was the role of a woman? Above all, she was expected to have a baby every year. Children made up half the population in most European countries. (In those days, most people didn't live beyond the age of forty.) Families were very large in those early times because less than half of all children lived to adulthood. Magdalucia, the Venetian wife of a wealthy merchant,

Francesco Marcello, gave birth to twenty-six children! (Thirteen survived to adulthood.) Sons were favored, in part because they continued the family name and, in the lower classes, because they could help out with the physical chores on the farm or in the workshop. The preference for male children can be seen in the records of babies abandoned at birth: the vast majority were girls.

Only the daughters of the wealthy received a formal education, and they generally learned only to converse well and play a musical instrument (and sing). They were taught at home, since respectable young ladies never left the house except to go to church. The number of noblewomen who actually read the classics were only a handful. The majority of women remained illiterate. Their lives were devoted to running the household, bearing and caring for the children, and making the family clothing.

A girl was expected to marry in her teens or to become a nun (if she was wealthy) or a servant (if she was poor). There were no other options. Marriage-bound daughters had to be provided with dowries (useful household materials as well as the ownership of property) in order to attract suitable husbands. A young maiden kept the linens of her dowry in a beautifully carved hope chest called a *cassone*, which was often passed down from mother to daughter. (Certain artists' workshops specialized in the production of the cassone.)

Marriages were arranged by parents for their own economic advantage, and love was seldom considered. (No sensible family would allow the acquisition of valuable property to be jeopardized by their daughter's lack of affection for her future spouse!) Since some middle class families could not afford dowries for all their daughters, the younger ones often ended up in convents against their wills. Imagine how terrible it must have been for a girl to be placed there if she had no religious calling. Actually, so many girls were forced to enter convents in sixteenth century Italy because they lacked suitable dowries (over twelve percent of the young women in Florence suffered this fate) that local communities began to establish special dowry funds. A sum of money was paid into the fund when a girl was born; at the age of fifteen she was repaid the sum with interest, and this provided her with a dowry.

Exceptional Women

Despite the subservient role assigned to the women of the Renaissance, a few noble souls charted their own course and accomplished great things. Among the more remarkable of these women was Isabella d'Este (1474-1539). She was born in the duchy of Ferrara and received an outstanding education from the best scholars of the day. She was extremely intelligent and clever, and she easily mastered Greek and Latin, memorized passages from Virgil and Terence, learned to play the lute with skill, perfected the steps of every new dance, embroidered beautifully, and could hold her own in a conversation with the ambassadors who visited her father, Duke Ercole.

Isabella married Gianfrancesco Gonzaga, the Marquis of Mantua, just before her sixteenth birthday. Although this was a political alliance, she got along well with her new husband. Together they reigned over a court that included such creative men as Leonardo da Vinci and Castiglione. The Marquis shared her enjoyment of music, and they commissioned lutes, organs, and clavichords to be made created specifically for their musical gatherings. Isabella wrote thousands of letters to artists, musicians, and government leaders. (She was, in fact, related by birth or marriage to almost every ruler in Italy!) Over 2,000 of her letters survive and tell us much about the thoughts of the leaders of sixteenth century European society.

Isabella was admired for her beauty, good taste, keen mind and political wisdom. Once Gianfrancesco was captured during a war with Venice, leaving Isabella in charge of Mantua. Her lively wit and diplomatic discretion enabled her to rule ably, even making allies of former enemies of the Marquis. When her husband returned home, he remarked, "It is our fate to have as a wife a woman who is always ruled by her head." Could he have been envious?

Isabella's study contained so many costly books and great art works it was called *Il Paradise*. (She was history's first female collector of great art.) On the ceiling were carved her name and motto: "Neither hope nor fear." (What do you think that means?) When she died (she lived into her sixties) her estate inventories revealed over 1,600 items, including bronze and marble statues, precious stone vases, gems, coins, and medals, cameos, enamels, crystal mirrors, and the paintings she had commissioned.

Lucrezia Borgia (1480-1519), the daughter of Pope Alexander VI, married three European rulers before she was twenty-two. Her father annulled the first marriage to Giovanni Sforza (because he quarreled with his Milanese family) and ordered the murder of the second husband (because he was a political foe). When Alexander died and her brother (Cesare) was killed in battle, a mourning Lucrezia donned a hairshirt (a garment of scratchy cloth worn next to the skin as a form of penance for past sins). She engaged in charity works and pawned her jewels to give alms to the poor. Eventually, however, she re-entered high society.

Her third marriage, to Alfonso d'Este, Duke of Ferrara (and brother of Isabella), was a happy one. She devoted the early years of this marriage to charitable works and the education of her seven children. Later, she made the court of Ferrara a brilliant center for artists, poets, and scholars.

Vittoria Colonna (1490-1547) was betrothed at the age of four and married at nineteen to Ferdinando d'Avalos, Marquis of Pescara. She deeply loved her husband (another exception to the rule), and after his untimely death she retired to a convent. Eventually, she settled in Rome. Like Isabella, she had many famous literary friends and correspondents, including Castiglione and Michelangelo (who addressed a number of poems and letters to her). Vittoria was a renowned poet in her own right. Her collection of Petrarchan sonnets in RIME were written, she said, to relieve the pain of her grieving for Ferdinando.

Beatrice del Sera (1515-86) became a nun because she had no dowry. She was so unhappy about being placed in the convent against her will that she focused her energies into the writing of morality plays. LOVE OF VIRTUE is a particularly moving protest against the conventional imprisonment of women by men. Indeed, weren't most women prisoners in one way or another? One character complains that women are not born for happiness but to serve others. The play is filled with symbolic images of rocks, walls, and towers, all of which confined most women born in those difficult times against their wills.

Beatrice Cenci (1577-99) was a Roman noblewoman of the late sixteenth century, whose experiences reflect just how terrible life could be for someone of her gender. She was the daughter of a violent and greedy man who was jealous of his own children. He imprisoned Beatrice and treated her so cruelly that she reluctantly decided to arrange his murder, with the aid of servants and members of her family. The crime was soon detected, however, and all involved were brought to trial, tortured and sentenced to death, despite pleas for leniency on their behalf.

The Roman people were divided in their reactions to the execution of Beatrice. (Like today, a public trial was eagerly followed by the local citizens.) While some considered her a liar and a cold-blooded killer, others saw her as a victim. Immediately after her death, the Cenci property was confiscated by the Church. (Many scholars accuse the greedy Pope Clement VIII of ordering her death to obtain the huge Cenci holdings.)

The debate and scandal associated with this case stirred the imaginations of the romantic writers of later centuries, including the English poet Shelley (whose tragedy THE CENSI appeared in 1819) and Italian novelist Alberto Moravia (his book, BEATRICE CENCI, was published in 1958).

REVIEW QUESTIONS:

1. Who was Baldassare Castiglione?

2. List five important characteristics of the ideal courtier.

3. What were the sumptuary laws?

4. Describe the attire of a typical courtier.

5. Describe the attire of a typical lady of the court.

6. What was slashing, and why was it so popular?

7. What were the typical roles of Renaissance women?

8. What did an unmarried woman do with her life?

9. In what ways (name five) was Isabella d'Este different than most of her peers?

10. How did the pope (probably) influence the trial of Beatrice Cenci?

FURTHERMORE:

1. In 1486 Giovanni Picco della Mirandola wrote THE DIGNITY OF MAN, an interesting work which acclaims the importance of mankind in the universe. He describes how Adam is created by God and made master of the earth. Mankind, he says, is to be granted whatever he wants and "can be whatever he wills." This was, of course, a basic theme of the humanists.

2. Isabella d'Este sat for a portrait by Titian when she was sixty years old. When he finished the work, she found it so unflattering that she commissioned him to do another one, making her look as she had appeared forty years earlier!

3. Even the wealthy people of the Renaissance had relatively few articles of clothing, but Lucrezia Borgia was an exception. Her huge wardrobe included fifty gowns, twenty hats, thirty-three pairs of shoes, sixty pairs of slippers, and twenty mantles.

4. Whenever a baby was born in Florence, a bean was dropped into an urn in the Baptistery - a black one for a boy and a white one for a girl.

PROJECTS:

1. Think about what is considered good manners in today's world. Make a list of ten rules that seem to apply. Do you think the same ones would have applied in Renaissance times. Why or why not? Write a short paper expressing your views.

2. Find a copy of THE COURTIER and read twenty pages (not necessarily in order). Report your findings to your class.

3. Reread the descriptions of the proper dress of a courtier and a lady of the court. Consult some other books about Renaissance attire, and find some appropriate illustrations. Then make a drawing of the typical courtier and his lady.

4. Choose one of the women described in this chapter. Do some research, using at least three other sources. Then write a report about her life and the contributions she made to Renaissance society.

5. Isabella d'Este had an equally fascinating sister named Beatrice. Find out what she did and write a short report.

6. The portraits of broken-nosed Federico da Montafeltra and his wife, Battista Sforza, were painted by Piero della Francesca. On the reverse side of their portraits are allegories of their virtues. Look for these famous portraits in an art book. Check out the allegories on the back. Which virtues are described for husband and wife?

PART II
RUSTLINGS AROUND EUROPE

Chapter VII
HAPPENINGS IN THE NORTH

While the city-states of Italy shaped their own destinies, much of western Europe was ruled by powerful monarchs. By the late Middle Ages the old ideal of a single Christian empire in Europe (controlled by the Pope) had given way to the reality of separate, competitive nation states such as England, France, Portugal, Sweden, Poland, and Russia. The rulers of these states depended upon large armies of mercenary soldiers to defend their territories. The middle class liked the idea of a strong monarchy, because it helped guarantee the law and order necessary for economic prosperity.

At the dawn of the fifteenth century the economies of the European nations were linked by a standard money system. As we have learned, Italian coins (the Florentine florin, as well as the Venetian ducat) had a fixed value throughout the continent, and Italian bankers had headquarters in all the major cities to issue checks, exchange currencies, and conduct other business transactions. Of course, the Medici banks were the richest and the most influential.

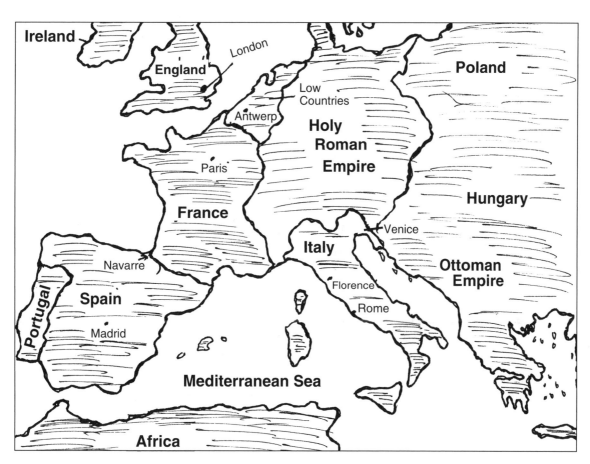

Figure 35: Europe in the Mid-Fifteenth Century

FLANDERS

From medieval times the lands bordering the English Channel that today make up Belgium and the Netherlands were known as the Low Countries. The name was an apt one, since much of this land lies at, or even below, sea level. Flanders was a county in the northern part of the region that became an important center of trade. Resourceful Flemish merchants imported raw wool from England, had it woven locally, and then transported the cloth either back to England or inland to the Champagne region of France, where it was sold at the large annual fairs held there. Venetian fleets frequently sailed from the Mediterranean up the Atlantic coast to Flanders to exchange their eastern products for woolen cloth. Over the years, Flemish cities, such as Antwerp, became extremely prosperous, and the more successful merchants began to live as comfortably as their counterparts in Florence.

FLEMISH ART

Flemish traders often carried Italian paintings home, and by the late fourteenth century the northern artists were well aware of the revolutionary techniques of their contemporaries in the south. However, the Flemish painters had their own artistic traditions, and they did not share the ties to the classical past that so inspired the Italians. Their principal interest was in depicting the natural world in the greatest possible detail. They were able to do this because oil paints had been available to them for some time.

Robert Campin was one of the first Flemish painters to abandon the flat medieval style and attempt to introduce elements of realism into his paintings. One panel of his well-known altarpiece shows the Annunciation (announcement to Mary that she will bear the Holy Child) taking place in the living quarters of an ordinary fourteenth century Dutch house. In this unusual blend of religious subjects and realistic settings, a white kitchen towel serves as a symbol of the purity of the Virgin Mary.

JAN VAN EYCK

The most innovative Flemish painter of the fifteenth century was Jan van Eyck (1390-1441). He was traditionally credited with the invention of oil paints (a myth perpetuated by Vasari), but although this is untrue, van Eyck was certainly the first to master the medium. He created subtle effects of light, depth, and texture by applying layers of translucent oil paint over an opaque background of tempera. Because he painted objects and clothing in almost microscopic detail, his pictures resemble modern color photographs. Most of van Eyck's figures stand or sit calmly in scenic or architectural settings. The artist often placed contemporary people among his biblical figures, just as Botticelli and Raphael would in later years.

Van Eyck's earliest known work is the huge Ghent altarpiece, which consists of twenty-six panels within a single frame. The paintings are filled with figures and symbols and are excellent examples of the artist's skillful use of color, his fastidious attention to detail (he recreated the embroidery of the clothing stitch by stitch), and his efforts to give the illusion of depth by painting distant objects with a greyish or bluish cast (as Leonardo later would). His most famous painting is the MARRIAGE OF ARNOLFINI - a portrait of a successful merchant and his bride. It, too, contains many symbols, such as a single burning candle, ripening fruit, and a faithful dog. Van Eyck and his assistant are reflected in the mirror on the rear wall, a clever device to immortalize their faces. The artist even inscribed below the mirror, "Jan Eyck was here."

Although he spent most of his time in Flanders, van Eyck was occasionally called upon to serve as a diplomat or court painter. Duke Philip the Good of Burgundy (a duchy in northwestern France) sent van Eyck to Portugal to paint a portrait of Princess Isabella. The Duke was engaged to Isabella, but he had never met her. Van Eyck's portrait was so pleasing that Philip quickly married the lady!

THE ITALIAN CONNECTION

The works of Jan van Eyck helped to advertise the many advantages of oil paint. Before long oils were being used in Venice and other Italian cities. Titian never could have achieved his miracles of color and brightness without the use of oil paint. But the artistic exchange went both ways. The Flemish painters of the sixteenth century were highly receptive to the techniques of the Italian Renaissance. Jan Gossaert, known as Mabuse, was the first Flemish artist to paint nude figures and mythological subjects, Quentin Massys studied Leonardo's subtle shading of light and darker tones and experimented with his methods of composition, while Bernard van Orley tried to emulate Raphael's realistic figures.

OTHER DIRECTIONS

Hieronymus Bosch (1450-1516) was a highly imaginative and eccentric Dutchman, whose paintings went beyond realism to reflect his nightmarish visions. He was in many ways a product of the Middle Ages, being obsessed with the wickedness of man and the punishments that lay beyond the grave. But the symbolism of his fantastic and macabre images is so irrational that much of it is not understood. Let's consider

his famous triptych (three panelled altarpiece) known as THE GARDEN OF DELIGHTS. Find a copy of it in one of the art books in your classroom.

Only the left panel has a subject that is easily recognizable. In separate scenes, God introduces Adam to Eve in the beautiful Garden of Eden, and then, after Adam is tempted by Eve, the couple is driven out of paradise. Above their heads winged angels are transformed into hideous insects and hurled from the heavens. The right panel depicts bizarre instruments of torture (including enormous musical instruments) and burning ruins, among which weird demons plague terrified men and women. One person is being crucified on the strings of a giant harp. This dark and dismal place is undoubtedly Bosch's vision of hell. But what about the center panel? Here, within a luscious landscape similar to that of the left panel, groups of nude men and women cavort about amid enormous fruits, flowers, birds, and marine creatures. Is this a depiction of the sinfulness of mankind?

Art historians have argued for centuries about the meaning of Bosch's weird and distorted imagery. Many wonder how much he was influenced by the gargoyles of medieval cathedrals and the monsters drawn in the margins of early manuscripts. Some suggest that his figures are simply the ultimate expression of a fascination with concealed religious symbolism that preoccupied so many northern artists of the period.

Pieter Bruegel the Elder (1525-1569) painted traditional biblical scenes in order to earn enough money to be able to focus upon what really interested him: animated, highly detailed scenes of the everyday lives of Flemish peasants. These are the works that made him famous. Bruegel often visited country fairs and sketched the people who gathered there to barter, socialize, and dance to the tunes of the flutes and drums.

The robust and hearty peasants who appear in his paintings have little in common with the handsome nudes of Michelangelo or the refined courtiers and philosophers in the frescoes of Raphael. They are ordinary men and women engaged in commonplace activities.

But there is also a hint of Bosch's eccentricity. Bruegel often placed the main subject of a painting in the distance or in the middle of a crowd of people. Sometimes an object seems terribly out of place, such as a windmill sitting atop a huge rock in the CARRYING OF THE CROSS. And there are usually a number of distracting activities going on at once, so you have to put some effort into figuring out what is the main subject. In THE FALL OF ICARUS the busy peasants don't even notice that the mythical hero has fallen into the sea. Is the artist suggesting that society cares little about the needs of the individual? Bruegel's pictures are at once pleasurable and unsettling. They reflect in many ways the turbulent times of the Reformation, which we will study in Chapter IX.

THE HOLY ROMAN EMPIRE

The Holy Roman Empire was a confederacy of over 300 fairly independent principalities and bishoprics in central Europe, including the Low Countries. It stretched from the Alps north to the Baltic Sea and from France in the west to Hungary and Poland in the east. The Empire had a population of nearly 20,000,000 in 1450, the largest in Europe. Most of the people spoke a dialect of German. The princes ruled their domains with great authority and even minted their own coins. The Emperor was elected by a powerful group of seven Electors: the Princes of Brandenburg, Bohemia, the Palatinate, and Saxony, and the Archbishops of Mainz, Trier, and Cologne. It was the Electors who held the real power. The

Emperor was virtually a figurehead: he derived no income from taxes and didn't even have a standing army. But he did have an impressive court.

THE HABSBURGS

During the Renaissance the Emperors were elected from the Austrian family of Habsburg. (The name Habsburg can be traced back to the family castle - *Habichsburg* - which was built in 1020 on the Aare River in Switzerland.) The Habsburgs had reigned almost without interruption ever since 1273. Maximilian I (ruling 1493-1519) was described in German folk legends as "the last knight." He was also a true Renaissance prince, who patronized a number of celebrated artists and scholars and found time to write autobiographical poems. His successors would be the greatest patrons in central Europe in the sixteenth century.

Maximilian married Mary of Burgundy in 1477, and their son Philip the Handsome married Joan the Mad, heiress of Spanish monarchs Ferdinand and Isabella. Maximilian's grandson (Philip's son), Charles, was born in Ghent, Flanders. He was a small, slight youth, with the jutting lower jaw that was characteristic of the Habsburgs. His habitually open mouth gave him a vacant expression, and the fact that he was not interested in books or administrative duties must have caused his advisors some concern. But Charles was an excellent warrior, and he was very anxious to win glory and honor on the battlefield. He became King Charles I of Spain in 1516 after the death of King Ferdinand.

When Maximilian died, the most likely candidate to succeed him as Emperor was Francis I of France. (Philip the Handsome had passed away in 1506.) Francis was not a Habsburg, but he had impressive political connections. Charles, however, was so determined to have the crown that he borrowed 800,000 florins (an enormous sum) and bought the necessary votes! He became Holy Roman Emperor Charles V on October 23, 1520. His vast empire stretched from Vienna, Austria to the Atlantic in a patchwork of kingdoms, counties, duchies, archbishoprics, electorates, and principalities. He ruled nearly one half of Christian Europe! He also inherited the Spanish overseas empire in America, which we will learn about in Chapter XIII.

More assertive than his predecessors, Charles would challenge the authority of the Electors and dominate European politics for forty years. Not since Charlemagne in the ninth century had one ruler controlled so much of Europe, and his Spanish holdings provided him with a formidable army. We learned earlier that Titian painted his portrait. If you look at a copy of it you will see that the young Emperor had quite an imposing presence.

Charles believed that he had been granted his vast empire so that he could unify Christian Europe and defend it against such heretics as the Turks (who were Muslims) and the Protestants (more about them later). He described himself as "God's standard bearer" and beneath his coat of arms appeared his motto, *plus ultra* (always further). Most of his reign was devoted to fighting his opponents - the Turks (who reached the gates of Vienna in 1529), the French, and later the German princes themselves. He has been described as a man desperately trying to extinguish fires in half a dozen parts of a large forest.

In 1556, exhausted by the burdens of his mission, Charles abdicated the throne, leaving his possessions in central Europe to his brother Ferdinand and the rest of his dominions to his son, Philip II of Spain. He retired to a comfortable villa near the monastery of San Yuste in the wooded hills north of the Tagus Valley in Spain. There he spent his final years in religious devotion, surrounded by his fine collection of paintings by Titian and other Renaissance artists. He often entertained himself by assembling and dismantling mechanical clocks, listening to music, eating fine foods, and dabbling (from afar) in political affairs. He died in 1558. Charles was the last Emperor to make any attempt to strengthen the authority of his title.

NUREMBERG

The overland trade route from Italy to the Low Countries passed right through the German-speaking regions of central Europe. Small towns sprang up along the route, where merchants could spend the night and take advantage of the local trade. In the fifteenth century the beautiful walled city of Nuremberg became very prosperous, thanks to its strategic location at the junction of two major trade routes (one linking Italy with the Low Countries and the other linking France with eastern Europe). Nuremberg was built on a hill above the Penitz River. Its winding streets and multi-storied buildings were dominated by the grand imperial palace (one of the Emperor's many residences). It was a lively, exciting center of merchants, furriers, cloth makers, and goldsmiths.

Nuremberg's close ties with Italy made it one of the leading centers of the northern Renaissance. In fact, some people considered the city the Florence of the north. Wealthy merchants established academies where they could gather with friends and talk about classical art and philosophy. They became so fascinated with the public baths of ancient Rome that they opened fourteen bathhouses of their own! Personal cleanliness became an important feature of life in Nuremberg (a refreshing change after centuries of unbathed, smelly, lice-infested people), and a certain portion of a man's wages was set aside as "bathing money." The city government hired laborers, known as "scavengers," to clean the city streets each day. The ethic of cleanliness even extended to food, and laws were passed forbidding the sale of the meat of animals that were not freshly killed.

A New Technology

The year 1450 marks a critical turning point in the communication of ideas, one that was as significant as the arrival of computers in the modern age. In that year the printing press was invented. Making multiple copies of a piece of written matter was not a new concept, even in those early times. Since about 800 the Chinese had been carving letters (characters) on wood blocks, inking them, and then pressing them onto large sheets of paper made from vegetable fibers. In the twelfth century Arab traders learned about the wood blocks and introduced the concept of printing into Europe.

Carving letters on blocks of wood and printing them on paper was certainly a lot quicker and less expensive than writing a book with pen and ink on parchment (dried animal hide). It took a monk about six months to copy a 200-page text, and the parchment required twenty-five sheepskins. The earliest known European woodblock was a picture of Saint Christopher done in 1423, and soon afterwards printers began to produce books by binding single printed pages together. Most of these were versions of the Bible. At first the paper was made from hemp and flax, but eventually old linen rags were boiled to make a pulp. This was strained through a flat sieve, and when the pulp dried, the fibers meshed and matted into a sheet of paper. Woodblocks were ideal for printing decks of playing cards (history's first), and these became popular in the courts of Europe. But although the new process was speedier and cheaper than the traditional method of copying books, a text could not be altered and the words were often unevenly printed.

Enter Gutenberg

Johannes Gutenberg (1399-1468) was a goldsmith living in Mainz, Germany. (We'll refer to the German-speaking section of the Holy Roman Empire as Germany.) He had learned about metalwork from an uncle, who, as master of a mint, knew how to cast coins from hot metal. In experimenting with molten metals, Gutenberg discovered an alloy of tin and lead that could be poured into molds and would not shrink or twist when it was cooled. So he made a set of letter molds or type. These could be laid out in a tray in even lines to spell words. The hard part was doing everything in reverse, since the letters were mirror images of what would be printed. But once the trays were ready Gutenberg could print a page by covering the letters with oil based ink and pressing them against a sheet of paper. After the page was printed, the letters could be reassembled to spell the words of another page. And they could be used thousands of times without noticeable "wear and tear." What an incredible breakthrough!

Gutenberg designed a printing press modeled upon an old wine press. This is how it worked. First he arranged the letters in the tray. Then, after placing a piece of paper over the letters, he slid the paper and the tray into the press. He lowered a flat wooden plate onto the paper by turning a huge wooden screw. This pressed the paper firmly down onto the inked type to print a page. Now he could remove the paper and print another copy. The pages were hung up on a line to dry. They were eventually put in order and attached to a leather cover with glue and thread to make a book. Gutenberg's press could print 300 pages a day, a dramatic improvement over woodblock printing and something of a miracle when compared to the time and labor involved in copying books by hand.

Gutenberg's *magnum opus* (great work) was his Bible, which he completed in 1456. It had 1,282 double columned pages, each one decorated by hand. (Gutenberg felt that people would only buy his books if they resembled the lavishly illustrated handwritten manuscripts of the day.) He printed 300 copies. The forty-eight Gutenberg Bibles that have survived are among the most valuable books in the world. Sadly, Gutenberg was a poor businessman, and he became involved in endless lawsuits over the patent of his press. But although he died a poor man, his invention would immortalize his name.

A New Industry

The demand for printed books was unprecedented. Presses were set up throughout the Holy Roman Empire, and before long they were appearing in cities all over Europe. Printing had become a major industry. More books were printed in the next few decades than had been copied by hand in several centuries. At first the type resembled manuscript writing, but this was eventually replaced by the more graceful, easily readable letters of the Romans. Italy was a fertile ground for publishing, given the large number of literate people living there. Immigrants from Germany printed the first books in Italy in the monastery of Sabiaco (near Rome) in 1465. These were, appropriately enough, a Latin grammar and a book by the Roman orator, Cicero.

Aldus Manutius (1449-1515) was an Ital-

ian scholar who established a printing press in Venice in 1494. His Aldine Press made widely available the first printed editions of nearly all the major Greek authors. Manutius invented several typefaces which became models for those in use today (most notably, the graceful Italic). He printed hundreds of books - everything from ancient classics to contemporary poetry. Many of the volumes were small and inexpensive enough for scholars to buy and to carry in their pockets. (These were the original paperbacks.) However, many well-to-do people looked askance at the new printed books. The Duke of Urbino refused to have any of them in his library, dismissing them as cheap imitations of his beautiful manuscripts.

But progress could not be held back. Thanks to Manutius, Venice became the leading printing center in Europe. Cheap editions of romances, histories and dialogues written in Italian were circulated among ordinary people, who had little interest in scholarly issues. By the end of the fifteenth century, over 150 printers were working in Venice, and forty per cent of all the printed books circulating in Europe were Italian. The earliest book catalogue was compiled in Venice, with prices listed beside the titles.

In England, a wool merchant named William Caxton translated French works into English as a hobby. Scholarship soon became his passion, and in 1475 he became a printer. After making copies of a translation of the story of the Trojan War, he published 107 new titles, many his own translations of ancient works. When he printed Geoffrey Chaucer's CANTERBURY TALES in the dialect spoken in London (and the royal court), he helped promote this as the standard English language. Until the invention of the printing press, most books had been written in Latin, the language of scholarship. The works of Dante, Petrarch, and

Boccaccio, as well as the poems of such humanists as Lorenzo de Medici, were notable exceptions. But times had changed, and people were now demanding books written in words they could understand.

Anton Koberger was the first major German publisher. He opened his workshop in Nuremberg in 1470 with forty presses and 100 employees. Within fifty years all the major works of Latin authors had been published in Germany. One of the earliest German best-sellers published was Sebastian Brant's satirical poem, SHIP OF FOOLS, published in 1494. It was the first modern work of poetry composed in German. This entertaining book satirizes the numerous foibles and follies of mankind by describing different types of fools. It was so popular that it was immediately translated from German into Latin, French, English, and Dutch.

At the dawn of the sixteenth century there were printing shops in more than 100 cities and towns in Europe, and several million books were in circulation. In the next century millions more would appear. Now readers could enjoy a wide variety of prose and poetry. They could easily consult encyclopedias, legal handbooks, maps, and even astrological charts. The first almanacs soon appeared, making predictions about the weather, the production of crops, and advice about daily living (often based on superstitions). These were the ancestors of our modern FARMERS' ALMANAC.

By the end of the sixteenth century 3,000 copies of a page could be printed per day. Broadsides (single printed sheets) came into being, the forerunners of daily newspapers. One of the main results of the explosion of available reading material was that people began to think for themselves and to debate many things they had once taken for granted, particularly the doctrines of the Church. We'll learn about the consequences of this in a later chapter.

THE FUGGERS

Some of the wealthy merchants of Nuremberg used their profits to found their own banking houses, just as the Medici had done in Florence. In time, Nuremberg became the major banking city outside Italy. Its major northern rival was the wealthy commercial center, Augsburg, which from the time of Maximillian was the headquarters of the two biggest banks in northern Europe: those of the Fugger and Welser families. The Fugger bank is the more famous.

Jakob "the Rich" Fugger took charge of his family trading and banking firm in 1485. In return for loans to the counts of nearby Tyrol and the Habsburg emperors (including Charles V), he obtained a monopoly of the mining of Tyrolese silver, Hungarian copper, and Spanish mercury. For sixteen years his profits increased annually at a rate of fifty-four percent! His trading interests extended from the Far East to the New World (America). The Fugger headquarters were in a magnificent building known as the Golden Counting House. The bank's agents in foreign cities wrote regular reports back to Augsburg, giving up-to-date information about the local economies where they were living. The company compiled the data in newsletters, which gave merchants better information about major commercial activities than any prince could obtain from his ambassadors or spies.

During the late fifteenth century and most of the sixteenth century the Fuggers were among the richest people in the western world. They spent much of their wealth on art, including portraits, buildings, and a family chapel in Augsburg. But things began going poorly for the family fortunes when the Habsburgs began demanding huge, risky loans to finance their wars. The bank was finally ruined at the end of the sixteenth century when the Spanish monarchy couldn't pay its sizable debt. Fortunately, the Fuggers still had their majestic country estates, to which they humbly retired.

ALBRECHT DURER

Albrecht Durer (1471-1521) of Nuremberg was the greatest German artist of the Renaissance. He was introduced to the process of printing by his godfather, Anton Koberger, and he developed a life-long interest in woodcuts. In 1494 Durer went to Italy, where he studied the works of Giovanni Bellini and Leonardo da Vinci, thought about the various techniques of creating a sense of depth in a painting, and closely examined the ancient statues. Was it possible, he wondered, to create figures as lifelike and animated as these statues in a woodcut? It was certainly a challenge, and when he returned to Nuremberg he got to work on a series of woodcuts depicting the Apocalypse - the biblical prediction of the end of the world. (Many people of the fifteenth century were convinced that the world was going to end in the year 1500!) Unlike the simple, linear designs of other woodcuts of the time, Durer's were of an unprecedented size, filled with intricate details, and charged with emotional drama. They were not simple book illustrations - they were magnificent works of art.

Fourteen full-page woodcuts appear in Durer's volume, THE APOCALYPSE - the first book to be designed, executed, printed, and published by an artist. The most famous of the prints is the allegorical FOUR HORSEMEN OF THE APOCALYPSE. Find a copy of it in an art book. The crowned rider with a bow on a white horse represents Conquest, the rider with a sword on a red horse is War, the rider with a set of scales on a black horse symbolizes Plague and Famine, and the scrawny rider on a sickly

pale horse is Death. The four horsemen are trampling everything in their path. What is Durer trying to say to us? All of the woodcuts in the volume are similarly filled with highly detailed forms, many of them symbolic. The major figures are highlighted by a dramatic flickering of light against the background darkness.

Like the Italian painters, Durer studied human anatomy to make his figures realistic. He often attended the public baths that had become popular throughout Germany and sketched the scantily clad bathers. His drawing of APOLLO AND DIANA shows his skill in depicting the human form. Durer, by the way, introduced the classic nude into German art.

He also painted numerous portraits, altarpieces, and scenes of nature. His SELF PORTRAIT painted in 1500 (one of several portraits he did of himself) reveals a confident and sophisticated gentleman in a fur-trimmed coat whose features bear an interesting resemblance to Christ. This is no lowly craftsman of earlier times. Durer's gaze is intense, and the details and lighting of the work reflect his technical genius (as well as the influence of Leonardo). In an effort to make the figures of religious scenes appear more human, Durer often gave them the expressive faces of the peasants he encountered every day (as Bruegel would) and placed them in German surroundings. Sometimes an artist's informal drawings become as famous as his finished works. The preliminary sketch of a pair of praying hands Durer made for an altarpiece has become a well-known symbol of the Christian faith.

Durer's portrayal of nature was, as you would expect, incredibly precise. The details of his watercolor A GREAT PIECE OF TURF are so accurate that modern botanists can easily identify the dandelions, meadow grass, yarrow, and plantains appearing in it.

Remember Sebastian Brant's SHIP OF FOOLS? Durer created a series of woodcuts showing the foibles of mankind to illustrate the book. In most of these man appears as a court jester engaged in such foolish acts as putting out his neighbors fire while his own house burns, or tending his sail while the ship breaks up beneath him! Despite the comic aspect of these prints, the figures and surroundings are convincing and believable.

In later years Durer pushed the technique of line engraving to its limits. Engraving was a new process for making multiple copies that originated in a goldsmith's shop in the fifteenth century. Cutting lines into copper plates allowed Durer to depict even greater detail than he had in the woodcuts. In NATIVITY the various ordinary objects of the old and decrepit farmyard - loose tiles, a broken wall, cracked mortar, even birds' nests - are so realistically depicted that they seem as important as the biblical figures in the scene.

His finest engravings are known as the Three Master Prints - THE KNIGHT, DEATH, and THE DEVIL (the knight represents the Christian faith), SAINT JEROME IN HIS STUDY, and MELANCHOLIA. Find them now in an art book. In the third engraving, Melancholia (the winged daughter of the Roman god Saturn) sits gloomily in her study amid the symbols of man's accomplishments: a compass, a book, a balance, and a hammer. She symbolizes the introspective (self-absorbed) intellectual. Is Durer suggesting that when thought is not directed toward practical ends it leads to despair? Or is he simply mocking the vanity of human knowledge? (The northern Europeans tended to exalt faith above intellectual pursuits.)

Durer was justly proud of his achievements, and on his engraving entitled ADAM AND EVE he wrote in Latin, *"Albertus Durer Noricus Faciebat"* (Albert

Durer Made This). Maximillian I appointed Durer his court painter and paid him 100 florins a year. When the Emperor died in 1519, the artist went to the Netherlands, where he studied Flemish painting and had his court position renewed by the new Emperor, Charles V. It was during this trip that he contracted malaria while examining a beached whale, so curious was he about the natural world. This condition would linger and weaken him considerably for the rest of his life.

Durer spent his last years back in Nuremberg, where he published three illustrated books on geometry, fortifications, and human proportions. He was Germany's answer to Leonardo da Vinci! Throughout his lifetime he experimented with a great diversity of media, styles, and subject matter, and when he died he left behind a rich legacy: six dozen paintings, over 100 engravings, 250 woodcuts, and 1,000 drawings. He did more than any other to popularize the classical revival in his own homeland. Some historians consider Durer the most important German artist of all time.

RESURGENT GERMAN NATIONALISM

Conrad Celtis (1459-1508) was perhaps the most exuberant of northern humanists and the greatest German lyric poet of the Renaissance. In 1487 Emperor Frederick III crowned him with a laurel wreath and conferred upon him the prestigious title of doctor of philosophy. (From then on Celtis haughtily insisted that he always be addressed as "Poet Laureate.")

Celtis taught classical studies in several universities and traveled widely. His voyages included a two-year visit to Italy, where he was deeply offended by his perception that the Italians considered themselves culturally superior to the "barbarians" of the north. He later gave a speech challenging his German countrymen to take up arms (literary ones) and rekindle the old spirit with which they had once terrorized ancient Rome. Celtis enthusiastically translated *GERMANIA* by the Roman historian Tacitus, a work that praised the culture of the Germanic tribesmen. He planned to write the first comprehensive geographical and historical survey of Germany, but he died in Vienna before its completion. His gravestone bore the words, *Vivo* ("I live").

Johann Reuchlin was a noted classical scholar who became interested in Jewish mystical literature. He believed that a study of the Hebrew language would bring him closer to God, since Moses and other Old Testament prophets had spoken in that tongue. He wrote a very reliable manual of Hebrew, and in his book ON THE CABALISTIC ART (1517) he tried to demonstrate that Greek and Hebrew values are compatible with Christian beliefs.

Reuchlin was attacked by those who feared that his theories might undermine traditional interpretations of the Bible, and in 1519 Emperor Maximillian I ordered that all Hebrew books be confiscated. Reuchlin protested by firing off short articles defending his beliefs, but the following year Pope Leo X condemned him to silence.

REVIEW QUESTIONS:

1. How did the presence of the Ottoman Turks affect western Europeans?

2. Describe the style of Jan van Eyck.

3. In what ways were the paintings of Bruegel Mannerist?

4. What was Hieronymous Bosch's obsession?

5. Who were the most powerful people in the Holy Roman Empire?

6. Why did Charles V finally abdicate?

7. Describe Nuremberg.

8. How did Gutenberg's press work?

9. What's so great about Aldus Manutius?

10. What was THE SHIP OF FOOLS?

11. What is Albrecht Durer most famous for?

12. How did Conrad Celtis feel about Italy?

FURTHERMORE:

1. According to legend, Antonello da Messina, a young Sicilian assistant to a Flemish painter, fled to Italy when his master died, taking with him the secret formula for oil paints. The enraged Flemish painters tried to stop him and even resorted to hiring a professional killer. But Antonello was not caught. He was among the first painters in Italy to use oil paints.

2. Charles IV of Bohemia (1346-78) one of the greatest patrons of the fourteenth century. His court in Prague attracted many scholars and artists (including, for a short period, Petrarch). Charles founded the University of Prague in 1348, where one thousand students were in attendance at the end of his reign. He also promoted the construction of St Vitus' Cathedral (in Prague), composed an autobiography, sponsored the writing of several chronicles of Bohemian history, and oversaw the translation of the Bible into Czech.

3. In 1045 Chinese printer Pi Sheng made the first movable type. He created a clay letter for each character. However, the idea of movable type never really caught on in his country, since the Chinese language has thousands of characters.

4. Johannes Gutenberg went by his mother's maiden name. His proper last

name was Gensfleish which means "gooseflesh." Can you blame him for not wanting to use his father's name?

5. Printers saved a letter by using the symbol "y" for the letters "th," so ye was the printer's abbreviation for the. Similarly, "double s" was represented by "f." These abbreviations appeared in printed works until the 18th century!

6. The first printed cookbook, *DE HONESTA VOLUPTATE*, appeared in Italy in 1475. Included among the recipes were bits of advice about maintaining good health, including warnings about the dangers of overindulgence.

7. A fad produced by the invention of the printing press was the "girdle book." This was a small leather covered volume that was worn suspended from a knot that passed through one's belt. It hung upside down, so it could be easily read without being detached. It was the perfect gift for someone who loved to read!

8. The Aldine Press is still publishing books. And it still has its original emblem, a dolphin and an anchor. The speeding dolphin is held back and controlled by the drag of the anchor. The dolphin represents inspiration and the anchor, reason.

9. Jacob Fugger used his riches to acquire a castle and even a title (he became a count). He was a shrewd and confident businessman. He once had the nerve to write a letter to Charles V, reminding him that he had used Fugger money to obtain his crown and advising him to make payment on a loan "without any further delay."

PROJECTS:

1. Part of Flanders later became a province of France. Is it still a French province? Find out more about this unique region. Also, find out where the Flemish language is still spoken today.

2. Albrecht Durer and Michelangelo had a great deal in common, starting with personality. Find out more about these two men and then write a short paper comparing and contrasting them.

3. Look in an art book and find illustrations of paintings by Raphael and Jan van Eyck. How are they similar and how are they different. Make a chart comparing these two Renaissance painters.

4. Find an illustration of Bosch's GARDEN OF DELIGHTS. Study it carefully. Then pick a theme and, using Bosch's style of art, make an intricate drawing (on poster board) to illustrate it.

5. Draw a family tree of the Habsburg family.

6. Find out more about the Fugger bank and write a short report.

7. Make a diagram of Gutenberg's printing press.

8. Compare Bosch's GARDEN OF DELIGHTS with Dante's description of the Inferno.

9. Find out more about Albrecht Durer. Select one of his works. Then write a report about it.

10. Write a paper comparing Flemish and Italian painting during the fifteenth century.

11. In medieval times money was used for exchange, but during the Renaissance money was used to make money. Think about this statement. Then write an essay explaining what it means. Use specific examples.

Chapter VIII
THE RENAISSANCE SPREADS TO FRANCE

The Valois family was the ruling dynasty in France from 1328 until 1589. During a long bloody conflict with England known as the Hundred Years' War, the *Estates General* (the elected French governing body) voted to allow King Charles VII to raise a tax (called the *taille*) to pay for soldiers whenever he needed them. This gave the French king tremendous power, while diminishing that of the Estates. Charles took advantage of the situation by building up a large professional army of *gens d'armes* (men at arms), which was his major legacy to his successors. One of these, Louis XI, was a shrewd and cunning monarch known to his enemies as "the Spider." He further strengthened his authority by restricting the privileges of the nobility and encouraged the growth of trade and industry. At the dawn of the Renaissance, the King of France was one of the most powerful men in Europe.

THE ITALIAN WARS

Let's return for a moment to fifteenth century Italy. As we learned in Chapter III, the Peace of Lodi, a mutual non-aggression pact among the five major powers of Italy (Venice, Milan, Florence, Naples, and the Papal Lands) was signed in 1454. Until the death of Lorenzo the Magnificent in 1492, the peace was maintained. But then new conflicts arose that had their roots in the preceding decade.

The problems began in Milan in 1480, when Francesco Sforza's second son, Ludovico, gained control of the government, ruling in the name of his young nephew. Ludovico was known as *Il Moro* (the Moor) because of his swarthy complexion. He was an able ruler and a well-educated patron of the arts. He married Beatrice d'Este of Mantua (the sister of Isabella, Marquise of Urbino) and presided over an elegant court. As we learned earlier, Leonardo da Vinci spent quite a bit of time designing theatrical sets for his courtiers. When Ludovico's nephew died in 1494, he proclaimed himself Duke of Milan. But there was another nephew who was the legitimate heir to this title, and he sought the support of his grandfather, the powerful King Alfonzo of Naples. Now Ludovico was really in a fix. So, to secure his position and preoccupy King Alfonzo, he encouraged Charles VIII of France to claim his ancient rights to southern Italy. (Charles, who succeeded Louis XI, was related to the ruling family in Naples through his great grandfather. Isn't it fascinating how most of the rulers of Europe were related to one another?) Charles marched his *gens d'armes* through Italy in 1494 and set into motion the Italian Wars, a long series of battles that would drag on for over half a century. These involved not only the Valois kings but also the rulers of Spain and the Holy Roman Empire. They would ultimately destroy the independence of the Italian city-states. The only good thing you can say about them is that they helped to spread the culture of Renaissance Italy to other parts of western Europe.

Charles led his French troops to Florence, which Piero de Medici immediately surrendered. (As we learned, the Florentines booted out Piero for betraying them.) Then Charles marched south, drove off Alfonzo, and had himself crowned King of Naples. When he returned to France, he left his army garrisoned in Italy. The presence of these soldiers was an unbearable affront to the Italians, and it prompted the five signers of the Treaty of Lodi (including Milan!) to look for another foreign ally. They appealed to King Ferdinand of Aragon, who obligingly sent his army down the Italian peninsula to surround the French soldiers. After some terrible fighting the French who survived fled home. But now there were Spanish soldiers garrisoned in Italy! The Italians were no better off than they were before.

But let's get back to Milan, where the problems began. In 1500 Louis XII of France (who succeeded Charles VIII) invaded Ludovico's city. (He had inherited a claim to Milan via his grandfather.) The city fell to the French. (Ludovico later ended his days as a prisoner in the French castle of Lorches.) Louis continued on to Naples but was driven back by the Spanish army. So now the French dominated northern Italy from a base in Milan, while the Spanish remained firmly entrenched in the south. Not much of the peninsula remained in Italian hands.

CESARE BORGIA

Cesare Borgia, the son of Pope Alexander VI, played a vital role in the politics of central Italy at this point. He was a ruthless and brutal man, one of the great villains of history, although he looked more like a hero. He was extremely handsome, with big shoulders, a slim waist, long, thick hair, and blazing blue eyes. Cesare was made a cardinal by his father in 1493, but he renounced his career with the Church five years later for a more active military life. He led an army against the rebelling Papal States and brought them back under the firm control of Rome. He was supported in his military campaign by Louis XII of France, who granted him the title of Duke of Valentinois. (By allying with Cesare, Louis cleverly extended the French influence in Italy further south.)

Now known to the local citizens as *Il Valentino*, Cesare set about conquering a territory for himself in central Italy. He used treason, murder, and intrigue to crush the noble families living there. He personally strangled and tortured many of them and even knifed a papal official, who had run to Alexander for refuge and was cowering in fear under the Pope's mantle!

In 1501 Alexander named his son Duke of Romagna, the state the young warrior had carved out for himself. Surprisingly, Romagna had a model government in which all subjects had equal treatment before the law. But Cesare had made many enemies, and the following summer several of his leading condottiere conspired against him. When he tricked the conspirators and slyly lured them to their deaths he earned the admiration, rather than the disapproval, of many Italians. In 1502 he swept down on Urbino and forced the rulers to flee. He appropriated the priceless art collection of Isabella d'Este, much of which he sold to pay his troops.

The death of Alexander signaled the end of Cesare's political career. Although the new pope, Pius III, supported him, he soon died and was succeeded by Julius II, a sworn enemy of the Borgias. Cesare was forced to give up his strongholds in the Papal States, and when it became clear that his life was in danger, he fled from Romagna to Naples, then to Spain. He was imprisoned by Ferdinand but escaped to Navarre. Cesare was killed in 1507 at the siege of Viana, fighting for his brother-in-law, the King of Navarre.

ENTER THE HABSBURGS

The Italian Wars intensified when Emperor Maximilian joined Pope Julius, King Louis XII, and King Ferdinand in the League of Cambrai (1508) against Venice, which was grabbing up large chunks of northern Italy. The League conquered all of Venice's mainland possessions, but quarrels over dividing up the spoils led to the formation of a new alliance, the anti-French Holy League between Julius, Maximilian and Ferdinand. Louis was forced out of Milan.

In 1515 the new French king, Francis I, led an army across the Alps and reconquered Milan. Soon afterwards both Ferdinand and Maximilian died, and Charles V became Holy Roman Emperor. So now Francis and Charles were the major players in the Italian Wars. In 1525 Charles defeated the French army at Pavia in northern Italy, capturing Francis himself and sending him to a prison in Spain. The French king was released the next year on condition that he surrender all the Italian territory he had claimed. But France was not yet out of the picture.

The new pope, Clement VII, was worried about the political ambitions of Charles, so he allied himself with Francis, as well as the cities of Florence, Milan, and Venice in the League of Cognac in 1526. In response, Charles sent an army to Italy. It conquered Milan and then marched on Rome in 1527, hoping to convince the Pope to quit the League. But the army commander was killed soon after their successful assault of the city and discipline completely broke down. The soldiers savagely sacked Rome for a week, murdering priests and looting churches and cathedrals. (This is when many of the artists and scholars fled to other cities, particularly Venice.) Clement took refuge in the strongly fortified Castel San Angelo before surrendering. Charles later released the Pope for a huge ransom and withdrew his men from Rome. The Emperor had proven his might and brought the Pope under his (temporary) control, but the sack of Rome shocked the Christian world. Was nothing sacred during these war-ridden times?

Francis continued to meddle in Italian affairs until political setbacks forced him to sign the Treaty of Cateau-Cambresis in 1559, by which he renounced all claims in Italy. That was the end of French involvement, although the imperial army was still firmly entrenched in Italy. The major consequences of the long and incredibly complicated Italian Wars were that, with the exception of Venice and the Papal Lands, the city-states were in the hands of the Spanish Habsburgs. Indeed, they would control much of Italy until the early eighteenth century.

MACHIAVELLI

Before moving on, we should take a moment to learn about the most original political thinker of the Renaissance, Niccolo Machiavelli (1469-1527). He was a Florentine diplomat and historian, educated in the humanist tradition, who lived during the turbulent times of the Italian Wars. As a young man he had observed how the city-states tried to protect themselves by playing off the larger powers against one another and by hiring armies of mercenaries, which they then had difficulty controlling. It was a dangerous era, marked by blackmail, violence, and political intrigue.

After the fall of Savonarola in 1498, Florence created a new republican government. Machiavelli held several top positions, and his high status enabled him to make numerous diplomatic missions abroad, where he met many of the most powerful political figures of the time, including Louis XII,

Maximilian I, Cesare Borgia, and Pope Julius II. But when the Medici returned to power in Florence in 1512, they unfairly accused Machiavelli of opposing them and ordered him imprisoned and even tortured. When he was released a year later, he returned to his country estate on the outskirts of Florence. There he spent most of his days socializing with his friends and former political colleagues, but each evening he retired to his study, dressed in the "regal and courtly garments" he had once worn so proudly as a public official, to work on his writings. He was particularly interested in analyzing the egotistical ways of mankind and the ruthless realities of political power. He was deeply troubled by the presence of the foreign armies in Italy. Machiavelli spent a good deal of time studying the writings of the ancients to learn how they coped with the crises of their era, hoping that perhaps he could apply their solutions to the crises of his own age. As it turned out, he came to very different conclusions about the responsibilities of leadership than they had.

His major work was THE PRINCE, a practical guide to running a government which became a landmark in political theory. The book was dedicated to Lorenzo the Magnificent's grandson (Lorenzo, Duke of Urbino) and was intended to advise the young man how to cope in the cut-throat world of politics. Machiavelli's bitter experiences had convinced him that morality and government were two separate things, and in THE PRINCE he discusses the sources of power without regard for their ethical (moral) content. In fact, Cesare Borgia, known for his cruelty and ruthless tactics, was a model for the book. Machiavelli admired the way Cesare welcomed his enemies as friends and then neatly strangled them! Like Il Valentino, the young Duke was advised, the cleverest deceiver always wins.

Machiavelli advises the Duke (who is addressed in the work as "the prince") to accept people as they are. Why waste time worrying about what they ought to be? So what are people really like? According to the author, they are ungrateful, undependable, false, and greedy. And a wise ruler should appeal to their selfish motives. Machiavelli glorifies the qualities of the lion (force) and the fox (slyness). A prince must be powerful and crafty; lies and deceit are totally acceptable if they accomplish a goal. Why be hampered by such noble values as honesty, justice, or honor? The end justifies the means. What works is good, what doesn't isn't. Above all, a prince's authority must be absolute and unquestioned, since "it is better to be feared than loved" (although, the author adds, it could be dangerous to be hated!). The treatise concludes with a plea for the rescue of Italy from the "barbarian forces" currently occupying it, namely the French and imperial armies.

THE PRINCE was not published until after the death of Machiavelli in 1532. As you might expect, it immediately drew tirades of criticism. Its fundamental concepts are very different from the political theories of Aristotle, who considered politics a branch of ethics (rules of conduct based upon principles of right and wrong). Most Italians, despite the obvious corruption of their own society, seemed to believe that government should be run in a fair and judicial manner. But didn't the humanists encourage everyone to open their eyes and minds to the real world? Artists like Giotto and Leonardo da Vinci tried to show how men really look. Machiavelli wanted to show how men really think.

Because of his political views, Machiavelli's name undeservedly became a byword for godlessness, cynicism, and treachery. Even today, "machiavellian" is a pejorative adjective applied to someone who does what is most practical, even if it is not ethical. Yet, THE PRINCE was closely studied by rulers like Charles V, and it is considered a classic treatise by political theorists in our own times.

ITALIAN CULTURE TRAVELS TO FRANCE

Many of the French officers serving in the Italian Wars were dazzled by the beautiful art they saw in the palazzos and churches of Italy, and they returned home laden with treasures they had seized. Louis XI had silkworms and even mulberry trees (their fruit is the favorite food of the silkworm caterpillar) imported from Italy to France, and in only a few years a silk industry was thriving in the French cities of Lyons and Tours. Charles VIII brought back twenty Italian artists, who passed on their techniques to local painters and sculptors. He also shipped from Naples 87,000 pounds of plunder, including tapestries, books, paintings, and sculpture. These further whetted the appetite of the French noblemen for Italian art, and it became fashionable to own pieces imported from Italy.

FRANCIS I

Francis I ruled France from 1515 until 1547. His repeated invasions of Italy aroused a keen interest in the Italian Renaissance, and he became one of the greatest patrons of art and literature in the history of France. He was a dashing, well-educated, and witty man, who modeled himself after the Italian princes and prided himself on the brilliance of his court. In 1516 Francis persuaded Leonardo da Vinci to spend his last years at his court. He also lured Benvenuto Cellini with the promise, "I will choke you with gold." (Remember the famous saltcellar Cellini made for the French

king?) It wasn't long before France was setting the style for other European nations to follow.

THE FIELD OF CLOTH OF GOLD

In June 1520 a historic meeting took place between Francis and King Henry VIII of England on the plain in Picardy (between the French villages of Guines and Ardres). The two kings, accompanied by huge numbers of followers, enjoyed three weeks of feasting and pageantry, each trying to outshine the other in the splendor of his retinue and the magnificence of his tent.

Henry's fabulous temporary palace at Guines covered nearly 130,000 square feet. Its windows were framed in gold and its walls were lined with silk. There was a chapel with a golden statue of the Apostles and altar cloths embroidered with pearls. Outside the tent a gilt fountain spouted wine! Not to be outdone, Francis occupied a gold brocade tent in neighboring Ardres. Its roof was adorned with astrological signs and stars made of gold leaf. Given the extravagant gilded decorations and golden silk of the tents, it's no wonder the plain was named the Field of Cloth of Gold.

The numbers of attendants were staggering. There were 4,000 in the English contingent alone. Splendid pavilions and arenas were set up for jousting, dancing, and feasting. Those who witnessed it called the spectacle the eighth wonder of the world! Thousands of cows, sheep, lambs, chickens, herons, and pheasants were imported to feed the courtiers, who were staying in smaller versions of the kings' magnificent tents. The extravagant banquet turned out to be a monumental waste of food. The participants conversed politely at the tables, but, because of the common fear of poisoning, they had all eaten earlier in the privacy of their own lodgings!

Despite the razzle dazzle, nothing much came from the meeting. Although it was staged as a show of friendship between the two rival monarchs (as well as a friendly competition of pomp), Henry's officials were already negotiating with Charles V, and England would join the Emperor's anti-French alliance the following year.

THE ARCHITECTURE OF THE FRENCH RENAISSANCE

During their occupation of Milan, the French had been captivated by the beauty of Certosa, an old church in the nearby town of Pavia. Although a medieval structure, Certosa had been given a new facade in the classical style of the Renaissance. (This was one of the pet projects of Ludovico Sforza.) Its ornate marble facing, intricate carvings of scrolls, shells, cherubs, and cornucopias, and columned galleries appealed to the French love of novelty and flamboyance. After the Italian Wars, the decorative features of Certosa were incorporated into a new French style of architecture.

Francis loved beautiful surroundings, and he ordered the "face-lifting" of older buildings and the construction of new ones. The medieval castle of Chambord in the Loire Valley was transformed into a majestic *chateau*. (*Chateau* is the French word for "castle.") It's crowded roofscape of chimneys, pinnacles, and dormers, all decorated with classical details, was clearly inspired by the roof of Certosa. This blending of the graceful and delicate features of French Gothic with classical design and decoration became known as the French Renaissance style of architecture.

Chambord was one of Francis' favorite residences. Its manicured grounds covered as much land as the city of Paris at that time! The chateau contains 440 rooms, which housed the king's ever-expanding court. That sounds like a huge number of rooms, but Francis' household had grown from the 318 people who served him at the beginning of the Italian Wars to over 1,000. Actually, the French king had more government officials than any other monarch in Europe. When his court moved from one chateau to

Figure 36: The Palace at Chambord

another, 18,000 horses were required to carry all the clothing, food, and other "necessities" of the courtiers.

In 1546 the Louvre in Paris, originally built as a royal fort in the twelfth century, was enlarged and made into a royal residence, with long arched colonnades and pillars. Sculptor Jean Goujon decorated the building with statues copied from Greek ones. Francis had a medieval hunting lodge in the forest of Fontainebleau torn down and hired Italian architects and artists to build and decorate an impressive chateau in the new style. The paintings and statues he amassed there, including some by Leonardo, Raphael, Titian, and Michelangelo, would later form the foundation of the outstanding collection of art housed today at the Louvre Museum in Paris.

Humanism in France

The French Renaissance in literature began before the reign of Francis with the work of humanist scholar Jacques Lefevre d'Etaples (1453-1536). He edited and translated the works of Aristotle, and in 1530 he completed the first French translation of the Bible. For a short while he was the tutor of the children of Francis I.

Guillaume Budé (1468-1540) was the most renowned humanist scholar of the early French Renaissance. Born in Paris, he served as secretary and ambassador to Louis XII. Budé's fluency in Greek and Latin enabled him to study the original versions of the great classical writers. Like Leonardo, he had an insatiable curiosity about all manner of things, including mathematics, philosophy, logic, law, and science. In fact, Budé introduced the word "encyclopedia" into the French language. In 1532 he published ABOUT PHILOSOPHY, which summed up all the major ideas of classical scholarship.

Budé was later appointed secretary to Francis I and master of the king's rapidly growing royal library. Francis had a keen interest in books and manuscripts, many of which he inherited from Charles VIII. To expand his collection, he enacted the Ordinance of Montpellier in 1537, which required that his library receive a copy of every book published in France. In addition, all foreign books sold in France were deposited there for examination and possible purchase (if they were considered important). Francis encouraged the translation of ancient and contemporary works into French, and his meals were often followed by readings from them. (Have you noticed how wealthy people loved to be read to during dinner?) Budé encouraged Francis to develop his idea of a university (the forerunner of the College de France), helping him to shape a curriculum based upon "the humanities."

François Rabelais (1494-1533) was the greatest comic writer of the French Renaissance. He was a jolly Franciscan friar who abandoned his religious pursuits to become a physician and Greek scholar. Rabelais hated the ignorance and immorality he observed in monastic life. He wanted to decipher the mysteries of the natural world without the hindrance of outdated rules and traditions. He expressed many of his ideas in his two satirical tales, GARGANTUA (1532) and its sequel, PANTAGRUEL.

The titles of the books refer to a giant philosopher king (Gargantua) and his son (Pantagruel). Both men have enormous appetites (a reflection of Rabelais' voracious curiosity and great love for learning.) Their mock heroic adventures serve as a vehicle for irreverently poking fun at the pretensions of various members of French society, including theologians, lawyers, and philosophers. The character of Friar John, for example, reveals the laziness and impiety of the monks when he remarks, "I never sleep soundly but when I am at sermon or prayers." In contrast to the corrupt and often outrageous individuals who appear in the books, Rabelais offers his version of an ideal society - the Abbey of Theleme. This is a monastic community that welcomes members of both genders and has for a motto, "Do what you wish." In this pleasant setting men and women pursue their intellectual interests in an ambiance of refinement and harmony reminiscent of the court of Castiglione. What was the author's main message? That although people have a variety of strengths and weaknesses, a humanist education brings out the best in everyone.

Rabelais' tales are an odd mixture of classical learning and bawdy jokes, and their earthiness offended many people. But although they were censored by the Church-controlled University of Paris, they were read and enjoyed by large numbers of people, including Francis I.

Speaking of the University of Paris, that hallowed institution attracted several young men in the early sixteenth century who later became celebrated poets and writers. They called themselves the *Pleiade* after a famous group of seven Alexandrine (from Alexandria, Egypt) poets of antiquity. Foremost among them were Pierre de Ronsard (1524-85) and Joachim du Bellay (1522-60). They had studied the major Greek and Roman poets as well as the works of Dante, Boccaccio, and Petrarch, and they believed that "modern poetry" should adhere to the forms, rhythms, and vocabulary of ancient verse but be written in the French vernacular. Their literary goals were expressed in DuBellay's DEFENCE AND ILLUSTRATION OF THE FRENCH LANGUAGE, a treatise that praised the beauty and precision of the French language and showed how effectively it could express the emotions and images of poetry.

Ronsard is considered the greatest poet of the group. He entered the court of Francis I in 1536 as a page to the royal family, but an illness left him partially deaf, forcing him to abandon his court career. This is when he began to study ancient poetry and met du Bellay and the other poets of the Pleiade. Ronsard was particularly inspired by the works of classical poets, Horace and Pindar, and by the sonnets of Petrarch. His lyrical verses contain simple truths about beauty, love, remorse, happiness, and the joys of the quiet life. One of the most famous, *"Mignonne allons voir si la rose..."* ("Little one, let's go see if the rose..."), uses the rose as a symbol of beauty that fades all too soon. English poet Robert Herrick must have been influenced by Ronsard when he wrote in the seventeenth century his famous lines, "Gather ye rosebuds while ye may."

LITERARY WOMEN

At the dawn of the Renaissance Christine de Pisan became the first woman to write professionally (and the first published feminist). Born in Venice, she moved with her family to France while still a child. Her father, who became court physician of Charles V of France, saw to it that his daughter was well educated. Christine learned to read French, Italian, and Latin before her marriage at the age fifteen to a young courtier. It was a happy marriage (an unusual situation in those days), but unfortunately her husband died suddenly in 1390. So, at the age of twenty-five, Christine found herself a mother of three children with no income and many debts. (Her father had also recently died.)

What to do? Few options were open to a woman of her class, so she decided to take the unprecedented step of pursuing a writing career to support herself and family. (Other women wrote verse, but not for a living.) After intensive studies of history, poetry, and science to prepare herself for the task ahead, she felt ready. At first she simply copied other books, doing her own illustrations, but then she began writing original poetry. This met with some success and brought her a commission to write the biography of Charles V. Encouraged by the positive reception of this work, she wrote a treatise on how to rule effectively, THE BODY OF POLICY (a worthy predecessor of Machiavelli's THE PRINCE), which was also highly regarded.

Christine de Pisan was the first to write in defense of the rights of women. She admired the heroism of Joan of Arc and wrote her narrative HYMN TO JOAN OF ARC in her honor. Her most important contribution to women's issues was THE BOOK OF THE CITY OF LADIES (1405), which describes an imaginary place where all the jobs required to run a city are performed efficiently and cheerfully by women. Christine called for other members of her gender to disregard the prejudices of men and to use their talents to achieve their potential. Remember, Europe in the days of the Renaissance was very much a man's world. She wrote a sequel, THE BOOK OF THE THREE VIRTUES, which was basically a practical guide to etiquette and survival for women from all walks of life.

Her literary accomplishments won Christine invitations to many of the courts of Europe, including those of Duke Giangaleazzo Visconti of Milan (this was before the times of the Sforzas) and King Henry IV of England. She refused most of them, although she later accepted King Charles VI of France as her patron. She spent her last years as a nun in the convent at Poissy, writing, of course.

Louise Labé (1520-1566) was another feminist and literary figure of the French Renaissance. Although the daughter of a ropemaker from Lyon, she received a fine education, something unusual for someone of her class. She urged other women to "rise their minds above their spindles" and find pleasure in study. Not the typical homebody, Louise was skilled in horseback riding and swordsmanship. Legend has it that she once fought in a battle disguised as a man! She married a wealthy rope manufacturer, a friend of the family. Her moving elegies and sonnets describe the joys and anguish of her love. She also penned a clever prose dialogue, THE DEBATE BETWEEN MADNESS AND LOVE.

Marguerite de Navarre (1492-1549) was the sister of Francis I. She was educated by her mother, who taught her French, Spanish, Italian, Latin and Greek. After the death of her first husband, Marguerite married Henri d'Albret, King of Navarre, and presided with her new husband over a circle of artists, poets, humanists, and religious reformers. Margaret wrote the HEPTAMERON, a collection of seventy-two tales of love and passion, influenced in form and tone by Boccaccio's DECAMERON. She also composed highly mystical poetry, the most famous collection entitled THE MIRROR OF A SINFUL SOUL. The future queen Elizabeth Tudor of England loved Marguerite's poems and translated them from French into her own language.

MONTAIGNE

Michel de Montaigne (1533-1592) was the most widely read author of the French Renaissance. He was the son of a wealthy merchant. For the first six years of his life he spoke only Latin, because his German tutor did not know the French language! He later became a lawyer and magistrate until his poor health forced him to retire at the age of thirty-eight to his country estate in Perigord. He wasn't sorry to give up his work, since he had plenty of money and didn't really enjoy what he later described as "the slavery of public duties." He had a large study in a tower of his chateau which housed his collection of 1,000 books. The ceiling was carved with Greek and Latin inscriptions, among them these words of Terence: "I am a man; I consider nothing human foreign to me." In this scholarly setting Montaigne pondered the meaning of life and wrote about his views.

His masterpiece was the ESSAYS, published in three volumes in 1580 and 1588. Montaigne is considered the inventor of the personal essay as a modern genre. The word "essay" is derived from the French *essayer* (to attempt), and Montaigne viewed each of his descriptive pieces as an attempt to express in writing his personal reflections. The essays deal with all sorts of topics from a strictly subjective (personal) point of view. They vary in length, structure, subject, and mood. Some are short and read like lists of things that interested Montaigne, while others deal with specific problems, such as the conduct of a siege or the use of judicial torture. The most interesting ones concern broader subjects, such as government, education, friendship, death, pain, human virtue, and the art of conversation. These include Montaigne's views on a "modern approach" of education that stresses judgment and reason rather than memory, his tips on how to deal with illness and to prepare for death, and his strategies for distinguishing between true and false friendship.

Most important, the book is a self-portrait of Montaigne, who appears as an endearing and interesting personality, full of questions and contradictions. (Actually, he once remarked that nothing is certain but uncertainty.) His curiosity about all things is reflected in his famous motto, *Que sais-je?* ("What do I know?"). Like the ancient Greek philosopher Socrates, Montaigne af-firmed the importance of first understanding himself in order to understand others. (Socrates also remarked that the more he knew the more he realized how little he knew!)

Montaigne's detailed observations of his own desires and longings are filled with insights that apply to every age and yet serve as invaluable records of French society in the late sixteenth century.

REVIEW QUESTIONS:

1. Why did Charles VIII of France invade Italy?

2. What two European powers dominated Italy in the early years of the Italian Wars?

3. List three adjectives that describe Cesare Borgia.

4. Describe the sack of Rome.

5. What was Machiavelli's principle piece of advice to the prince? (his basic idea)

6. What happened at the Field of Cloth of Gold?

7. Who was Guillaume Budé?

8. Who was Pantagruel?

9. Who is considered the most important poet of the French Renaissance?

10. Why did Christine de Pisan turn to writing for a living?

11. Who was Marguerite de Navarre?

12. What was Montaigne's motto?

FURTHERMORE:

1. The Borgia family had great power and influence in the late fifteenth and sixteenth centuries. They earned an unsavory reputation for immorality, treachery, nepotism, and greed. The founder

of the family fortune, Spaniard Alfonso, became Pope Calixtus III. He made his nephew, Rodrigo, Cardinal. Rodrigo later became Pope Alexander VI, and he schemed to advance the fortunes of his illegitimate children, Cesare and Lucrezia. But not all Borgia's were evil. We already learned about Lucrezia in the last chapter. Saint Francis Borgia (1510-72), a great grandson of Alexander VI, was the third general of the Jesuits (more about them later). He did much to redeem his family's reputation. He founded the university of Gandia, and his generosity led to the foundation of Gregoriana at Rome, a Jesuit College founded in 1551 by Saint Ignatius Loyola and made into a university by Pope Gregory XIII in 1584.

2. Francis I loved fine French wine, but he disapproved of drunkenness. Anyone who over-imbibed in his court was punished according to the following rules: for the first offense he was put in prison for a short time and fed only bread and water; for the second offense he was whipped and then put in prison (on bread and water); for the third offense he was whipped publicly (very humiliating); and for the fourth offense his ears were cut off and he was exiled from France.

3. Clement Marot was a poet in the court of Francis I. He introduced many of the poetic forms into the French language and composed some of the earliest French sonnets. Maurice Scève was the leader of a group of poets in Lyons, France. He made his name in the literary world with his alleged discovery of the tomb of Petrarch's Laura at Avignon. Scève wrote a number of collections of poetry, many of them influenced by Petrarch and Plato.

PROJECTS:

1. Machiavelli said that the Prince should imitate the lion and the fox. What did he mean by that? Write a skit showing how these two animals use their special talents to survive. (Use Aesop as your model, if you like.)

2. François Villon (1431-1464) was the greatest French lyric poet of the fifteenth century. He wrote several long poems and forty ballads and rondeaux that revealed his innermost thoughts, yearnings, and fears more honestly than any previous poet had done. Find out about him and write a short report.

3. Cesare Borgia's ambition was reflected in the mottos he had engraved on his sword: "Either Caesar or nothing" and "The die is cast." Consult an encyclopedia about Julius Caesar. Then write a paragraph explaining why Borgia chose him as his idol. Also, explain when (and why) Caesar uttered the famous words, "The die is cast."

4. Charles always had three books beside his bed: the Bible, THE COURTIER, and THE PRINCE. What does this tell you about the man? Write an essay explaining your views.

5. King Alfonso I of Naples (he ruled 1442-1458) read the writings of Roman authors Livy and Seneca every day. He spent 20,000 ducats a year patronizing artists and scholars. Find out more about this humanist king and write a short report.

6. Silkworm eggs were brought to Constantinople in 550 from China. Although the Byzantines tried to monopolize the silk industry, silkworms were smuggled to many distant ports. Find out more about how silk cloth is made and write a short report.

7. Obtain a copy of Pisan's BOOK OF THE CITY OF LADIES from your library. Read three chapters and then make an oral report to your class about what you've learned.

8. It has been proposed that the distortions and eccentricities of Mannerism reflect the unease of the local artists living during the unsettling Italian Wars. What do you think? Write several paragraphs discussing your views. Be sure to include examples of Mannerist art to support your ideas.

Chapter IX
THE REFORMATION

Despite the efforts of popes like Nicholas V and Julius II to restore the grandeur of Rome and improve the image of their office, many Christians were dissatisfied with the way the Catholic Church functioned. The number of abuses within the church community was astonishing. For starters, many parish priests were illiterate and hardly knew how to perform ordinary services, monks and nuns often violated their vows of poverty and chastity, and cardinals seemed more concerned about their material possessions than saving anyone's soul.

The sprawling network of church dioceses (districts) required a great deal of money to run, and the necessary funds were gathered in numerous ways. The Church demanded an annual tribute from kings and emperors, and it required fees for the appointment of high officials such as bishops. It levied separate taxes among the Christian community for the building of churches, the fighting of wars, and countless other activities. Every Catholic man was required to contribute one tenth of his wages (known as a tithe) to his parish priest. Another fund-raiser was the sale of important ecclesiastical positions to the highest bidder (a practice known as simony). Qualifications for the job didn't seem to make any difference!

All these devices for collecting money made the Church extremely rich. During the Babylonian Captivity, the popes residing in Avignon collected an income three and a half times greater than that of the King of France! When the Papacy was restored in Rome, the popes were the wealthiest men in the world, living like kings amid the splendors of the papal court.

Although they grumbled a lot about the abuses and financial demands of the Church, few people actually complained to the high authorities, fearing that to do so might jeopardize their chances of eternal happiness beyond the grave. But there were some who dared to demand reform. Among the fiercest critics of the Church at the dawn of the Renaissance were John Wycliffe in England, John Huss in Bohemia, and, a bit later, the fiery Girolamo Savonarola who caused Lorenzo the Magnificent so much grief. Neo-Platonist philosophers (such as Ficino) took a different approach, questioning the Church attacks upon the paganism of the ancients. They claimed that the teachings of the classical Greeks were consistent with the doctrines of Christianity. They even proposed that a person could seek God directly without relying upon a priest as intermediary. (This must have made the Pope cringe!) Other humanists, who studied the works of early theologians, shuddered at how worldly and materialistic the clergy had become since the times of the Apostles.

In the fifteenth century the political authority of the Papacy came under fire. The Pope had long justified his supremacy in the secular (non-religious) world by citing the Donation of Constantine. According to tradition, Roman Emperor Constantine was cured of leprosy when he was baptized by Pope Sylvester I. In gratitude, Constantine had transferred his capital to Constantinople so that the Bishop of Rome (the Pope) would be free to govern the western half of the Roman Empire without his interference. This was his famous

Donation, and it was described in a document that was considered authentic by medieval scholars. The Church claimed the Donation guaranteed the Pope's power over everyone else in western Europe, king and emperor alike. But in 1440 Lorenzo Valla exposed the document as an eighth century forgery by pointing out that certain words in the text were not in use at the time of Constantine. He went on to state that the awesome power of the Church had no foundation in the Scriptures.

GROWING DISCONTENT IN GERMANY AND THE NETHERLANDS

As we have learned, fifteenth century Germany was made up of many principalities, duchies, and other German-speaking territories lying within the borders of the Holy Roman Empire. Although they were fairly independent, these states were nominally (in name but not in fact) ruled by the Emperor. The humanists living in Germany and the Low Countries tended to concern themselves more passionately with religious questions than the Italian scholars, and some were moved to vehemently protest the abuses of the Church. They accused the Church of having forgotten its moral duties as well as the spiritual mission of Jesus. In their eyes, inner piety had been replaced by lavish ceremonies, and the religious leaders were little more than ambitious politicians.

Sebastian Brant ridiculed the materialism of clergymen in his popular satire, THE SHIP OF FOOLS, and then (vainly) called upon Emperor Maximilian to do something about the situation. When Conrad Celtis wrote about Germany's distinctly unclassical past, he asked his countrymen why a nation that was never conquered by the Romans in earlier times should now accept the rule of a Roman pope. This evolving sense of national identity was an important factor in the growing demand for religious reform in Germany.

ERASMUS

Desiderius Erasmus (1469-1536) of Rotterdam (a city in the Low Countries) was the most respected scholar in northern Europe in the sixteenth century. As a young priest he enrolled at the College of Montague in Paris, but he was dismayed by its "stale eggs and its stale theology," referring to its poor food and outdated scholasticism. (Scholasticism, remember, was a method of logical argument to prove the validity of certain religious concepts, including the existence of God.) In 1499 Erasmus went to Oxford, England. There he met humanist John Colet, whose historical interpretation of the Bible inspired him to devote his talents to a study of the ancient world and the early years of Christianity. This, he hoped, would enable him to better understand the fundamentals of Christian belief.

In 1500 he published ADAGES - a collection of Greek and Roman proverbs accompanied by references to the classical authors. This extremely popular book introduced non-scholars to the wit and wisdom of the ancients. His HANDBOOK OF THE CHRISTIAN SOLDIER was a plea to revive the simplicity of the early Church. He later began work on his own translation of the New Testament into Greek (so that it could be read in the language in which it was originally written).

Erasmus' satire, IN PRAISE OF FOLLY, is his most famous work. It was composed in Latin at the home of English humanist Thomas More, to whom it is dedicated. (Its Latin title, *ENCOMIUM MORIAE*, is a pun on More's name.) The book begins with the goddess Folly (folly means foolishness) addressing her disciples and congratulating herself for having such influence over the lives of mortal men. Erasmus held folly, the opposite of reason, responsible for the ills of humanity. Like THE SHIP OF FOOLS, his work pokes fun at the ignorance and superstitions of contemporary society, belittling the self-serving behavior of princes, courtiers, statesmen, scholars, poets, lawyers, and philosophers and then zeroing in on the clergy. His biting wit even attacks the Papacy, calling it the "disease of Christendom" and presenting an amusing image of Pope Julius trying to bully his way into heaven!

Erasmus remarks how those who have a reputation for wisdom (namely the theologians) are the most totally in Folly's power, and he contrasts their "petty ceremonies and silly absurdities" with the true religion expressed in the New Testament. He chides the Church's cult of saints which, he says, reinforces superstition and encourages dependence upon the priesthood. He questions the practices of fasting, relic-worshiping, celibacy, indulgence-selling (more about this later), pilgrimages, confession, and the burning of heretics. Then he dismisses the roles of monks, abbots and friars, pointing out that these "holy brothers" are not even mentioned in the Bible! The alternative to the presently corroded values of the Church can be found, he says, in the simple, pious way of life advocated by Jesus.

IN PRAISE OF FOLLY was a best-seller. Forty-two editions appeared in Erasmus' lifetime. The Latin text was translated into French, German, and English in the years following its original publication. (No one was surprised when the Pope placed the book on his list of forbidden books in the 1560's.) But although he attacked the corruption of the clergy, Erasmus remained loyal to the Church. He sought reform from within the organization and relied upon his talents of reason and persuasion to achieve it. And yet, his writings laid the groundwork for changes he never envisioned.

THE MATTER OF INDULGENCES

In 1514 Pope Leo X launched a massive campaign to rebuild Saint Peter's Cathedral in Rome. Leo, the worldliest of the Renaissance popes, was constantly soliciting funds from his subjects to support his extravagant life style and to finance his art and architectural projects. He once remarked, "All the world knows how profitable this fable of Christ has been to us and ours." His means of raising money were often highly questionable. For example, he arrested a group of cardinals whom he accused of plotting against him. He had one strangled, then offered to set the rest free if they paid him the sum of 150,000 ducats! He later created thirty-one new positions of cardinal and offered them to anyone willing to pay the price: over 300,000 ducats apiece.

When Albrecht of Hohenzollern was appointed Archbishop of Mainz in Germany, he had to borrow 10,000 ducats from the Fugger bank to pay the fees. Pope Leo then authorized him to sell indulgences to pay his debts. What is an indulgence? It's an official pardon from the Pope. According to Catholic doctrine, a person who committed a mortal sin (such as robbery or bodily assault) had to do penance in order to be forgiven. This could involve anything from saying a certain number of extra prayers to making a pilgrimage to a shrine where the remains of a famous saint were kept. (The most popular shrines were those of Saint James in Spain and Saint Peter in Rome, as well as the Church of the Holy Sepulcher in Jerusalem.) An indulgence, written upon a slip of paper and signed by the Pope, instantly forgave all sins, and even those that might occur in the future, in return for repentance (or a financial payment). This release from penance even extended beyond the grave. As we know from our study of Dante, Christians believed that after death the souls of bad people went directly to hell, those of the pious ascended into heaven, and the souls of those whose sins were not yet forgiven floated around in a misty, dreary intermediary place called purgatory. An indulgence enabled the soul of a loved one to leave purgatory and go to heaven. In the Middle Ages an indulgence was a reward for an exceptionally pious deed, but by 1500 great numbers of them were being sold throughout Europe to anyone who could afford them to raise money for the Pope's personal projects.

In 1517 Dominican friar Johann Tetzel was ordered by Pope Leo to travel about northern Germany urging people to buy indulgences to support the construction of Saint Peter's Cathedral. (Half of the proceeds would go to the Archbishop of Mainz to help pay off his debts.) Tetzel was a talented and persuasive salesman. His strategy was to set up a large cross and gaudy rostrum, decorated with the arms of the pope, in the marketplace of a town. Beside the rostrum sat a representative of the Fugger bank, holding a golden vessel into which the citizens could drop their coins to buy an indulgence. Tetzel would chant from the rostrum, "As soon as the coin in the coffer rings, the soul from purgatory springs!" Small wonder that the friar was known to some as a "peddler of paradise passports."

MARTIN LUTHER PROTESTS

One of Tetzel's "sales pitches" was attended by a thirty-three-year-old lecturer on Biblical Studies at Wittenburg University. His name was Martin Luther, and he didn't like what he heard. Six months later (on All Saints' Eve 1517), Luther sent a letter of protest to the Archbishop. It contained ninety-five theses (statements) arguing against the sale of indulgences and pleading for reform within the Church. Luther even suggested that the Pope was wealthy enough to build Saint Peter's new church with his own money! He nailed a copy of the letter to the door of the Wittenburg Cathedral. (In those days there were no newspapers, and it was customary to post opinions in some public place.) His protests would launch a reform movement of a magnitude far beyond his wildest expectations.

YOUNG LUTHER

Martin Luther was born in 1483 in Eisleben, Saxony (a German principality) on the eve of the feast day of Saint Martin, the patron of drinking and merriment. (He was, of course, named after the saint.) Although the son of a copper miner, Luther received a fine formal education and then went on to the University of Erfurt to study law. But he was always troubled about his own salvation. How could he be certain that his soul would go to heaven? The answers given by the Church didn't satisfy him. He couldn't figure how visiting a shrine or living on bread and water should gain him "points." In 1505, while returning to law school from a visit home, he was caught in a violent thunderstorm and was nearly struck by a bolt of lightning. In a state of panic, he vowed to Saint Anne (the patron saint of miners) that he would become a monk if she protected him. Two weeks later he dutifully entered the Augustinian monastery at Erfurt, Saxony. Now he had plenty of time to devote to questions about salvation.

Luther's superior at the monastery recognized his brilliant mind, and he encouraged him to continue his academic studies at the University of Wittenberg after he was ordained. In 1510 Luther received his doctorate in theology there and became one of the university's most popular professors. Although he was familiar with the abstract logic of scholasticism, he was more interested in the study of the Bible, especially the epistles of Saint Paul. Like the humanist scholars we have studied, Luther was amazed by the difference between the ideas revealed in the Scriptures and the traditional beliefs of the Roman Catholic Church. The more he analyzed the original sources, the more he came to disagree with the views of the Church.

Luther now totally dismissed the notion that a person could gain entry to heaven simply by performing certain tasks or paying a sum of money. God was not an accountant to be bargained with! What saved a Christian was his faith. Attendance at church rituals and ceremonies, a certain number of prayers, or pilgrimages should have no effect upon the fate of one's soul. Furthermore, Luther became convinced that the cult of the saints and their relics smacked of polytheism (the worship of multiple gods). We've already encountered similar ideas expressed by Erasmus, but IN PRAISE OF FOLLY did not appear in print until later (1520). Given his rather revolutionary ideas about religion, it is not surprising that Luther condemned Tetzel's sale of indulgences.

THE POPE REACTS

Luther's friends circulated copies of the Ninety-Five Theses (as his list of complaints came to be known) among themselves and then passed some on to the printers for wider distribution. Had Luther lived in earlier times, his ideas would have had a small effect upon the Catholic Church. But the printing press enabled his protests to be circulated throughout Germany in two weeks, and all of Europe was buzzing about them within a month.

At first Leo ignored the commotion, dismissing Luther's arguments as a "monkish squabble." But when the young reformer began writing treatises and pamphlets attacking Church policies, the Pope summoned him to Rome. This is when Duke Frederick III (the Wise) of Saxony stepped in. He was one of the seven Electors of the Holy Roman Empire and a leading lay (secular) Christian. He used his authority to convince Leo to hold a hearing concerning Luther's activities in Augsburg. (Frederick suspected that going to Rome might lead to Luther's imprisonment or even death.) On the appointed day the Pope's emissary (Cardinal Cajetan) asked Luther to recant. Instead, Luther quoted Scriptures supporting his belief that Christians can achieve salvation through their faith and not by the purchase of indulgences. The Cardinal lost patience and walked out. Everyone wondered what would happen next. When it looked like his arrest was imminent, Luther escaped to Nuremberg.

MORE WRITINGS

Beginning in 1520 Luther published twenty-four books and pamphlets (written in German, not Latin). One of his pamphlets sold 4,000 copies in five days, an amazing number for those early times. Three hundred thousand copies of his writings were printed in the next three years. Luther had become the best-selling author in Germany.

His message was clear. The Church needed to be reformed and a council should be convened to carry out the changes. Luther denied that the clergy had any special privileges, and he proposed a common priesthood of all believers. He demanded the abolition of indulgences and pilgrimages to Rome, urged that the clergy be allowed to marry, and called for an end of the numerous saints' days (acknowledged by most serious people as an excuse for riotous drinking and gambling). He claimed that the Bible, not the Pope, was the source of truth, and he insisted that Christians had the right to pray directly to God without the aid of a priest. Above all, he reiterated his belief that a Christian could be saved from eternal damnation by his faith alone.

Three of Luther's books personally attacked the Pope, calling Leo "the devil incarnate" and referring to the Papacy as the devil's church. The Pope responded by calling Luther a wild boar that had invaded the Lord's vineyard! On June 15, 1520 Leo issued a papal bull condemning forty-one of Luther's declarations and ordering the rebellious cleric to recant and return to the fold. Not a chance! And when Luther heard that his books were being burned in Rome, he turned the tables on Leo and joined with his students in burning the university's library books on canon (church) law in a huge bonfire, dramatically throwing in the papal bull itself. (Does this remind you of Savonarola's Bonfire of the Vanities?) Luther was given sixty days to come to Rome to explain his actions. When he didn't appear, he was excommunicated (deprived of the Church sacraments). All Christians were forbidden to listen to him, to speak to him, or even to look at him. He was now a fugitive, whom Leo described as "a dangerous and notorious heretic."

Soon after the book burning, young Emperor Charles V (he was only twenty-one at the time) stepped in to help settle the dispute. Charles had an obvious bias, given his mission to defend the Church. But he did not wish to offend Luther's protector, Duke Frederick, or the other German princes, whose support he needed for his wars against the French and the Ottoman Turks. His compromise was to arrange for a new hearing at the Imperial Diet (government) meeting in Worms (a German city on the Rhine River).

Luther had hoped that he would be able to discuss his views at this session, but when he appeared he was simply ordered to abandon all objections to Church policy. He refused to do so unless proven wrong by the Bible or by clear reason, so he was declared an outlaw throughout the Empire, deprived of all civil and legal rights. According to the Edict of Worms, anyone could kill Luther without fear of punishment. It was illegal to buy, sell, read, preserve, or print any of his writings. But the papal policy backfired. Because he had bravely stood alone before the might of the Empire and the Papacy and had stuck to the truth as he saw it, Luther became a popular hero.

At this point Frederick, fearing for the safety of the rebellious cleric, arranged to have him taken to his mountain fortress, the Wartburg. There Luther remained in hiding for eight months. He grew a beard and let his hair get long, wore the clothes of a knight, and adopted a pseudonym (Knight George). In this disguise he wrote more pamphlets and worked on his German translation of the New Testament of the Bible.

RETURN TO WITTENBURG

Luther's ideas were on everyone's lips. He had brought into the open many of the questions that had been troubling people for years. Now nearly every aspect of Church doctrine and policy was subject to debate. The Reformation of the Catholic Church was well underway, and there was nothing the Pope could do to stem the tide of change that was sweeping over Europe.

Many of Luther's followers in

Wittenburg acted upon his ideas while he was in Wartburg. They replaced the Latin Mass with a service conducted entirely in German, threw away their priestly robes, and even took wives (as did numerous monks). But not all changes were peaceful ones. Groups of university students began rioting and destroying religious pictures and statues in the churches. This spate of violence caused Luther to return to his home city. His mere presence there brought about a return to peace. For the next twenty-five years he would live in Wittenburg, writing pamphlets, sermons, treatises, biblical commentaries, and thousands of letters. Always busy, he once remarked, "If I rest, I rust!"

He completed his translation of the entire Bible into German and had it published in 1534. Its highly readable text made the Saxon dialect the standard language for all German-speaking people. The printing press that had helped to spread his message now made the Bible widely available. It ran through 430 editions in his lifetime, selling over 100,000 copies. Although Germany had a low rate of literacy, books were commonly read aloud to large audiences in community gatherings. Now ordinary people could discuss among themselves the messages of the Scriptures, and they no longer required the services of the parish priests.

THE NEW PROTESTANT CHURCH

Luther set about organizing a new kind of church (later called the Lutheran Church) that would conform to his ideas. He abolished many traditional practices, including confession and private Mass. He encouraged priests, monks, and nuns to marry, as the convents and monasteries were abandoned. Luther himself married an ex-nun, Katharina von Bora. He met her when she and eight other Cistercian nuns were fleeing from the convent where they had been placed because they lacked dowries. Luther agreed to help them find them husbands. He succeeded in finding eight, and, seeing no other candidates, he nobly married the last nun (Katharina) himself. He allegedly remarked that he hoped the marriage would satisfy his father, spite the devil, and upset the Pope! They had six children and later took in eleven orphans.

As more and more people left the Catholic Church to form new Protestant communities, the reform movement lost the support of Erasmus. Although the Dutch scholar agreed with Luther's basic ideas (hadn't he said many of the same things?), he refused to endorse the establishment of a separate church. He once said, "I laid a hen's egg, but Luther hatched a bird of quite a different species." Erasmus wanted all Christians to stand as one, and he tried (in vain) to create a moderate middle ground between strict Catholics and those seeking reform.

In 1525 the leaders of the reform movement met at the Council of Nuremberg to expel Catholic priests, assume control of ecclesiastical appointments, and establish a training college for Lutheran ministers. Nuremberg was the major city of the Holy Roman Empire, and by officially adopting Lutheranism it placed the Catholic Habsburgs in an uncomfortable position. Other cities, including Hamburg and Strasbourg, followed suit, replacing their priests with ministers who performed no sacraments (religious ceremonies) apart from those of Baptism and Communion - the only two Luther endorsed.

In 1529 Charles V sent an order to the Diet at Speyer demanding the traditional forms of Catholic worship in the Empire. Six princes and fourteen cities protested his demand and became known as the Protesting Estates. This is the source of the word "Protestant," which was then applied to anyone who left the Catholic Church. And many people certainly did. Within a decade two thirds of all imperial German cities were Lutheran. In 1530 the Protestant leaders presented the Augsburg Confession to the Diet of that city. Written by Philip Melanchthon, a close colleague of Luther, it became the basic statement of Lutheran doctrine.

Martin Luther lived to an old age. In his final years he was the patriarch in a large house crowded with grandchildren, student lodgers, and famous visitors from abroad. Late in 1545, he was asked to settle a dispute in Eisleben. In spite of the icy winter weather, he traveled there and settled the dispute. But the strain was too great for him, and he died the next day, probably of a heart attack. So ended the life of one of history's greatest men. His legacy was the Reformation of the Catholic Church and the establishment of the Protestant religion. His doctrines, especially those concerning salvation through faith and the final authority of the Bible, were adopted by other reformers and are shared by many Protestant denominations today.

In 1555 Charles V signed a treaty (the Peace of Augsburg), which entitled each prince or city to choose the religion, Lutheran or Catholic, for his (its) subjects. Those citizens who were unhappy with the choice could migrate to regions where their religion was the dominant one. The next year Charles abdicated his throne and retired to the monastery in Spain.

PROTESTANTISM SPREADS TO SCANDINAVIA & SWITZERLAND

Within a few years of Luther's death, Europe was divided between the Protestants in the north and the Catholics in the south. The Scandinavian countries were among the first nations outside of Germany to adopt the Lutheran faith. King Gustavus I of Sweden confiscated much of the Church property and introduced Protestantism into his country as well as Finland (then under Swedish authority). In 1536 King Christian of Denmark made the Lutheran faith his state religion. This extended to Norway, which was then a Danish province. In most other cases, the Reformation spread rapidly as a popular movement, making dramatic inroads in Poland, Bohemia, Moravia, Hungary, and Transylvania.

Huldrych Zwingli was the leader of the Swiss Reformation. (Switzerland lay within the Holy Roman Empire.) Zwingli would carry out reforms more rigorous than any even Luther had proposed. In 1519 he became a priest in Zurich, where he preached moving sermons stressing the messages of the New Testament and attacking clerical abuses. He inspired the citizens of Zurich to demand reform. Zwingli eventually abandoned his allegiance to the Pope and broke his priestly vow of celibacy by marrying. He replaced the Catholic Mass with his own brand of Communion (called "the Lord's Supper") and rid his city's churches of crucifixes, statuary, chalices, and other Catholic objects. His SIXTY-SEVEN ARTICLES (1523) formed the basis of the Swiss Reformed Church. He worked actively to spread his ideas until 1531, when he was killed by a pike on the battlefield as the Catholic cantons of southern Switzerland attacked Zurich.

JOHN CALVIN

John Calvin (1509-1564) led the second generation of reformers in Switzerland. It has been said that if Luther sounded the trumpet for reform, Calvin orchestrated the score by which the Reformation became a part of western civilization. But there were many differences between these two religious leaders. A major one was their image of God. Luther believed in a loving and merciful Father of mankind, while Calvin conceived of an intolerant, somewhat forbidding deity.

Calvin was born and educated in France. While studying at the College of Montague in Paris, he came into contact with some of the finest minds of the time, including Guillaume Budé and François Rabelais. He was moved by their arguments for religious reform, and he gradually distanced himself from the Catholic Church until he finally converted to Protestantism. France was a staunchly Catholic country, although King Francis I varied in his treatment of Protestants (depending upon the political circumstances). When Calvin's friend Nicholas Cop, the Rector of the University of Paris, gave a public address supporting reform, the Parisian clergy became so incensed that Calvin feared for his own safety and fled to Basel, Switzerland.

In 1536 he published the first edition of his greatest work, THE INSTITUTES OF THE CHRISTIAN RELIGION. This began as a small book of six chapters summarizing the major doctrines of the Christian religion. Like Luther, Calvin considered the Bible the source of Christian belief, and he stressed faith above ceremony. Over the years he expanded his views and added them to his book so that the last edition (1559) contained seventy-nine chapters. This monumental work presents every detail of what a Christian should believe, and it defines a code of religious behavior that later united the followers of Calvin and made their organization strong.

Central to Calvin's theology is predestination, the belief that God assigns some people to salvation and others to damnation. Although Adam and Eve passed on original sin to all humanity, and everyone is naturally wicked and deserves to go to hell, the lucky few selected by God go to heaven. Since no one can be certain who is chosen, a person can demonstrate his fitness for salvation by being law-abiding, industrious, sober, and thrifty. So Calvin instructed his followers to lead a godly life and to be ever on the alert for temptations to commit a sin. He warned that any unpious people should be cast out before they corrupted everyone else.

After writing the INSTITUTES, Calvin decided to devote his life to the study of religion. On a trip to Strasbourg in 1536 he was forced to detour through Geneva, Switzerland. A year earlier the citizens of Geneva had voted to abandon the Catholic Church in favor of their Protestant beliefs, and the city became a center for religious refugees from Catholic France and Italy. When Calvin arrived there, a charismatic reformer named Guillaume Farel convinced him to remain and work with him (threatening him with a curse from God if he didn't!). But the Genevan citizens were not ready to accept the preachers' demands for austerity, and so they expelled them in 1538. Calvin returned to Strasbourg, married a widow, Idelette de Bure, and lived happily as the pastor of the local Protestant church.

In 1541 he was summoned back to Geneva (the city was now more receptive to his ideas), and he spent the next fourteen years there. He established the first Protestant church to be governed by a council of ministers, who interpreted God's will as expressed in the Bible and elected leaders (elders from the church membership). Mass was replaced with prayer, extremely long sermons, and the singing of hymns. The interiors of the churches, stripped of all paintings and statues, were very plain.

John Calvin ruled the city with such a heavy hand that he came to be known as "the Pope of Geneva." His authority was more uncompromising than that of the Papacy it opposed! A government that is run by a religious organization is known as a theocracy, and Geneva is an excellent example. Calvin tolerated no criticism, considering opposition to his views to be the handiwork of the devil. Anyone who defied his edicts or who did not attend church regularly had to repent and do penance (recite a series of prayers begging for forgiveness) before the entire congregation or else be expelled from Geneva. Ministers and elders sought out wrongdoers and inspected every household at least once a year to make sure everyone was leading a pious life. They had the power to order members of the congregation to account for their actions and, if necessary, to excommunicate them! Calvin banned plays and encouraged the reading of religious pamphlets and the singing of psalms in Geneva's taverns! The church even published a list of acceptable Christian names for newborn babies.

Calvin was no harder on others than he was on himself. He preached as many as five sermons in one day. He carried on a wide correspondence with other theologians and wrote dozens of books and treatises. He introduced sanitary regulations that gave Geneva a cleanliness and neatness for which it is noted to this day, and he founded the Genevan Academy (later the University of Geneva) to train men for the ministry. His clearly stated theology and well-organized churches had an enormous influence on other northern nations. In Scotland, John Knox would carry out his own version of Calvin's reforms. Not everyone supported his views, however. Rabelais called him a "mad devil."

THE REFORM MOVEMENT IN FRANCE

The French were a very traditional people, so most of them remained loyal to the Catholic Church. The Sorbonne (University) had long been a strong supporter of Catholic theology and scholasticism. (Luther dismissed its teachers as "the moles and bats of Paris.") Nonetheless, Protestantism was growing even in this inhospitable environment. For years, Calvin had been sending ministers trained in Geneva to convert his former countrymen to his beliefs. The French Protestants were known as Huguenots.

In 1516 Francis I made a treaty with the Pope, known as the Concordat of Bologna, which gave him the right to appoint men to high church positions. He used these appointments to reward officials and courtiers for their services. This convenience, as well as the substantial income he received in Church taxes, made Francis a supporter of the Catholic Church. But he was also an opportunist, who shifted his political alliances as it suited his interests. When he needed the aid of the Pope, he lashed out at the Huguenots; when he sought favor with the German princes, he tolerated Protestant activities.

In 1534 Francis found it politically expedient to forbid Protestant worship in his kingdom, so the Huguenots were in big trouble. When he died, one of the first royal acts of his son, Henry II, was to create a special government committee (called the "Burning Chamber") to suppress heresy (non-Catholic forms of worship) in Paris. But despite the widespread persecution of the Huguenots that followed, by 1550 one tenth of the population of France was Protestant. Among their numbers were many members of the nobility, including the king's cousins.

Henry had married Catherine de Medici, the daughter of Lorenzo, Duke of Urbino, when she was only fourteen. Catherine blossomed into a refined and energetic woman, and she made a great splash at the French court. She had loved the beautiful geometrically landscaped gardens of Italy, and she used them as models when she designed the Tuileries Gardens in Paris. Catherine also introduced fine cuisine to the court. (Her favorite dishes were cocks' combs, kidneys, and artichoke hearts.) Before she came to France, the women of the French court had dined on broth, because the movement of their jaws seemed to deform the contours of their lovely faces! Catherine changed this sorry situation so that the ladies shared "real meals" with the courtiers, to the accompaniment of music.

Her marriage was not a happy one, however, since the king gave his affections to his former tutor, Diane de Poitiers. (An elegant woman, who always dressed in black and white, she was twenty years older than the king!) Henry gave Diane the majestic chateau at Chenonceaux in the Loire Valley. She hosted many festive events there.

In 1559 Henry signed the Peace of Cateau-Cambresis, ending years of hostility with Spain. To demonstrate his goodwill, he gave his daughter Elizabeth in marriage to Spain's King Philip. (The Spanish king was recently widowed by Queen Mary of England). A tournament was held to celebrate the marriage. Henry himself participated in the jousting and was struck in the eye by a piece of his opponent's shattered lance. He died soon afterwards. The crown was then passed to his son, Francis II. But the new ruler was a sickly youth, and he, too, died. In 1560 Henry's next eldest son,

nine-year-old Charles, became king, with his mother Catherine serving as (a very meddling) regent. One of the first things Catherine did was to take back Chenonceaux from Diane de Poitiers!

For the next decade the conflict between Huguenots and Catholics was played out in a series of terrible religious wars. Finally, in 1572 Protestants and Catholics vowed to end the bloodshed with the signing of the Peace of Saint Germain. The new tolerance was marked by the marriage of Catherine's daughter, Marguerite of Valois, to the leader of the Huguenots, Henry of Navarre. By now Charles had come of age, but Catherine was still running the show.

Plans were made to celebrate the wedding as well as the new era of peace in Paris on Saint Bartholomew's Day: Sunday, August 24. The festivities attracted thousands of Huguenots from the provincial cities of France. Among them was an important Protestant leader, Gaspard de Coligny. On the eve of the big occasion he was attacked by a group of Catholics, who falsely accused him of being involved in a conspiracy against the Duke of Guise (a Catholic nobleman). Coligny escaped unscathed, but the attack was an omen of things to come.

The next morning, as the bells in the churches rang to announce the saint's day, a group of officers were ordered by King Charles (prompted by Catherine) to kill Coligny. Most historians believe that Catherine had decided to take advantage of the gathering of Protestant leaders to wipe out the main sources of opposition to the Catholic Church. Coligny was decapitated, and his head was sent to Rome. (The current pope, Gregory XIII, happily received it and ordered a commemorative medal to be struck celebrating this triumph for the Church!)

Meanwhile, word of the attack rapidly spread among the crowds of Catholic Parisians, who took this as a cue to murder every Protestant they could find. Before the day was over, thousands of Protestants had been slain. The slaughter set off other massacres throughout France that continued until October. Henry of Navarre escaped death by promising to convert to Catholicism. He was held for three months by a group of fanatics and then escaped to the countryside to rally the surviving Huguenot forces.

Two years after the massacre in Paris, Charles died and was succeeded by his brother, Henry III. The new king was considerably more vigorous and independent than his two elder brothers. He delighted in throwing lavish parties at the chateau at Chenonceaux. Costumed young men and women would emerge from the woods to greet the guests, while singers and musicians entertained them from boats on the river. In 1576 Henry agreed to a truce that recognized the legality of Protestantism. But this act so angered the Catholics that they formed the Catholic League, with support from Spain and the Pope, to continue the fight against the Huguenots. Once again the religious wars began to rage. They would drag on for decades, spawning the worst sectarian violence to appear in Europe during the Reformation.

The War of the Three Henries, named after its three major leaders (King Henry III, Henry, Duke of Guise, and Henry of Navarre), began in 1587. It seems that Henry of Guise was angered when the king failed to send him royal reinforcements in his battles against the Huguenots in the northeast, so he marched on Paris and forced Henri III to flee. Guise was proclaimed "King of Paris." A bit later, the real king invited Guise and his brother to a secret meeting and then had them murdered as traitors to the crown! When the Catholic League denounced the king as a tyrant he fled into the camp of his Protestant rival, Henry of Navarre, whom he agreed to accept as his heir.

Now the two remaining Henries made plans to retake Paris, but before any action was taken, the king was assassinated. With his two rivals gone, Henry of Navarre declared himself the new King of France (Henry IV). He was a practical man who realized how difficult it would be to govern a country divided between Protestant supporters and the Catholic League, so he did the logical thing: he converted to Catholicism, the religion of ninety per cent of the French, remarking that "Paris is worth a Mass." This conversion took the wind out of the sails of the Catholic League. (Why should they fight a Catholic king?)

Henry IV became one of the most popular monarchs in French history. He signed the Edict of Nantes in 1598, which made Catholicism the national religion in France but allowed Protestants to worship as they wished. In 1600 he married Marie de Medici of Florence, continuing the alliance of French royalty with the elite of that prosperous Italian city.

THE COUNTER-REFORMATION

The Catholic Church took a long time to recognize the threat of the Protestants. Remember how Pope Leo X dismissed Luther's criticisms as "a monkish squabble"? But by the 1530's reformers within the Church began calling for drastic changes. Pope Paul III heeded the demands by making conscientious appointments of learned and pious bishops and by maintaining strict discipline at the papal court. He had spent time at the court of Lorenzo the Magnificent and developed a taste for art. When he became the Pope he was eager to follow the lead of such men as Julius II in beautifying the Vatican. (It was Paul who commissioned Michelangelo to paint the LAST JUDGMENT in the Sistine Chapel.)

In 1545 Paul summoned the Council of Trent (a city on Italy's northern border) to discuss other reforms that might revitalize the Catholic Church. The Council defined and clarified the official Catholic doctrines as precisely as Calvin had done for the Protestant church. It banned the sale of indulgences and tightened the discipline of clergy. It instructed each diocese to build a seminary (a college of religious instruction) to educate its priests. It drew up an Index of books forbidden to Catholics (a act intended to protect parishioners from the words of dissenters), and it promoted sending missionaries to distant parts of the world.

Beyond these steps, the Council reaffirmed almost every doctrine Luther had attacked. It emphasized the need for magnificent ceremonies, calling for the worship of God in a setting of pomp and splendor. The cult of the Virgin and the saints was to be exalted in the decoration of church interiors. The elaborate carvings, beautiful chalices, and jeweled crosses that graced the cathedrals of the sixteenth century certainly contrasted with the spartan interiors of the Protestant churches. The Council reaffirmed the role of good works and pilgrimages in obtaining salvation, and it stated that since salvation could be obtained only through the Church, the assistance of the priest was essential. (In 1547 the dark confessional box was introduced so priests might no longer be tempted by beautiful penitents!) Furthermore, only the Church could interpret the Bible, and Mass was to be given exclusively in Latin.

The Council of Trent dramatically ended the perilous decline of the Catholic Church by its determined efforts to counter the Reformation. Although the Church would never have the same power it enjoyed in earlier times, the Pope in all his regal splendor was once again recognized as the supreme authority in Christendom by all Catholics. The spread of Protestantism was now held in check in southern and eastern Europe.

THE BAROQUE PERIOD

In an effort to promote its new image and to revive the appeal of its spiritual doctrines, the Catholic Church commissioned some of the leading Italian artists of the day to create vivid and inspirational religious paintings. Titian and his protégé, Tintoretto, brought new power and emotion to Catholic art with their spectacular use of color and brush stroke. Michelangelo da Caravaggio and Annibale Carracci painted religious scenes that struck an emotional chord by their dramatic interplay of light and darkness (chiaroscuro). Many of the other paintings of the period depict weeping figures, who make exaggerated gestures of repentance, their eyes turned piously toward heaven.

Known as the Baroque, the new style of art would flourish for over a century in predominantly Catholic countries like Italy and Spain. An interesting aspect of the new movement was the sense of modesty that compelled Pope Paul IV to order the nudes in Michelangelo's LAST JUDGMENT to be covered with drapes. Perhaps this modesty symbolizes the Church's attempts to clean itself of all past scandal and corruption!

THE JESUITS

The Society of Jesus was a driving force of the Catholic Counter-Reformation. This organization of priests, known as the Jesuits, was founded by Ignatius de Loyola, a Spanish nobleman and former soldier. Loyola was born in the family castle in the

Basque province (near the Pyrenees Mountains) and educated in the court of Castile. His leg was fractured by a cannon ball while he was fighting in Navarre against the French. He had not been particularly religious, but the boredom of his convalescence prompted him to read about the life of Christ, the only book available to him. This reading inspired him to re-examine the meaning of his own life. Ultimately, he decided to transform his military ardor into religious zeal.

At the Benedictine monastery of Montserrat Loyola dedicated himself to God. He was convinced that salvation could be achieved by a rigorously ordered spiritual life. He expressed his ideas in a book, SPIRITUAL EXERCISES, which might be viewed as the Catholic response to Luther's pamphlets. From Spain he set out as a mendicant on a pilgrimage to Rome, Venice, and finally Jerusalem.

Upon his return to Spain, Loyola studied Latin in Barcelona and then philosophy in Salamanca. In 1528 he began his theological training at the University of Paris, where he met six other students who were drawn to his views. In 1534 the group donned the black robes of monks and took vows of poverty and chastity at the altar of the cathedral on Montmartre. They lived simply, following the strict code of discipline outlined by Loyola. After they were ordained as priests in 1537, the seven men placed themselves at the disposal of Pope Paul III, to whom they swore obedience. Paul recognized the Society of Jesus as an official order of the Church in 1540. Loyola became its first leader (known as the General of the Order), who was responsible only to the Pope. During the Council of Trent, several Jesuits served as consulting theologians.

The order of the Jesuits grew so quickly that upon Loyola's death in 1556 its members numbered nearly 1,000. Jesuit priests were persuasive writers and speakers, who used reason and their own moral behavior to defend the Catholic Church against the criticisms of the Protestants. Loyola had tapped the order's strong interest in scholarship by founding the *Collegium Romanum* (the College of Rome). It was made into a university in 1584 by Pope Gregory XIII, who changed its name to Gregoriana. It was the earliest modern seminary and the model for other Jesuit schools, which became renowned for their high standards of education.

Many graduates of the Jesuit schools helped to establish a vast network of foreign missions to spread their religion to other parts of the world. (Remember how the Council of Trent promoted missionary work?) In this way, the Jesuits spearheaded a resurgence of Catholicism in Europe, especially in Poland, Bohemia, Hungary, Germany, and France (where they were instrumental in halting the spread of Protestantism). They also brought Christianity to places as distant as India, China, and Japan.

REVIEW QUESTIONS:

1. What are three ways that the Catholic Church made money before the Council of Trent?

2. What was the Donation of Constantine?

3. What was the main message of IN PRAISE OF FOLLY?

4. What was an indulgence?

5. What did Luther most dislike about the Catholic Church?

6. Why did most Germans support Luther?

7. What is the derivation of the word "Protestant?"

8. Who was Zwingli?

9. What is a theocracy? Give an example of one.

10. Who were the Huguenots?

11. What caused the Massacre of Saint Bartholomew's Day?

12. Who won the War of the Three Henries?

13. Name three decisions made by the Council of Trent.

14. Describe Baroque art.

15. List three adjectives that describe a typical Jesuit.

FURTHERMORE:

1. The seven sacraments of the Catholic Church are believed to be outward visible signs of spiritual grace to which the promise of Christ is attached. They are Baptism, the Eucharist (Communion), Confirmation, Confession, Anointing of the Sick, Marriage, and Holy Orders. The Council of Trent declared that they were all instituted by Christ. Protestants accept only Baptism and the Eucharist as instituted by Christ. However, the Anglican Church accepts the other five as sacramental rites that evolved in the Church. Some Protestant groups, such as Quakers, do not use sacraments at all.

2. In the sixteenth century an ecclesiastical appointee was obligated to send to Rome one half of his income the first year, then one tenth each year after that. Archbishops paid a huge amount for that prestigious position. When a clerical office holder died, all of his money went to the Church.

3. The Latin Bible that Martin Luther used to translate Christianity's holy book into German was found in 1995 after being lost for more than two hundred years. The volume, signed by Luther and covered with notes he made in its margins, was among thousands of Bibles stored at the Wuerttemberg State Library in Stuttgart, Germany. Luther translated the New Testament from Latin into German in 1522 and the rest of the Bible in 1534. By 1574, 500,000 copies of his Bible had been printed.

4. Lutherans and other Protestants encouraged community life and stressed the importance of the family. Education was highly regarded. They encouraged industriousness, thrifty living, and careful management of material things. This attitude came to be known as the Protestant Ethic. It had a significant effect upon the growth of industry and commerce in later years.

5. Pope Paul IV was a stern, pious man who contrasted with the cynical, pleasure-loving Renaissance popes. He once said, "If my father were a heretic, I would burn him." Never again would religious devotion be ignored by a leader of the Church.

PROJECTS:

1. "While others complained of corrupt behavior in the Church, Martin Luther focused his energies upon corrupt teaching." Do you agree with this statement? Write a short essay explaining why you agree, or why you don't. Be sure to include several examples to back up your argument.

2. "An appeal of Protestantism was the defiance of authority." Think about this statement. Then write a few paragraphs explaining what you think it means. Be sure to include examples.

3. Martin Luther wrote the hymn "A Mighty Fortress Is Our God." Find the hymn in a modern Protestant hymnal.

With a group of classmates, sing it to the class.

4. "The Renaissance united Europe, but the Reformation divided it." Explain the meaning of this statement. Point out the similarities between the two movements and the basic differences.

5. Michelangelo's LAST JUDGMENT was clearly a forerunner of Baroque art. Compare this painting to Raphael's SCHOOL OF ATHENS. Make a list of the similarities between the two and a second list of the differences. Then write a few paragraphs about your observations and what they suggest about the art of these two periods.

6. El Greco's paintings are typical of Baroque art. Find a book with illustrations of his major paintings. Then write a few paragraphs explaining what made him a Baroque artist.

7. English people who followed John Calvin were called Puritans. They were opposed to the Anglican Church because it was episcopal (governed by bishops). They preferred the presbyterian form of church government (rule by ministers and elders). Find out more about the Puritans and write a short report.

8. Inspired by the Counter-Reformation, new orders of monks, like the Capuchins, took vows of poverty and chastity and poured their energies into creating hospitals and schools. Find out more about the Capuchins. Then make a poster illustrating their appearance and main activities.

9. Teresa of Avila, an aristocrat like Loyola, gave up her worldly goods and founded an order of Carmelite nuns. Find out more about her and write a short report.

Chapter X
TUDOR ENGLAND

Politics had a lot to do with the spread of Protestantism. We have seen how the German princes who embraced Luther's reforms were partly motivated by a desire to stand up against the authority of the Emperor and the Pope. In England, too, conflict with papal authority would lead to a break with the Catholic Church.

There had been resistance to particular doctrines and beliefs of the Church in England since medieval times. In the fourteenth century John Wycliffe denied the authority of the Pope, calling upon the English king to reform the Church according to the interests of his subjects. He considered Christ to be the true head of the Christian community and, reasoning that the people would have no need of priests if they could read the Bible for themselves, he translated the Scriptures from Latin into English, completing the task in 1382. Nonetheless, England remained within the fold of the Catholic Church.

THE NEW TUDOR DYNASTY

The second half of the fifteenth century was a time of political instability in England. A series of civil wars known as the Wars of the Roses raged for thirty years between the noble houses of York (whose emblem was the white rose) and Lancaster (represented by the red rose). Each side was vying for the throne. The conflict ended when Henry Tudor (a Lancaster) defeated Yorkist Richard III at the Battle of Bosworth Field in 1485. Henry resolved the family feud by wedding Elizabeth of York (a niece of Richard).

The new king, who became Henry VII (1457-1509), founded the Tudor royal dynasty. He devoted his energy to binding together the greatly divided nation. He was a shrewd politician, who reined in the power of the nobles by expanding the political role of the middle class. He arranged a marriage between his eldest son Arthur and Catherine of Aragon, daughter of King Ferdinand and Queen Isabella of Spain. He hoped that this alliance would give England more clout with the other European powers. Henry encouraged trade, particularly the export of English wool. (There were allegedly three sheep to every person in England!) He also expressed an interest in distant markets by sending John Cabot across the Atlantic Ocean to explore the uncharted lands there in 1497. (We'll learn more about this voyage in Chapter XIII.)

In those days England was a small nation of 4,000,000. There were twice as many Spanish, four times as many French, and five times as many Germans as there were English subjects. Yet, with a population of nearly 100,000 people, London was one of the largest cities in Europe. (The world's population has increased dramatically in modern times. Currently about 15,000,000 people live in New York City alone!)

Henry's death provided the occasion for an important work by Florentine sculptor Pietro Torrigiano, Michelangelo's old rival. (Remember how he once broke Michelangelo's nose?). Torrigiano was the first artist of the Italian Renaissance to work in England. He was commissioned to sculpt the figures on the tombs of Henry and his wife Elizabeth in Westminster Abbey. The haughty artist found the local people unsophisticated by Italian standards, and when he returned to Florence he sneeringly referred to Henry's subjects as "those brutes, the English!"

ENTER HENRY VIII

Henry VIII (1491-1547) came to power in 1509. He was a popular and energetic young man educated by humanists. He danced elegantly, sang well, and played a number of musical instruments, including the recorder (for which he composed music of high quality). He also dabbled in astronomy, wrote lyrical verses of poetry, and excelled at sports. He looked like a storybook prince, being tall and muscular, with a ruddy complexion, sparkling blue eyes, and wavy red hair.

Henry's goal as a young king was to achieve a political status equal to those of Emperor Charles V and King Francis I. (Do you remember how he tried to outshine Francis I at the Field of Cloth of Gold?) He began building up a navy that would make England one of the world's greatest sea powers. During his reign the English royal court acquired a refinement and splendor that rivaled many of those of the Continent. Hans Holbein (the Younger) came to England from Augsburg to become the court artist. Holbein, one of the greatest portrait painters of the German Renaissance, combined the techniques of northern detail with southern perspective and color. His full-length painting of Henry depicted as the mythical hero Hercules astride the world gives us an idea of the young king's ambitious plans to be a major player in European affairs!

Earlier monarchs had spent most of their time in London, but Henry preferred to stay there only during the cold, damp winter months. Each spring he moved his court to one of his country estates. He spent a fortune building new palaces, such as None-such in Surrey, which he hoped would rival Chambord in splendor. (Sadly, the palace has not survived to our times.) He also up-dated the existing estates, like Richmond and Windsor. By the end of his reign he would have fifty-five palaces to choose from!

GOINGS ON AT OXFORD

Oxford, one of the world's oldest universities, was founded in England in the twelfth century. About a century later the first of its thirty-five self-governing colleges was built. Humphrey, Duke of Gloucester, was the earliest conspicuous example of an English patron of learning. His donations, beginning in 1411, enabled Oxford to have a library of its own. When he died, he left to the library his personal collection of manuscripts, including Latin versions of Plato and Aristotle, Italian poetry by Dante, and Latin prose by Petrarch and Boccaccio. Unfortunately, many of the manuscripts were dispersed throughout England during the years of civil war. In 1598 Thomas Bodley, an English diplomat and scholar, hunted down as many of the lost works as he could and refounded the library, known today as the Bodleian Library. By the seventeenth century it would own a copy of every book printed in England. (Today it contains over two million books and 50,000 early manuscripts.)

Lady Margaret Beaufort, mother of Henry VII, was an enthusiastic supporter of humanism and a generous patroness of art. She established funds to pay the salaries of teachers at Oxford and Cambridge (a second renowned university formed by a group of dissident Oxfordians). Cardinal Thomas Wolsey, one of Henry VIII's advisors and a graduate of Oxford, financed the establishment of Cardinal College. After Wolsey's fall from power (we'll learn about that later), Henry renamed it King's College. Eventually, the college was given its present name, Christ Church. A bell in its towers is called "Great Tom" after the Cardinal who founded the school.

Many of those who studied or taught at Oxford would go on to do great things. Thomas Linacre traveled to Italy in 1485 with a group of fellow Oxford students, among them Giovanni de Medici, later to become Pope Leo X. When Linacre became a famous scholar, he dedicated one of his classical studies to Leo in memory of "the happy times" when they were together at Oxford. Linacre is best known for founding the College of Physicians (forerunner of the Royal College of Physicians). William Grocyn, a friend of Linacre, delivered the first public lectures on Greek at Oxford in 1491.

John Colet was a student and later a teacher of Greek and Biblical Studies at Oxford. To gain a better understanding of life in ancient times, he compared the words of Saint Paul in the New Testament with accounts of Roman historian and biographer Suetonius. Erasmus studied at Oxford with Grocyn and Colet. We learned in the last chapter how Colet inspired Erasmus to focus upon biblical history. He was later appointed to a Greek lectureship at Cambridge, and it was while teaching there that he completed his Greek version of the New Testament.

Thomas More also studied Greek at Oxford and became friends with Colet and Erasmus. He went on to hold several official posts that brought him into contact with Henry VIII. He accompanied the King to the Field of the Cloth of Gold, where he met the famous French humanist, Budé. More used his position at court to promote "the new learning" in England. It was More who brought Hans Holbein to Henry's court. In 1529 he was made Lord Chancellor, the key advisor to the king.

More was concerned about the plight of the poor and the greed of the upper classes in England. He expressed his ideas in a social and political satire entitled UTOPIA. Written originally in Latin, the book is the journal of a fictitious Portuguese sailor named Raphael Hythlodaye. (In Greek, his name means "skilled in talking nonsense." More was having a bit of scholarly fun with words, while writing about a subject that was quite serious.) The sailor describes his three voyages to America and, most particularly, his visit to the (imaginary) island of Utopia (a word meaning "nowhere").

In the true spirit of humanism, the men and women of Utopia are well educated and enjoy the pursuit of knowledge. Everyone does his share of the community work and all property is commonly owned. No one works more than six hours a day, so that the rest of the time can be devoted to leisure activities involving art, music, and poetry. In this ideal world there is no poverty, crime, or political corruption, and war occurs only as a matter of self-defense. All religious views are tolerated, and the government is based upon what seems most reasonable. Unlike Machiavelli, More believed that rational people could build a strong society without having to resort to trickery or deceit. His vision of Utopia was inspired by the ideal kingdom of Atlantis described in the writings of Plato. (Not everyone realized that these are mythical places. People have been looking for Atlantis for centuries, and a sixteenth century missionary said he would go to Utopia, if only he could find it on a map!)

Erasmus arranged the publication of UTOPIA in Louvain in 1516. It was enormously popular from the moment it appeared in print. By the middle of the sixteenth century the book had been translated into German, Italian, French, English and Dutch. Today the word "utopia" refers to any ideal place or state of mind.

THE KING'S "GREAT MATTER"

Henry VIII had been raised a loyal Catholic, and when he became king he banned Luther's works. He even published his own personal refutation of "the heresy" of the German reformer (THE ASSERTION OF THE SEVEN SACRAMENTS). For this gesture of support, Pope Leo X gratefully rewarded the young monarch with the title of "Defender of the Faith."

In 1527, however, Henry's relations with the Papacy turned sour. The source of the conflict was the king's desire for a male heir. Eighteen years of marriage to Catherine of Aragon had provided him with no son. Catherine, as we know, was the daughter of Ferdinand and Isabella of Spain, and she was also the aunt of Emperor Charles V. Her marriage to Henry's older brother, Arthur, was short-lived, since he died young. After marrying Henry, she gave birth to a number of babies, but only one, a frail, introspective girl named Mary, survived infancy.

Determined to have a son, Henry turned to his current Lord Chancellor, Cardinal Thomas Wolsey, for help in ending his marriage to Catherine. Wolsey was an arrogant and ambitious man who loved fine living. He spent his leisure time on the grand estate he built outside London at Hampton Court. His pompous manner made him the major target of the satirical barbs of court poet John Skelton. But despite his inflated ego, Wolsey was a skillful politician. Henry hoped he could obtain an annulment for him, on the grounds of the biblical teaching that a man shouldn't marry his brother's widow. Although divorce was considered sinful in the eyes of the Church, Pope Clement VII might have granted Henry a settlement. (The English king was, afterall, the Defender of the Faith.) However, Charles V strongly opposed anything that might sever the link he had with England through his aunt. So ob-taining a separation for Henry proved an impossible task even for Wolsey.

The years dragged on until Henry fell in love with Anne Boleyn, a flirtatious dark-eyed lady-in-waiting to Catherine. Exasperated over Wolsey's failure to grant him the freedom to marry someone else, Henry stripped his counselor of his office. Wolsey desperately tried to win back the king's support by offering him his estate at Hampton Court. Henry gladly accepted the property (he later expanded the palace), but Wolsey was still arrested. He died of a heart attack on his way to London to answer to charges of treason.

Henry replaced Wolsey with Thomas More and appointed Thomas Cranmer, an ambitious young cleric sympathetic to the reformist movement, as Archbishop of Canterbury (the highest ecclesiastical post in England). Cranmer used his power to officially pronounce the dissolution of Henry's marriage to Catherine. Soon afterwards, Henry married Anne Bolyn, and on September 7, 1533, Anne gave birth to her first child, Elizabeth. Despite Henry's belief that only a son made a suitable heir, Elizabeth would become the greatest monarch in English history, as we will soon see.

To show that he was in charge of his own destiny, Henry persuaded Parliament to pass the Act in Restraint of Appeals, which denied the authority of all foreign powers (including the Pope) in English affairs. Clement responded by excommunicating Henry and declaring his marriage to Anne invalid. Thomas More, who had long felt torn by his feelings of loyalty to the king and the Pope, resigned his office in protest over Henry's latest policies. However, Henry had the support of his people and seemed unconcerned about the rumblings in Rome.

In 1534 Parliament passed the Act of Succession, which established Henry and his successors as supreme rulers of the Church of England. Once again the authority of the Pope was denied, and once again Thomas More protested. Henry had had enough of More's complaining, and he had the scholar locked up in the Tower of London. Everyone was amazed by More's calm acceptance of his fate. He even managed to write his finest English work, A DIALOGUE OF CONFLICT AGAINST TRIBULATION, while awaiting his trial. Ultimately he was convicted of treason (the evidence was perjured, or falsely sworn to) and executed. More's severed head was prominently displayed on London Bridge as a warning to any other subject who might oppose Henry's will. But many admired More, and he became a legendary example of a man of courage who places his own conscience above the policies of his government. In 1935 he was made a saint by the Catholic Church.

The Acts of Restraint and Succession established the Reformation in England. In 1536 the Act of Dissolution completed the process of dismantling the Catholic Church in the island kingdom by closing 560 monasteries, ceding their lands, as well as those belonging to the Catholic dioceses, to the crown. Seven thousand monks were suddenly homeless. They were given the option of joining the few monasteries that were allowed to remain or entering the secular (non-monastic) priesthood. Much of the land was sold to Henry's friends, as well as to well-off merchants and prosperous farmers, at bargain prices. This led to the creation of a dynamic new class of landowners. In the process, many of the monastic buildings were destroyed, including the majestic abbeys of Fountains and Rievaulx, which now lie in ruins. Cartloads of stones from the monasteries were taken to Hampton Court, where they were incorporated into the palace Henry was expanding.

The monasteries had long played a central role in the social, economic, educational, and medical welfare of the rural communities in England. After their dissolution many people, particularly those living in the conservative northern counties, mourned their great loss. Large numbers demonstrated their frustration in 1536 in an open rebellion known as the Pilgrimage of Grace. But this protest was poorly led and easily put down by the king's soldiers. The leaders were pardoned, but they were executed the following year when a new uprising began.

By dissolving the monasteries, Henry also destroyed the workshops where artists and sculptors had labored for the last eight centuries. In these cloistered rooms, generations of monks had lovingly created beautiful illuminated manuscripts, priceless golden jeweled chalices, and intricately sculpted crosses. The royal court, which could have compensated for this loss by patronizing English artists, lacked the sophistication of the courts of France and Italy and took little interest in art. Making matters worse, religious paintings and statues were now forbidden in the Protestant churches. (As in Switzerland, this removal of elaborate works of art was a reaction against the Catholic influence.) Since they had no sponsors for great works of art that might have rivaled those of the Italian masters, the artists of Tudor England limited their efforts to those genres that did attract customers, such as portraiture and tomb sculpture.

MORE MARRIAGES

Meanwhile, Henry's marriage was on the rocks. Anne had a miscarriage, and the fetus turned out to be a deformed male. Could this be an omen? Henry became convinced that he was being punished for his second marriage. Besides, he was tiring of his young wife, so he charged her with treasonous adultery and had her executed in the Tower of London. Now he could begin again with a clean slate! Remember, having a male heir was what mattered most to him. Henry's next wife, Jane Seymour, turned out to be his one true love. She presented him with a son, the future Edward VI, but she died shortly after his birth, a common occurrence in those days of primitive medical practices.

It was a relief to finally have a son, but Edward was quite frail. Henry needed more sons in case this child should die. Having heard about the eligible eldest daughter (Anne) of the Protestant Duke of Cleves in the Netherlands, he sent Hans Holbein abroad to paint her portrait. The artist's portrayal of an attractive young woman so enchanted Henry that he immediately dispatched ambassadors across the Channel to negotiate a marriage. But when Anne later arrived in England, neither she nor the bridegroom were pleased with what they saw. Holbein's portrait had not shown Anne's pocked complexion (a result of smallpox) or her ample figure. (Henry sarcastically referred to her as the "Flanders mare.") But neither was Henry the slim and athletic rogue he once was. A leg injury in a tournament years earlier had never healed, preventing him from getting much exercise. And he loved to eat! In fact, feasting at his court had become the scandal of Europe. In one day he and his courtiers consumed eleven double sides of beef, six sheep, seventeen hogs and pigs, 540 chickens, fifteen swans, six cranes, 384 pigeons, 648 larks, seventy-two geese, four peacocks, 3,000 pears, and 1,300 apples! Needless to say, the king had filled out considerably since his youth, and in time his waist measurement would expand to fifty-two inches. The last suit of armor that was made for him (currently on display at the Tower of London) would easily fit Santa Claus! Henry went

ahead and married Anne, but their union was soon annulled and she was packed off to a castle in the north of England. The two former spouses had enjoyed one another's company, however, and in later years Anne was known as "the king's sister."

Not about to give up his campaign for male heirs, Henry tried marriage again. This time he chose a high-spirited young lady of his court named Catherine Howard. But alas, her flirtatious activities with the courtiers led to her destruction: Catherine, too, lost her head. The following year Henry

Figure 37: Henry VIII, from a portrait by Holbein

married a sensible and matronly widow, Catherine Parr. She proved to be a fine companion for the aging king and a caring stepmother to his three children. Catherine survived Henry when he died in 1547.

Although it seems Henry spent much of his time wedding and then disposing of his wives, he was actually married to Catherine of Aragon over half of his adult life, more years than all the time spent with his later wives put together. English children remember the fates of Henry's wives by chanting the jingle, "Divorced, beheaded, died, divorced, beheaded, survived."

HENRY'S SUCCESSORS

Henry was succeeded by his ten-year-old son Edward, who ruled with the aid of a council of regents. But, as we've learned, Edward was a frail youth, and in 1553 he died of tuberculosis. The crown was passed on to his eldest sister Mary, daughter of Catherine of Aragon. The new queen was a devout Catholic, and this, of course, led to all sorts of religious turmoil. Mary's determination to restore her mother's faith in England caused most of the Protestant leaders to flee to the Continent. She canceled the acts passed in Henry's and Edward's reigns and replaced them with others that persecuted non-Catholics. Papal supremacy was restored in England. Mary appointed her Catholic cousin, Cardinal Reginald Pole, as Archbishop of Canterbury, replacing the Protestant Thomas Cranmer. Cranmer (who had annulled her mother Catherine's marriage to Henry) was arrested for treason and burned at the stake as a heretic. The Queen exacted a high price of revenge. During her six-year reign, 287 other Protestants were executed, earning her the title of "Bloody Mary."

Despite the national dislike for Catholic Spain, Mary married her cousin Philip II, son of Emperor Charles V. (She was one of his four wives.) Philip was unable to spend much time in England, and Mary died childless in 1558. Cardinal Pole expired the very same day. These two staunch Catholics had not lived long enough to permanently reestablish the Roman Church in England. In fact, by persecuting all those Protestants, they made life very difficult for the Catholics who survived them.

ELIZABETH

Henry VIII's younger daughter Elizabeth (1533-1603) was crowned soon after Mary's death. She would reign nearly half a century, transforming England from an unsophisticated, inward-looking land on the western periphery of Europe into a formidable international power. Elizabeth had a keen mind and was well educated by Roger Ascham, a distinguished Cambridge scholar and humanist. Ascham wrote THE SCHOOLMASTER (published posthumously in 1570), a major landmark in educational theory. Elizabeth particularly enjoyed the study of languages, learning to read Greek and Latin and to speak French, Spanish, and Italian fluently. As queen, she often surprised foreign ambassadors by responding to them in their own tongue.

Elizabeth planned a magnificent coronation that lasted four days, hoping to dazzle her subjects and win their support. It was a great treat for the people, who had grown weary of the oppressive reign of Mary. After a series of spectacles, a stately procession made its way through the streets of London. The houses were decorated with banners and silk tapestries shining with gold and silver thread. The citizens watched in awe as hundreds of officials and courtiers paraded by in their finest clothes. Elizabeth was carried in a jewel-encrusted palanquin (a fancy litter) shaded by a crimson velvet canopy and carried on the shoulders of four dapperly dressed servants. She looked like a goddess in her gold and silver robes.

From the beginning of her reign, Elizabeth demonstrated her skills of leadership. She chose gifted councilors to help her govern. Her closest colleague was the brilliant political strategist, Sir William Cecil; together they basically ran England. The Queen had a talent for getting along with the rival factions within her government, never siding totally with one group and ultimately winning the loyalty of all.

She displayed her practical nature in her dealings with the religious issue. Not about to resort to the extremes of Mary, she sought a solution to the religious divisions of her kingdom that would satisfy the majority of her people. She assumed her father's title as Head of Church and State (in the Act of Supremacy of 1559). The Act of Uniformity of the same year established the Protestant Anglican Church as the official church of England, but it allowed Catholics to worship as they wished. The Anglican Church was built on compromise, taking matters of doctrine (such as justification by faith) from Luther, while retaining the rituals of Catholicism. The THIRTY-NINE ARTICLES (1563) presented the basic teachings of the Anglican Church in a manner that was so vague that they could be interpreted as primarily Protestant or Catholic, depending upon the reader. Bishops in the dioceses continued to handle daily affairs in their communities, but they were answerable to the Queen, not the Pope.

But not all members of society were satisfied. The Puritans were Protestant extremists who wanted to "purify" the English church, ridding it of all traces of Catholicism. They wanted to abolish the bishops and let the local congregations appoint their own ministers. In the following century groups of Puritans would leave England and establish their own religious communities in Massachusetts.

GLORIANA

The years of Elizabeth's reign are often described as England's Golden Age. Rather than rule through fear or intimidation, as her father had often done, Elizabeth transformed herself into a cult figure, "Gloriana." Among her courtiers were poets, painters, and musicians, as well as playwrights - all of them ready and eager to express the virtues of the Queen through their art. While often hinting at the possibility of marriage, Elizabeth held all suitors - courtier and European prince alike - at a distance. In fact, she used her eligibility as a powerful weapon in diplomatic negotiations until she was well into her fifties. Because she never married, she is known as the Virgin Queen. (The state of Virginia was named after her.)

The Queen set the style of dress for the women of her court. Like her father Henry, she had red hair, which she wore in a frizzled style. As she aged, her hairline receded. This was the signal for the other women to shave the hair above their foreheads so that they, too, would have a receding hairline! As we learned earlier, a high forehead became fashionable throughout Europe. This is how it got started! A remarkable feature of Elizabethan dress was the huge ruff that had evolved from a simple lace collar. Worn by both genders, it was often embroidered with gold and silken threads. The fork became a popular utensil in England mainly because it prevented spotting of the ruff during meals! The Queen wore a tight, uncomfortable corset and a metal hoop under her skirt to present the image of an hour-glass figure. Over this she often wore a brocade dress decorated with pearls and jewels. Even the courtiers wore tight corsets, seeking "the look" of a narrow waist between their thickly padded doublets and short padded breeches.

Figure 38: Elizabethan Dress

Throughout her reign Elizabeth kept in contact with her people by making frequent processions through London, just as she had done during her coronation. The lavish costumes of the Queen and her attendants and the magnificent carriages drawn by high-stepping horses made a lasting impression upon every man, woman, and child who stood along the way. Occasionally Elizabeth dropped her mask of royal aloofness and ordered her carriage drawn close to the crowds, where she extended her hand and personally thanked the wide-eyed bystanders for their loyalty.

Each summer she closed down her court and led the entire royal household on leisurely "progresses" through the countryside as far as Derby, Dover and Bristol. Sometimes she stopped at one of her favorite country estates. On other occasions she simply made herself a guest at the home of one of her wealthier subjects. Her hosts had to spend huge sums entertaining her and her large retinue. At one banquet, the court was served 300 different dishes, and, so that "every man might feed on what he likes best," all of the main courses were set out at one time! Despite her frequent travels, the Queen never ventured more than 100 miles from London.

Elizabeth's reign was a time of prosperity for England. Huge amounts of wool were produced and turned into fine cloth which was sold throughout western Europe. But a major source of revenue came from overseas. We'll learn about the activities of the English "sea dogs" in the next chapter. The sound economy led to a building boom, as wealthy subjects replaced their timber houses with handsome new ones of brick or stone. The printing press made available illustrated books on architecture, and classical designs became popular among the English elite. The estates built during this period often had an E-shaped ground plan: the formal entrance was at the short stroke of the E, while the two long strokes were wings of rooms which protruded at right angles from the main section. (Try to envision the E-shaped design.) This over-all plan of balance and symmetry remained in style in England for a very long time. A grand staircase and a long gallery were fashionable interior features, and the fireplaces were elaborate stone structures, often inlaid with colored marble tiles imported from Italy. Even the humble abodes of the peasants improved during Elizabethan times, as the old smoke holes in the roofs were replaced by proper chimneys. Now most English subjects could look out of their homes through glazed windows, sleep in beds (rather than on mats), and dine on plates of pewter instead of wood. Another popular item was the pillow. Previously used only for childbirth, the down-filled pillow was now available for everyone's sleeping comfort!

CREATIVE MINDS

Elizabethan England is known as the Golden Age primarily because of the achievements of its poets and playwrights. (The most famous literary spirit was William Shakespeare, whom we'll learn about in Chapter XV.) The Areopagus was a society of poets whose mission was to reform English poetry along the lines of the ancients. (The name of the group comes from the northwest slope of the Acropolis, where the tribunal of ancient Greece once met.) In the late 1570's the Areopagus included two aspiring young poets - Edmund Spencer and Philip Sidney.

Edmund Spenser is best known for THE FAERIE QUEENE, a narrative poem left uncompleted at his death. This was Spenser's attempt to provide England with an epic comparable to Virgil's ancient work, THE AENEID. The story takes place at the court of Gloriana, Queen of Fairyland, during a twelve day feast. (Spenser was referring to Elizabeth and her court, and this is the origin of the Queen's "cult" name.) Each day a stranger appears and asks for help against some enemy - in the form of a dragon, giant, or other monster. And each day a different knight, who represents one of the twelve moral virtues described by Aristotle, is assigned to help out. The twelve virtues include such qualities as courtesy and justice. Together, they define the ideal Elizabethan courtier. In each episode Prince Arthur appears, symbolizing magnificence or "greatness of soul." But the poem has other purposes beyond idealizing the virtues of Gloriana and her court. Many scholars consider it an allegory of the English Church struggling to free itself from the Papacy. (Spenser was a Puritan.)

Philip Sidney is famous for his pastoral romance ARCADIA, which is written in prose interspersed with lyrical passages. Arcadia was a remote, mountainous region in southern Greece often described by Virgil, and during the Renaissance it came to symbolize the ideal country landscape. Sidney's poem describes the adventures of two princes, Musidorus and Pyrocles, who search for love in a tranquil setting of woods and meadows as sheep and gentle shepherds look on. This rustic image became so popular at court that festivals were held at which the courtiers and ladies dressed as shepherds and shepherdesses!

MARY QUEEN OF SCOTS

Elizabeth's cousin, Mary Stuart of Scotland, was a staunch Catholic. Her life was filled with intrigue and, ultimately, despair. Mary was educated at the French court and in 1558 she married the future Francis II. But Francis died young, so Mary returned home to Scotland. There she tried to rule as the Catholic queen of a primarily Protestant country, not an easy thing to do. At first she was able to maintain peace, but her marriage to her Catholic cousin, Lord Darnley, enraged the Protestants. Calvinist preacher John Knox led an unsuccessful movement to dethrone her.

The marriage soon cooled, and after the two separated, Mary gave birth to a son (the future James VI of Scotland). She then turned to the Earl of Bothwell for sympathy and support. In 1566 Darnley (her husband) murdered Mary's secretary and confidant, David Rizzio. Then Darnley himself was assassinated! To this day, no one knows who killed him, although most think the plot was orchestrated by Bothwell, whom Mary then married.

The Scottish nobles had had enough. They were outraged not only by the Queen's marriage to a Catholic but by her widely suspected involvement in Darnley's death. So they rebelled and imprisoned Mary at Lochleven Castle. Bothwell managed to flee to safety. On July 24, 1567, Mary was forced to abdicate in favor of her baby son, James.

A few faithful friends helped the former queen to escape, and she sought refuge in England with her cousin, Elizabeth, who she hoped would help her win back her crown. Instead, she was imprisoned again, this time for nineteen years! Elizabeth was worried about a Catholic movement to make her cousin Queen of England. Mary was ultimately beheaded in 1587 at Fotheringhay Castle after being accused of conspiring in the Babington plot to assassinate Elizabeth. Most people believe she was involved, but what a terrible way to end her days!

Elizabeth had been excommunicated in 1570, but she did not seem to mind. Now, after the execution of Mary, the Pope and King Philip II of Spain devised a plan to rid England of the Protestant Queen and restore the Catholic religion. In the next chapter we'll learn whether or not they succeeded.

REVIEW QUESTIONS:

1. What was the War of the Roses?

2. Who were Henry VIII's main rivals in continental Europe?

3. What is the Bodleian Library?

4. What is the plot of UTOPIA?

5. What was the king's "great matter?"

6. What was the Act of Supremacy?

7. How did Henry's dissolution of the monasteries affect English society?

8. How did "Bloody Mary" get her nickname?

9. How did Elizabeth win support from her ordinary subjects?

10. Who was "the faerie queene?"

11. What did "Arcadia" symbolize?

12. Why did Elizabeth have Mary Queen of Scots executed?

FURTHERMORE:

1. Henry VII kept artillery in the Tower of London to protect himself against murder plots. He also founded the Yeomen of the Guard (popularly known as "the Beefeaters") as his personal escort. Today, modern Beefeaters wear the livery (uniforms) of the Tudors as they guard the Tower. They are well loved by visiting tourists.

2. Thomas Wyatt was a poet and diplomat educated at the "other university" - Cambridge. He introduced the Petrarchan sonnet form to England. His son, Thomas the younger, was executed for instigating Wyatt's Rebellion, an unsuccessful protest against Mary's proposal to marry Philip II.

3. After Henry's announcement of the imminent dissolution of monasteries, Tewkesbury Abbey in Gloucester was bought by the local townspeople for 453 English pounds. Dorchester Abbey in Oxfordshire was bought by Richard Bewfforeste for 140 pounds and left in his will to the people of his community.

4. Bess of Hardwock was the daughter of a country squire. She married a wealthy (but short-lived) neighbor and used her

inheritance to transform her single estate into a vast collection of properties. Bess had a fine business sense, and acted as banker and mortgage holder for much of her region. She developed the local lead mines and iron works and built country houses that outshone most royal palaces in magnificence. She remarried several times and outlived husbands even richer than the first. Along the line, she acquired the title of Countess of Shrewsbury. What a woman!

5. Many Jesuits flocked to England to reverse the reformation of the Catholic Church that had taken place there. In response, Parliament made it a capital offense for Catholic priests to enter the country. From 1580 until the end of Elizabeth's reign, 180 priests were executed for treason.

PROJECTS:

1. Sir Walter Raleigh - diplomat, soldier, adventurer - was a favorite courtier of Elizabeth. He spent his last years imprisoned in the Tower of London writing his HISTORY OF THE WORLD. Find out more about him and why he ended up in the Tower.

2. THE PRINCE AND THE PAUPER is a fine older movie about Edward VI. Obtain a copy, watch it, and then make a report to your class.

3. In 1483 two young boys who were in line to inherit the throne were murdered in the Tower of London. They were the nephews of King Richard III. Did he kill them? If not, who did? Find out more and write a short report.

4. On poster board make a family tree of the Tudors.

5. Find a copy of THE FAERIE QUEENE. Read about three of the knight's adventures. Then choose excerpts to read to the class, as well as Spenser's description of the court of Gloriana.

6. Read a biography of Mary, Queen of Scots.

Chapter XI
HABSBURG SPAIN

The Spanish kingdom ruled by Philip II in the days of Elizabeth had a long and interesting history. In the eighth century Arab Muslims from Morocco (or Moors, as the Christians called them) had settled in southern Spain and gradually conquered all of the Iberian peninsula. They called the region where they lived *al-Andalus,* and they built a number of prosperous cities there. (Most of Europe was rural and fairly primitive at this time.) The Muslim rulers were tolerant of other religions and welcomed cultural diversity. They highly valued scholarship, and their capital, Cordova, became a center of mathematics, medicine, law, philosophy, and music. The city had a library housing over 400,000 volumes, as well as a great university, where scholars studied the wisdom of the ancients and translated it into Arabic. These scholars helped preserve much of the intellectual heritage of Greece, since many of the original works were eventually lost.

Over the years the Christian kingdoms of Castile, Aragon, Navarre, and Portugal were established in the hillier regions of Spain. Beginning in the eleventh century a long series of wars occurred between the

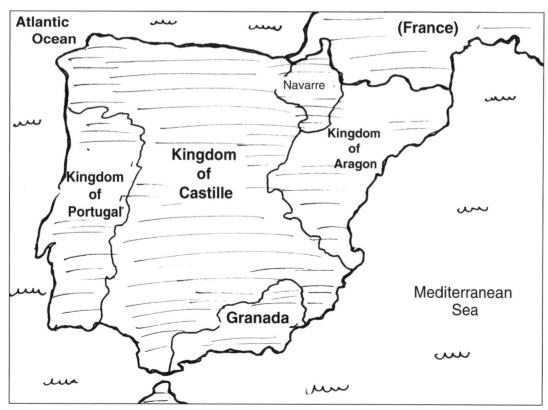

Figure 39: The Kingdoms in Spain in the Early Middle Ages

Christians and the Muslims. (The Christians launched a campaign to drive the "infidels" out of Europe.) In 1236 the King of Castile won a decisive victory and Cordova fell into his hands. The Moors were driven south and confined to the small southern kingdom of Granada, where they remained until 1492.

FERDINAND AND ISABELLA

In 1469 Princess Isabella of Castile married Prince Ferdinand of Aragon, thus uniting the two most powerful Christian kingdoms in Spain. King Ferdinand maintained order in Spain with a well-armed police force known as the Holy Brotherhood (*Hermandad*). In 1492 Ferdinand and Isabella's armies conquered Granada and drove the last Moorish ruler from Spanish soil. Now the region that had once been known for its tolerance became the most intolerant nation in Europe. The Spanish Inquisition, a tribunal set up to weed out heretics, ordered all Jews living in Spain to convert to Christianity or leave the country. In 1502, the same order was given to all Moors, and then to anyone who wasn't an actively practicing Christian. Pope Alexander VI recognized the Spanish monarchs' loyalty to the Church by proclaiming them "the Catholic Kings." It was Ferdinand who established Spanish dominance in southern Italy during the Italian Wars, gaining possession of Naples in 1504.

While Isabella is remembered for her piety, Ferdinand was a cold, calculating, and often devious fellow. Machiavelli, however, admired him and used him as one of his models for THE PRINCE, writing that "he may rightly be called a new prince because he has transformed himself from insignificance into the greatest monarch in Christendom."

THE INQUISITION

The Spanish Inquisition was presided over by a High Council and a Grand Inquisitor. The first Grand Inquisitor, Tomas de Torquemada, was so cruel, narrow-minded, and fanatical about his religion that his name has become synonymous with these traits. The Inquisition controlled a vast network of secret police, spies, and informers who sought out heretics. A suspect was summoned to an interrogation, where the inquisitors tried to obtain the confession necessary for conviction. Those who insisted upon their innocence or demanded religious freedom of choice (this was unthinkable!) were hounded with questions and subjected to all kinds of physical torture (such as stretching the limbs on a rack, burning parts of the body with hot coals, or squeezing fingers and toes) until they "confessed" to heresy (or died). Even Ignatius Loyola, who later founded the Jesuits, was brought before the Inquisition for his untraditional manner of preaching, but he was released.

If a person "confessed" to heresy and was willing to repent or join the Church, he was prescribed certain penances, such as flogging, fasting, saying prayers, paying a fine, or making a pilgrimage. However, even those "infidels" who vowed to become Christian remained suspect. The *Marranos* (converts from Judaism) and the *Moriscos* (converts from Islam) were often arrested again and accused of adhering to their original faiths. Refusal to confess or persistence in the heresy resulted in life imprisonment or execution (and total confiscation of one's property). Because the Church was not permitted to shed blood, a sentenced heretic was burned at the stake.

Prisoners were sentenced at a ceremony called an *auto-da-fe*. They marched in a procession wearing special sulphur-colored gowns (*sanbenitos*), their heads covered with hoods decorated with portraits of the devil. After the sentences were read, those found guilty of unrepentant heresy were solemnly cursed and immediately executed before the attending clergy and townspeople.

EARLY ATTEMPTS AT REFORM

The religious intolerance and cruel repression of the Inquisition alarmed many of the clergy. Some of them believed that success in the war against heresy had to start with ending the abuses within the Spanish Church. People should want to join the Church, not run from it. The first to take action was Jimenez de Cisneros, a Franciscan friar who served as Queen Isabella's personal confessor. In 1495, with the Queen's backing, he became the Archbishop of Toledo, a position that made him the most powerful man in Spain next to the monarchs.

Cisneros used his authority to enact measures to reform the clergy. He cleansed the Spanish monasteries of corruption, and in 1508 he founded the University of Alcala, which became famous for its high standards of scholarship. Despite his accomplishments Cisneros remained a humble and pious man. When Pope Alexander VI required him to wear the luxurious robes appropriate for someone of his station, the friar reluctantly complied, but underneath all his finery he wore his Franciscan habit and under that, a hair shirt!

THE EARLY RENAISSANCE IN SPAIN

Spain was less receptive to the ideals of the Renaissance than the other European nations because of the tight grip of the Catholic Church and the persistence of me-

dieval traditions there. But certain inroads were made.

The country had its first taste of humanism in the early fifteenth century when Inigo Lopez de Mendoza, Marquis of Santillana, amassed a huge library of manuscripts in his palace at Guadalajara. He headed a circle of writers and noble patrons, who promoted the study of Italian and classical works at the court of John II of Castile. Santillana commissioned Spanish translations from local scholars of such classical texts as Homer's ILIAD and Virgil's AENEID, as well as Dante's DIVINE COMEDY and Petrarch's CANZONIERE. A talented poet, he was the first to experiment with the Petrarchan sonnet in Spanish.

Santillano was also a renowned knight. His nephew praised him for his ability to "wear the breastplate and the toga" with equal ease, an allusion to the soldier-citizen of ancient Rome. Royal chronicler Gomez Manrique referred to Santillano as a Hannibal (a great general of antiquity) in war and an Apollo (the classical god of music and poetry) at court. He became the model of a new ideal in Spanish society: the chivalrous *hidalgo* (soldier poet) who ably combined arms and letters. This image was celebrated in the heroic literature, portrait painting, and sculpture produced in Spain in the sixteenth century. It is, of course, the Spanish version of the Renaissance Man.

Antonio de Nebrija was a Spanish humanist who published the first sound Latin grammar book in Spain (INTRODUCTION TO LATIN) in 1481. It was a vast improvement over the old medieval text and was used everywhere. The book revolutionized the study of Latin and made Nebrija the best known Spanish humanist in Europe. He later translated it into Spanish for Queen Isabella. Nebrija also compiled a Latin-Spanish dictionary and published a grammar of a European vernacular language

(Castillian). He was one of the first Spanish scholars to take advantage of the printing press. His contributions to the field of language led him to proudly proclaim himself "the vanquisher of barbarism."

Ferdinand and Isabella were generous patrons of religious art, hoping that in return for their support the artists would glorify and justify the absolutism of their regime. During their reign there evolved in Spain a new style of architecture known as Isabelline (after Isabella). It is noted for the elaborate detail on the outer surface of the buildings.

CHARLES I TAKES CHARGE

Queen Isabella died in 1504, and twelve years later Ferdinand, too, passed away. He was succeeded by his grandson, Charles. We've heard a great deal about Charles in an earlier chapter. As you will recall, he was raised in Flanders (he spoke no Spanish when he came to the throne), and when he became king he added the Low Countries to his Spanish holdings. Charles was the first Habsburg ruler of Spain, and when he also became Holy Roman Emperor he ruled much of western Europe. When he abdicated in 1556, the German part of his territory went to his brother Ferdinand, while Spain (and the rest of the western part) was acquired by his son Philip.

PHILIP II

Philip II (1527-98) became the most powerful ruler of late sixteenth century Europe and a central figure in a series of religious wars. His sprawling empire included (in addition to Spain, Naples, and the Low Countries) Milan, Sicily, Sardinia, Corsica, and the Spanish holdings along the coast of Africa and in the western hemisphere (more about this later). Philip made Madrid his capital and, in 1580, he annexed Portugal (claiming it was rightly his by marriage). He strengthened his alliances with other European powers through his other marriages. (As we've learned, Philip had four wives, Mary Tudor being the second. But, unlike Henry VIII, he only remarried after his present spouse died!)

Philip was a brooding, melancholic person who disliked socializing. Needless to say, he had no glittering court! Like his father, Charles, he always dressed in black. Although he traveled to Italy, Germany and the Netherlands as a young man, he later preferred the seclusion of El Escorial, the austere monastery-palace complex he had built in the mountains near Madrid. From his study there he directed his viceroys in the governing of his provinces. They brought him lengthy, detailed reports of their activities. Philip allegedly read (and enjoyed!) 400 documents a day.

His desk looked out upon beautiful formal gardens, where he often puttered around planting flowers and even weeding (a highly unusual activity for a king). Philip enjoyed his own company (his marriages were little more than political alliances), and he spent much of his time reading his wide selection of books or listening to music. He continued his father's patronage of Titian and two other Italian artists, Leone and Pompeo Leoni (father and son). The elder Leoni painted a portrait of Philip and collaborated with his son on the larger-than-life bronze statuary exhibited today at El Escorial.

One artist who failed to win Philip's patronage was El Greco (Domenikos Theotokopoulos). He was the most outstanding Spanish artist of the sixteenth century and the last great artist of the Renaissance. He studied under Titian in Venice during the 1560's and developed from him a taste for bright color. According to legend, he was asked to leave Italy when he offended the Pope by asking to repaint Michelangelo's LAST JUDGMENT! He settled in Toledo, Spain (a center for painters and poets) and began to develop his own unique style. It was at this time that he became known as *El Greco* - "the Greek one" - among the local artists. (He was born in Greece.)

Philip commissioned him to paint THE ADORATION OF THE NAME OF JESUS for El Escorial, but he was bothered by the harsh colors and emotional intensity of El Greco's painting (which he considered inappropriate for religious devotion), and he never commissioned anything else from him. Nonetheless, El Greco found plenty of other patrons in Toledo. His style was evolving, as little by little he rejected the three-dimensional space and solidly depicted figures of the Italian masters, preferring the elongated figures and flat backgrounds of Mannerism. His later works have a hallucinatory quality. Excellent examples are the mystical THE BURIAL OF COUNT ORGAZ and THE AGONY IN THE GARDEN. Take a look at them in an art book, and then turn to his VIEW OF TOLEDO. This is a gloomy, visionary landscape dominated by dark greens and greys below a stormy sky. Doesn't it make you feel uneasy? What demons do you suppose were causing El Greco such distress?

PHILIP'S MISSION

But let's get back to Philip. Like his father, he was a deeply religious man, and he took it upon himself to combat Protestantism and restore the power of the Catholic Church throughout Europe. Apart from its spiritual offerings, he believed that the Church was essential for maintaining social order. But in the end, his obsession with religious matters would help to bankrupt his country.

One of the first things Philip did as king was to order the Inquisition to double its efforts to "purify" Spain. Among his chief targets were priests who abandoned their calling. He ordered the executioners to mutilate their bodies, cutting the skin from their hands and skulls with a piece of glass and removing the flesh from their lips in order to wipe out the imprint of the holy oils of their ordination! Luis de Leon was a professor of biblical studies who was imprisoned on the grounds that his study of Hebrew and his advocacy of vernacular versions of the Bible were heretical. So close-minded was Philip that Spaniards were not allowed to study in foreign universities (lest they be corrupted), and only the books on an approved list could be read. Being caught with a smuggled book could bring a death sentence!

Like his predecessors, Philip believed in the absolute authority of the Spanish monarchy (he had little interest in democratic principles), and he used the Inquisition to support this power. Once, when his favorite minister, Antonio Perez, was accused of a conspiracy to assassinate one of the king's enemies, Philip avoided being linked with the plot by arranging for Perez' imprisonment and torture by the unforgiving tribunal. Perez later escaped to Paris and wrote a series of letters (the RELATIONS), which implicated Philip in the plot, casting his entire monarchy in a terrible light. The king, meanwhile, confiscated Perez' fine collection of paintings and had them hung in his palace. He was unphased by Perez' attacks.

THE REVOLT OF THE LOW COUNTRIES

The Low Countries were the richest part of Philip's empire, thanks to the commercial enterprises of the Flemish merchants. His father Charles, having grown up in

Flanders, had been popular with his northern subjects. Philip, however, was not liked because of his ruthless persecution of heretics. (Remember, most of northern Europe was Protestant.) Making matters worse, Philip had little regard for people who made their money in trade. He prized wealth, but wealth to him meant land. For centuries the Spanish nobility had shunned and despised those involved in any sort of business, considering them their social inferiors. (This out-dated medieval attitude would later cause Spain to squander its riches rather than invest them.) So when the Dutch merchants complained about the new taxes Philip had ordered, he ignored them. Nor did he acknowledge their objections to his appointment of Spanish officials to government and Church positions in the Low Countries. This act was especially intolerable for the northern cities, which had been efficiently running their own affairs for a very long time.

In 1566 a group of Dutch nobles, led by Prince William the Silent of Orange, presented a petition to Philip's regent in the Low Countries, Margaret of Parma. The petition, known as the Compromise of Breda, called for an end to the Inquisition in the region and summoned a council to deal with the religious question. When one of the Spanish officials scornfully dismissed the petitioners as *un tas de gueux* (a mass of beggars), bloodshed was inevitable. The nobles and their followers, who now proudly referred to themselves as the Gueux ("the Beggars"), attacked the Catholic clergy and the churches. (The money belt and the food bowl of a beggar became the symbols of their protest.)

Philip retaliated by sending 10,000 troops (mostly Spanish and Italian mercenaries) led by the cruel "Iron Duke" of Alva to whip the rebels back into line. Alva spent the next six years seeking out heretics and having them tried by the "Council of Blood," which sentenced the guilty to death. (Needless to say, few were found innocent.) His victims numbered in the thousands. When Prince William's friend and co-leader of the Gueux, the Count of Egmont, was publicly beheaded, William fled to Germany, where he raised an army of 25,000 men. Then he returned to lead a forceful resistance. William was aided by Dutch privateers known as the Sea Beggars, who raided the coastal towns and crippled the Spanish communications network as well as Philip's shipping enterprises. Alva was soon recalled to Spain in disgrace.

When ten of the southern provinces of the Low Countries avowed their loyalty to Philip and the Catholic Church in 1579, William organized the seven northern provinces into the Protestant Union of Utrecht. In 1581 these seven claimed their independence as the Republic of the United Netherlands, with William as their leader. Their new government, although mostly Calvinist, was tolerant of other religious faiths. Of course, Philip didn't acknowledge their independence and kept sending soldiers to fight them. When the Prince was assassinated in 1584 by a religious fanatic (Philip had maliciously offered a reward for William's head), his sons took up his fallen standard.

ENGLAND BECOMES INVOLVED

But let's back up in time. At the beginning of the revolt the Dutch rebels had appealed to Queen Elizabeth for support. The Low Countries were less than 100 miles from the English coast, and the thought of a nation dominated by Spanish Catholics so close to her doorstep convinced Elizabeth to spring into action. In 1568 she ordered the seizure of a fleet carrying pay for the Spanish armies that were fighting in the

Low Countries. The Dutch Protestants were so pleased by this gesture of the Queen's support that they offered her the regency of their struggling state. She declined the offer (and returned the fleet to the Spanish) but then lent the rebels large sums of money. She even encouraged 7,000 English mercenaries to aid them. After the northern provinces announced their independence, Elizabeth sent an army of 6,000 men commanded by her favorite courtier, the Earl of Leicester. Under the leadership of Maurice of Nassau (William's son), the combined English and Dutch forces succeeded in driving the Spanish out of the United Netherlands.

THE SPANISH ARMADA

The fighting in the Low Countries was only one of the issues dividing England and Spain. Philip had tried in vain to court Elizabeth after the death of his wife (and her sister) Mary, but the Queen refused him. In 1570 Pope Pius V issued a papal bull excommunicating Elizabeth and calling upon all good Catholics to work toward her downfall. Philip gladly complied by backing numerous plots to depose her in favor of her Catholic cousin, Mary, Queen of Scots. As we know, it was his mission to restore the Catholic Church to those places where Protestantism had become firmly established, and England was the leading Protestant power in the sixteenth century.

Of course, Philip's antipathy toward Elizabeth increased when she aided his rebellious subjects in the Low Countries. He was further infuriated when he heard that she was supporting English privateers, known as "Sea Dogs," who plundered colonies in the West Indies held by Spain. She even knighted one of them, Francis Drake, for sailing around the world in a ship laden with stolen Spanish gold! But the execution

of Mary, Queen of Scots was the final straw. Philip declared Elizabeth's Catholic cousin a martyr and swore to avenge her death.

The Spanish King announced to the Pope his plans to invade England. Unfortunately for Spain, this information was not kept secret, and before long a network of English spies were sending home frequent reports on the status of the Spanish navy. In May of 1587 Elizabeth sent off Sir Francis Drake for a surprise attack upon the harbor of Cadiz in southeastern Spain. Drake destroyed twenty-four Spanish ships and captured four vessels loaded with provisions. His mission, popularly known as "the singeing of the King of Spain's beard," forced an embarrassed Philip to delay his attack upon England.

Finally, in 1588, he was ready. His plan was to send an armed fleet to the Low Countries, where it would pick up the Spanish troops and then set sail across the Channel to England. Because Philip considered this to be a holy war, he insisted that every soldier, sailor, and slave confess his sins to a priest before setting out. No one would be allowed to swear or gamble on board, and every crew member had to say prayers before the mainmast each morning and evening.

The commander of the Spanish fleet was the inexperienced Duke of Medina Sidonia. The English were led by the very competent Lord Howard. The English had other advantages, too. While the Spanish ships were rather heavy, with tall decks and square-rigged sails, Elizabeth had remodeled her own fleet with smaller and faster vessels. These were crewed by expert sailors, and they carried larger and more long-range guns, as well as more ammunition than the Spanish ships.

Just before his fleet left Spain, Philip had a detailed description of his "Invincible Armada" distributed throughout Europe. No one knows why - perhaps he intended to frighten the English. But now Elizabeth knew exactly what she was contending with: 130 ships, 20,000 soldiers, 10,000 sailors, 2,000 slaves, and 2,000 guns. She certainly wasn't frightened, having 190 sleek ships of her own. Many of her vessels were captained by privateers, who were given royal permission to seize and plunder any enemy ships they could. Dressed in full armor, Elizabeth met with her home-guard troops on the English coast at Tilbury and swore that she would lead them into battle if the Spanish should ever land on their shores. (A nice gesture, but something she certainly never could have carried out!)

After the Armada anchored off the coast of Calais to await the arrival of the troops from the Low Countries, the English set fire to eight of their own small vessels and sent them toward the enemy. Worried that the approaching vessels were filled with gunpowder and would explode upon impact, the Spanish cut their anchor cables and broke formation in a desperate attempt to escape. But then their ships began to drift before the wind and started crashing into one another. One ended up on the rocks and was torn apart. At daybreak the English moved in for the kill, as Sir Francis Drake led an attack upon the disorderly fleet. The English gunners crippled many Spanish ships that tried to resist and blasted others full of holes as they struggled to flee.

Contrary winds made it impossible for any Spanish vessels to escape via the English Channel, so they headed into the North Sea. Medina Sidonia hoped to circle around Britain and then return to Spain. But the weather was stormy, and many of the ships were lost on the rocks off the Irish coast, their crews captured and slaughtered by the local people. It took about a month for the ninety surviving ships to struggle home. They finally reached Spain after sailing 2,500 difficult miles. The "Invincible Armada" was a sorry sight, led by a flagship whose ruptured timbers were lashed together with rope. Medina Sodinia was so weak and ill that he couldn't sit up. Many people unfairly blamed him for the disaster. When he traveled home to Cadiz, children threw stones at his carriage. He later wrote Philip that he'd rather die than go to sea again. Spain had lost about sixty ships. (England had lost only the ships purposefully set afire.) Nearly every noble family had lost a father, son, or close relative. The entire country went into mourning.

The defeat of the Armada foreshadowed Spain's declining influence in Europe and England's emergence as a great power. In 1604, after Philip and Elizabeth were both dead, their two kingdoms finally signed a peace treaty. England remained a strong Protestant nation.

In 1609 Spain agreed to a twelve-year truce with the Low Countries. In 1648, the independence of the Protestant provinces was formally recognized. This region is now known as the Netherlands. The southern provinces remained loyal to Spain and the Catholic Church. They make up modern Belgium.

REVIEW QUESTIONS:

1. Describe the Moorish culture.

2. What was the purpose of the Spanish Inquisition and how did it function?

3. In what ways was Iniga Lopez de Mendoza the Spanish version of the Renaissance Man?

4. What parts of Europe were ruled by Philip II?

5. How was El Greco's painting different from that of Michelangelo?

6. What was Philip's mission?

7. Why did the Low Countries rebel?

8. Why did Philip want to attack England?

9. What advantages did the English fleet have over the Spanish Armada?

10. After the Armada, what was the strongest nation in Europe?

FURTHERMORE:

1. The hidalgo and indeed the entire outmoded code of chivalry would be ridiculed in the seventeenth century by Miguel de Cervantes in his comic prose masterpiece, DON QUIXOTE. In this epic novel the elderly hidalgo Don Quixote, who has gone mad from reading too many chivalry romances, sets out in search of adventure with his foolish squire, Sancho Panza. He is so deluded by his idealistic beliefs that he mistakes windmills for giants and peasant girls for princesses.

2. The Spanish Inquisition survived until the nineteenth century, when it was suppressed by Napoleon in 1808.

3. There was so much religious zeal in sixteenth century Spain that nearly one quarter of the population was enrolled in monasteries and convents! And more people were hunted down and burned as witches in that period than any time before. Witchcraft became heresy in 1484 when Pope Innocent VIII issued a papal bull stating, "Thou shalt not suffer a witch to live." A few years later a text was added to describe how to recognize and punish witches. What was a witch? Supposedly it was someone who made a bargain with the devil: the witch got certain powers (such as control of the weather and influence over the actions of other people) but was denied salvation. Because a confession was required for conviction, those accused of witchcraft were tortured horribly to make them "confess." If they confessed, they were imprisoned. If they refused, they were burned at the stake.

4. William of Orange was once a page to Habsburg Emperor Charles V. He was well educated (he spoke seven languages) and was later known as William the Silent because he kept his own counsel. Although a wealthy man, he died penniless, having sold most of his possessions to raise money to fight the Spanish.

5. Many objects from the Armada have been recovered in the last thirty years from wrecks off the coast of Ireland, including silver candlesticks, gold pendants, silver forks, gold rings, pewter plates, gold and silver coins, and lots of ammunition and guns.

6. Spain and England each seemed to believe that God was on its side when the Armada sailed north. One of the Armada's officers, when asked how the Spanish hoped to defeat the superior English fleet, replied, "we are sailing against England in the confident hope of a miracle." The English responded in a similar vein when a storm broke the formation of the Spanish fleet, announcing, "God breathed and they were scattered."

7. Pietro Torrigiano, the Italian sculptor who produced the tomb of Henry VII of England, settled in Seville, Spain during the 1520's. He was imprisoned by the Spanish Inquisition and starved himself to death.

PROJECTS:

1. Philip II was a staunch opponent of the Turks. His forces checked their expansion at Lepanto in 1571. Find out more about this battle.

2. Bloody Mary and Philip II certainly had a lot in common. For starters, both were grim, unsociable, and fanatically religious. Think about what you've learned about them (do some additional research if you like) and then write a short play about an event in their lives as husband and wife. It can be humorous!

3. Find out more about the Spanish Inquisition and write a short report.

4. The Moorish culture was a rich one and Corvova was a very special city. Consult several encyclopedias about the intellectual accomplishments of the Muslims living in Spain during the Middle Ages. Make a poster illustrating some of them.

5. Do an in-depth research project on the Spanish Armada.

6. Write a play about an encounter between Elizabeth and Philip. It can be humorous!

PART III
NEW VISTAS

Chapter XII
EXPLORING THE WORLD OF NATURE

Why does water freeze? How does a bird fly? What happens to the sun at night? These are the kinds of questions curious people of the early Renaissance asked themselves. Of course, we know the answers to them, because our scope of knowledge has grown at an incredible rate over the last five hundred years, accelerating even more dramatically in the most recent decades.

But let's get back to the times when Europe was slowly emerging from the close-minded culture of the Middle Ages. Remember how the Church had all the answers, and how good Christians were not supposed to question what they were told by their local priests? If something strange or terrible or wonderful happened, it was viewed as an act of God. And anyone who disagreed with Church doctrines was considered a heretic. Imagine how exciting, and perhaps a bit unsettling, it must have been for the priestly scholars who first encountered, through the writings of the ancients, a world where people were actually encouraged to ask questions and to make their own decisions. What a breath of fresh air!

When the works of Aristotle became available, the humanists were amazed by how much he seemed to know about the natural world, and they viewed him as the final authority on scientific matters. But then they did some investigations of their own, and the more deeply they probed the mysteries of the universe, the more they dismissed the Greek belief that everything could be explained by a few general theories. The world is extremely complex, and the study of something like the movement of the stars surely requires a different approach than the study of animal species.

Direct observation seemed to be the best way to figure out why something happened the way it did. So inquisitive scholars put aside the old books and set out to find the answers for themselves. Leonardo, of course, is famous for his diagrams and inventions, but there were many others who also "caught the bug" of scientific investigation. Their methods involved observing natural phenomena, conducting experiments to test theories, and accepting nothing unless it could be proven. Their efforts would ultimately lead to the scientific revolution of the sixteenth century.

Of course, the Catholic Church discouraged any type of scientific speculation that might bring into question its fundamental beliefs about the creation of the universe. But it could no longer keep a lid on the activities of its more curious parishioners. We'll soon see how the Pope responded to their discoveries.

MEDICINE

One area where Renaissance scientists made great progress was in the field of medicine. Compared to modern times, medieval medicine was quite primitive, being a mixture of superstition and religion with just a smattering of serious observation. Half of the children born in those days died before their first birthday, and few people lived beyond the age of forty. (Anyone older than that was considered quite elderly.) The presence of death was always lurking nearby, waiting to seize a victim through disease, malnutrition, or the injuries of war. In hopes of warding off these calamities, most people wore magical charms around their necks and bracelets engraved with mysterious symbols intended to please "Dame Fortune."

The first medical school in Europe was founded in Salerno, Italy in the eighth century to train both men and women physicians. In later centuries other schools sprang up in Bologna and Padua (Italy) and Montpellier (France). Until the sixteenth century the teaching of medicine was based upon the writings of Galen, a Greek physician and anatomist who once served the Roman Emperor, Marcus Aurelius. (Of his 500 books, eighty still exist.) Galen ably described the workings of the nervous system and explained the functions of the brain. However, many of his statements about human anatomy are inaccurate, since his dissections were limited to Barbary apes. Galen fallaciously believed that human organs are similar to those of other animals. A major inaccuracy was his proposal that there are tiny holes in the heart through which blood passes from the right to the left ventricle. He also suggested that the blood ebbs and flows through the body, somewhat like the ocean tides.

The dissections performed by medical students were also restricted to apes and other animals (cats, dogs, and pigs), because it was considered sinful to cut open a dead human body. The Church stood in the way of progress until the fourteenth century, when Italian universities began conducting autopsies on cadavers. In 1316 Mondine di Luzzi wrote the first anatomical treatise based upon the dissection of humans.

But let's get back to Galen. He devised a complex, although totally erroneous, theory of disease. He believed that the human body is created from four elements (fire, earth, water, and air) which form the four bodily humors (yellow bile, black bile, phlegm, and blood). These humors must be kept in balance. Illness occurs when they are out of balance. It is the physician's task to restore them to their original harmonious state.

During the early years of the Renaissance, many physicians attempted to restore the balance of the humors through diet, rest, and herbal medicines. Of course, many people with minor illnesses did improve following such practical measures, but those who were seriously ill did not. Sometimes a vein was cut with a knife to let out excess blood. Leeches were a useful alternative to the knife. As many as twenty of the slimy critters were often applied to a patient's body to gorge themselves with his blood!

But despite the theories of Galen and the investigations of medical students, disease remained pretty much of a mystery, and many doctors concocted their own remedies to combat it. Much of the medicine commonly prescribed contained such unlikely ingredients as powdered human skull, live buttered spiders, and crabs' eyes! The treatment for baldness was to shave the head and then cover the scalp with the fat of a fox. Of course, none of these medications were effective, and some were harmful. However, a potion made from boiled toad actually reduced the symptoms of heart disease. This is because a toad's skin contains a chemical similar to digitalis, the modern drug used to prevent heart attacks. Folk remedies made from herbs were often effective against minor physical ailments, and these were published in "Herbals," books listing plants and their medicinal uses. In 1498 Florentine physicians, in an effort to filter out "quack remedies" from more serious medicine, prepared lists of approved "drugs." It was known as a *pharmacopoeia* (from which our word "pharmacy" is derived).

The most serious diseases were influenza, smallpox, and bubonic plague. Infection was worst in the cities, where large numbers of people crowded together in filthy conditions. Since no one really understood the cause of disease, most people resorted to their own superstitions for explanations. When the plague struck Milan in 1576, the clergy blamed "servants of the devil," who had supposedly put poison in the holy water in the local churches! One of the worst illnesses to inflict Tudor England was a lung disease known as the "sweat." Once infected, a victim broke out in a heavy sweat (which explains the name), developed a high fever and rash, and soon died. In 1528 40,000 people in London contracted the disease, and most of them perished. To avoid contagion, Henry VIII changed residences every other day.

Theophrastus Philipus Aerolus Bombastus von Hohenheim was a sixteenth century German physician who discarded Galen's theory of the four humors, reasoning that disease was a specific rather than a general condition. In fact, he publicly burned Galen's works in a large bonfire. (Bonfires again!) He called himself Paracelsus, and so we will, too. This epithet implies that he surpassed Celsus, a Roman physician of the first century who wrote widely about the medical advances of his day. (In Greek *para* means "beyond," so *Paracelsus* means "beyond Celsus.")

Paracelsus believed disease was caused by external agents that attacked the body. Therefore, therapy should be directed against these agents. He proposed the use of chemicals rather than herbs to treat a sickness. This was a respectable concept (it is the rationale of modern chemotherapy), but given the limitations of Paracelsus' knowledge his remedies (which included powerful poisons like mercury and antimony) killed as many patients as their diseases did.

Girolamo Fracastoro was an Italian physician who proposed that some diseases were spread by invisible *seminaria contagium* (contagious seeds). But his critics asked why, if this was true, did some members of a family die of the plague while others didn't? Besides, how could disease be caused by something invisible? Fracastoro was clearly too far ahead of his time.

Andreas Vesalius was an anatomist who lived in the sixteenth century and helped to clear the slate of many of the false theories of Galen. While studying at Padua University, he performed dozens of dissections. He collected human remains to examine from graveyards, public gallows and mortuaries. Vesalius became a world-famous lecturer while still in his twenties, and students came from all over Europe to study with him. Rather than simply read Galen's description of the organs while a surgeon located each one (which is how medical classes were traditionally taught), Vesalius used the scalpel himself and pointed out the errors in Galen's thinking. At the University of Pisa so many crowds came to watch him at the dissection table that the theater built specially for the occasion collapsed!

Vesalius was the son and grandson of physicians who practiced at the imperial court. He decided to follow the family tradition and left his teaching to serve at the courts of Emperor Charles V and later King Philip II. In 1543 he completed a vast anatomical text, ON THE STRUCTURE OF THE HUMAN BODY, with 270 detailed illustrations printed from his own engravings. These accurately show the composition of muscles, bones, and organs and indicate how veins run through the body. Vesalius did make some errors. For example, since he worked on dead bodies, he concluded that arteries carried only air. Nonetheless, his book provided the first comprehensive and (relatively) accurate description of human anatomy. It became the standard work on the subject for years, and

Vesalius became known as the "father of anatomy."

Unfortunately, the Church objected to Vesalius' practice of dissection, and the Inquisition sentenced him to death for "body snatching." This sentence was later reduced, and he was required make a pilgrimage to the Holy Land. He died in mysterious circumstances while returning from this trip and was buried on the Ionian island of Zakynthos.

Ambroise Paré was a French army surgeon of the sixteenth century. In those days there was a big difference between a physician and a surgeon: a physician was supposed to understand the functioning of the body and treat illness, whereas a surgeon was more like a craftsman who specialized in cutting out or off certain infected parts. Sometimes surgery was performed by a barber, who was then known as a barber surgeon. (Did you know that the red and white stripes on a barber's pole represent blood and bandages?) But let's get back to Paré. One of the major problems he faced was treating the terrible wounds caused by the firearms that had been recently introduced into warfare. He learned that using dressings and a cord called a ligature to tie off bleeding arteries was more effective than the traditional method, cauterization (sealing a wound with a red-hot iron). And it was certainly more comfortable for the patient! This innovation is common medical practice today, but in early times it was a big step forward. Paré took little credit for his efforts and once humbly remarked about a patient, "I treated him, but God cured him." Religion and science now walked hand in hand. Paré is considered the father of modern surgery.

Girolamo Fabricus, a professor of anatomy at Padua, discovered the valves in human veins, but he didn't understand their function. Later, in 1628, his pupil William Harvey would observe that the heart pumps blood around the body and explain that the valves are part of the process. Harvey was the first to understand and describe the circulation of blood, the working of the heart, and the function of blood vessels. Medicine had certainly come a long way from the theories of Galen!

ALCHEMY

At the same time that advances were being made in medicine, many scholars focused their energies upon the "pseudoscience" of alchemy. For centuries it had been a well-known fact that certain substances in nature change over time. (Think about how a plant grows from a seed, blossoms, and then wilts.) Furthermore, some substances change when heated or cooled. (Consider what happens to water.) Alchemists were convinced that base metals such as lead could be turned into gold, if only they could figure out how to do it. The pseudoscience of alchemy dates back to Aristotle, who said that all matter was composed of four elements: water, earth, fire, and air. (He was the source of Galen's theory of the four humors.) Different materials supposedly had different ratios of these elements. So, the theory went, by proper treatment an ordinary metal could be transformed into gold.

The alchemists of the Renaissance wasted most of their time looking for the "Philosopher's Stone" (a magical substance that would help change ordinary metals into gold) and the "Panacea" (a magic potion that would cure all disease and prolong life indefinitely). But along the way they learned a great deal about the properties of certain substances, and they discovered how to make new chemicals, including some acids. They also invented laboratory instruments, such as funnels, delicate scales, and crucibles (containers for heating substances). All of this knowledge would lead to a new field of science: chemistry.

ANCIENT ASTRONOMY

As early as the sixth century BC, a Greek philosopher named Pythagoras declared that the earth was round and that it was constantly in motion. A century later his countryman, Anaxagoras, theorized that lunar eclipses were caused by the moon passing between the earth and the sun. And in the third century BC the Greek scholar Aristarchus proposed that the earth and planets revolve around the sun. His view is known as the heliocentric theory of the solar system. Unfortunately, the people of his time were not ready for such a radical concept, and they continued to accept the words of Aristotle (he lived in the fourth century BC), who claimed that everything moved around the earth. This is the geocentric theory, and it was accepted by most scholars for almost two thousand years.

In the first century AD, Greek astronomer Claudius Ptolemy wrote (in his treatise, ALMAGEST) that the universe is made of a series of clear spheres. The planets and stars are embedded in these spheres, which are arranged one inside the other, all revolving around the earth. His theory of an earth-centered universe was derived from Aristotle's writings. The Church liked Ptolemy's ideas and incorporated them into its theological concept of the makeup of the universe. According to Catholic doctrine, the heavens are arranged in a circle (the most perfect shape), at the center of which is the earth (and the Church). This vision was not challenged during the medieval period when the Church held such sway over European society.

COPERNICUS

Nicholas Copernicus was a Polish priest and mathematician who lived in the sixteenth century. He observed the heavens from the tower of the Frauenberg Cathedral and studied the writings of Ptolemy. His observations that the planets sometimes appear to move backward led him to doubt Ptolemy's theory that they move in circles around the earth. He made a number of mathematical calculations and eventually concluded that the earth was one of many planets, all of which revolve around the sun. (He had rediscovered the heliocentric theory.)

In 1530 Copernicus completed a long book describing his theories of astronomy, ON THE REVOLUTION OF THE CELESTIAL SPHERES, but he kept the manuscript hidden for thirty-six years. He worried about how his ideas spoiled the neat arrangement of the universe described by the Church. The book was finally published in 1543. Copernicus saw the first copy just a few hours before he died. He had humbly dedicated the work to Pope Paul III, hoping to appease him, and he belittled his discoveries by adding that his book was only a hypothesis intended for the computation of heavenly bodies.

But the Pope was not pleased, and Catholics as well as Protestants (including Martin Luther and John Calvin) strongly opposed Copernicus' revolutionary conclusions. Some objected that if the earth moved buildings would collapse and a stone dropped from a person's hand would not fall directly to the ground. Others quoted the lines from the Bible in which Joshua told the sun, not the earth, to stand still (Joshua 10:12-13). The Catholic Church put all of Copernicus' writings on its Index of forbidden books. And that wasn't the end of it. Seventy years after his death the Church declared Copernicus a heretic.

THE COPERNICAN THEORY IS CONFIRMED

Giordano Bruno was one of the leading philosophers of the Italian Renaissance. He rejected the geocentric theory and supported the ideas of Copernicus. In his book, ON THE INFINITE UNIVERSE AND WORLDS, Bruno described a rotating, orbiting earth and went on to suggest that the planet and humanity were only the accidents of a single living world-substance. He even ventured to propose that "there are innumerable suns, and an infinite number of earths revolve around these suns, just as the seven we can see revolve around the sun close to us." Bruno was arrested in Rome and burned at the stake for heresy.

Tycho Brahe was a Danish astronomer who established an international reputation with his observation in 1572 of the first ever "new star" to be recorded in the west. His report on the finding, ABOUT THE NEW STAR, was taken by many as proof of the inadequacy of the old theories of concentric spheres dating back to Aristotle. Brahe built the finest observatory of his day, where he calculated (with the naked eye) the position of nearly 800 stars with (until then) unparalleled accuracy. He also made careful observations of the movements of Mars. Surprisingly, he did not accept the heliocentric theory. However, his student, Johannes Kepler, later used his observations to confirm the Copernican system in THE NEW ASTRONOMY (1609). Kepler also noted that planetary orbits are ellipses (ovals), not circles.

GALILEO

Galilei was an Italian professor of mathematics at the University of Padua. He heard about how a Dutch spectacle maker had put two glass lenses together in a tube to make a telescope, enabling him to see distant objects clearly. In 1609 Galileo copied the design and made himself a telescope to study the heavens. With his new instrument he discovered the mountains and valleys of the moon, four of Jupiter's moons, Saturn's rings, and sunspots. He confirmed Copernicus' heliocentric theory, and he discovered that the stars are more numerous and farther from the earth than had previously been assumed. In 1610 he published his book, THE STARRY MESSENGER, which describes his observations and even suggests that the universe might be infinite.

In 1611 Galileo traveled to Rome to explain his discoveries to the Pope. Many supported him and his views, including the head mathematician of the Jesuits as well as Cardinal Maffeo Barberini, who would later become Pope Urban VIII. But others were offended by his ideas.

In 1616 he was denounced by the Roman Inquisition (yes, Rome had one, too), which warned him to abandon his views. He refused to do so, and in 1632 he published in Florence CONCERNING THE TWO CHIEF WORLD SYSTEMS, PTOLEMAIC AND COPERNICAN. The Pope was so angry he summoned Galileo to appear again before the Inquisition. This time the astronomer was ordered to publicly renounce all his theories and discoveries and to declare as erroneous the Copernican claim that the earth moves around the sun. The alternative was torture. So he swore an oath of renouncement, but according to legend, after he did so he whispered, "and yet it (the earth) does move." Forced to retire, Galileo spent the rest of his life under arrest in his villa at Arcetri, where he wrote a long treatise on the nature of motion.

ADVANCES IN MATHEMATICS

The Renaissance was a transitional period in the history of mathematics. Johann Muller was perhaps the most accomplished mathematician of the mid-fifteenth century. Much of his work was inspired by his careful reading of ancient Greek scientific texts. His *DE TRIANGULIS* is one of the earliest works of modern trigonometry. Luca Pacioli was a Franciscan monk who published one of the earliest printed mathematical texts in 1487. His second work, *DE DIVINA PROPORTIONE*, focused upon geometry and was illustrated by his friend, Leonardo da Vinci.

Niccolo Tartaglia was a self-educated Italian mathematician who became fascinated by algebra. He established his reputation by claiming to be able to solve any cubic equation in the form $x^3 + qx = r$. He proved his ability to do so in a competition in Venice in 1535. He was persuaded to reveal his general solution of cubic equations to fellow mathematician Girolamo Cardano. Despite swearing an oath of secrecy, Cardano disclosed the result in his *ARS MAGNA* (1545), the first modern algebra text. (Tartaglia received no credit.) Raffaelle Bombelli worked with equations using imaginary roots, publishing his ideas in ALGEBRA in 1572.

At the end of the century Simon Stevin of Bruges (in the Low Countries) introduced decimal fractions into western mathematics and John Napier of Scotland did the same with logarithms. (Napier, a fanatical Protestant, also predicted that the world would come to an end between 1688 and 1700!) French mathematician Francois Viete demonstrated the values of the symbols +, -, and = and the use of letters to represent unknowns. His innovations in notation helped to make possible the great advances in mathematics in the seventeenth century.

GEOGRAPHY

After the Roman Empire collapsed, many of the achievements of Greek geographers were recorded and preserved by the Muslims in Arabic. (Remember the academic community in Cordova, Spain?) However, the Christian view of the world prevailed throughout Europe. Many medieval cathedrals displayed large copies of the *Mappa Mundi* (Map of the World) which showed the earth's surface (limited, of course, to Europe and parts of Asia, and Africa) with Jerusalem at the center. (East rather than north was located at the top of the map.) Geography was not a major interest during those difficult times, when few people traveled beyond their own village, apart from those who made a pilgrimage, joined the Crusades, or were involved in trade.

The situation changed dramatically when the ancient texts of Strabo and Ptolemy became available. Strabo was a Greek geographer and historian who lived in the first century AD. His seventeen-volume GEOGRAPHY records his observations made while traveling around the eastern Mediterranean regions and summarizes the geographical knowledge of his times. Ptolemy, the same man who proposed the theory of concentric spheres surrounding the earth, wrote an eight-volume GUIDE TO GEOGRAPHY. It was basically a list of all the known places of the world, tabulated according to longitude and latitude (a grid system for locating places on a map that he popularized). Ptolemy also drew many maps, including a large one of the then-known world which was remarkably accurate. However, he badly underestimated the world's size, fallaciously believing that the land masses of Africa, Europe, and Asia were surrounded by a relatively small amount of open seas. As we will see, his faulty estimates led Christopher Columbus to make some major mistakes.

When Ptolemy's work was translated into Latin in 1406, it unleashed a flurry of interest among scholars in the measurement of the earth's surface. In 1477 the first printed edition of GUIDE TO GEOGRAPHY, illustrated with a series of maps, appeared. This was history's first world atlas (although, of course, it included only a portion of the earth). It was widely circulated and popularized the art of map-making in Europe.

Portuguese sailors began exploring the western coast of Africa in the fifteenth century, mapping the regions they sailed past and thus extending their geographical knowledge of that part of the world. In 1457 King Alfonso V of Portugal commissioned Italian cartographer Fra Mauro to make a circular world map, based upon information drawn from the voyages of the medieval globe-trotter Marco Polo (more about him later) and the more recent explorations of the Portuguese vessels. The map, which has a diameter of about six feet, can be seen today in Venice.

In 1492 Martin Bechaim, a Nuremberg merchant, made a globe to represent the earth, thus introducing the third dimension to the science of cartography. In 1507 German cartographer Martin Waldseemuller produced a map of the world that clearly indicated both North and South America, the first to do so. (We'll find out how he knew about America in the next chapter.)

Flemish cartographer Gerhard Kremer (known as Mercator) developed a technique for drawing a spherical world on a flat surface and published a series of maps that surpassed in accuracy anything previously produced. This included a world navigation chart (printed in 1569), which introduced the map design bearing his name with its grid of parallels of latitude and meridians of longitude. However, it is not easy to portray something round on a flat surface. Imagine taking the skin of an orange and stretching it out. The top and bottom will be quite jagged. Mercator, in flattening the globe to create a map, filled in the jagged parts of the extreme north and south. As a result, the land in these regions appears disproportionately large on his maps, although those areas near the equator are quite accurate. (To check this out, compare the size of Greenland on a map in your atlas with its more accurate representation on a globe.)

Mercator spent his later years consolidating his maps into a series of publications, most notably his ATLAS. (He was the first to actually use the word "atlas" to define a book of maps.)

NAVIGATION

Until the fifteenth century European sea trade was confined to the inland seas (particularly the Mediterranean) and along the Atlantic coast. Navigators depended upon their knowledge of familiar landmarks, as well as written records of prevailing currents and winds and underwater hazards. They carried maps drawn in ink on goatskin, but these lacked detail and were fairly inaccurate. Of course, they also studied the heavens, noting the positions of the sun, stars and planets in order to determine the direction in which to sail.

The earliest vessels had no navigational equipment, except perhaps the sounding pole that was used to measure depths in shallow water. In the late twelfth century the magnetic compass was introduced to Mediterranean seamen by the Arabs, who learned about it from the Chinese. The compass consisted of an iron needle rubbed against a piece of lodestone (magnetic rock). Once magnetized the needle would point north. (The earth is like a giant magnet with two magnetic poles - north and south - so a needle of magnetized iron will always point toward one of them -the closest one - if allowed to swing freely.) In the earliest compass the needle floated on a piece of cork in a bowl of water. Imagine how difficult it must have been to take a reading as the ship tossed and turned at sea! By the fourteenth century the magnetized needle of the compass swung around an upright pin attached to a card marked with the four cardinal directions. The only problem with the device was that the needle could be affected by iron weapons or tools nearby.

The first known navigational book, THE COMPASS OF NAVIGATION, appeared in 1296. Around the same time, THE PISAN MAP was made, representing the earth in terms of compass points. However, navigators were still unaware of the fact that the magnetic north of the earth is not the same as true north (the location of the North Pole).

In the fifteenth century Portuguese cartographers began making greater use of the imaginary lines of latitude, which mark the distance from the equator. Navigators at sea determined their latitude by measuring the angle of the Pole Star above the horizon. The star remains constantly in the north, and as a ship sails north, it appears to climb higher in the sky. When sailing south, of course, it sinks lower.

The quadrant was an instrument designed to measure the height of the Pole Star. It consisted of a quarter circle (this explains its name) made of wood or brass, with degrees from zero to ninety marked on the curved edge. (The equator lies at 0° latitude; the North Pole is 90° north latitude, while the South Pole is 90° south latitude.) One straight edge had sights at each end, and a plumb line (a piece of weighted cord) hung from the topmost point (the apex). Holding the quadrant vertically, a naviga-

tor simply lined up the sights on the star. The plumb line, which hung straight down, would then cross the curved edge at a particular point, indicating the height of the star in degrees and thus giving the latitude. This instrument was fairly accurate and easy to use, but it required a calm sea. (Imagine how the plumb line would swing back and forth in a storm.)

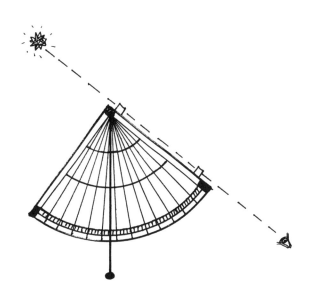

Figure 40: A Quadrant

Unfortunately, the Pole Star disappears completely near the equator, so ships sailing south along the coast of Africa needed another means of determining their latitude. Some navigators resorted to tables that measured the sun's altitude, but most turned to an instrument called the *astrolabe* (a Greek word meaning "star finder"). This ancient device (used as early as the first century BC) measured the height of the sun or another star above the horizon. More complex than the quadrant, it consisted of a flat circular disk, originally made of wood but later of brass, that had degrees marked around the edges. Attached to this was a rotating arm with a small eyehole at each end. The astrolabe was suspended from a thumb-ring in a vertical position. A navigator placed the ring on his thumb and lifted it high, then turned the rotating arm until he lined up the star between the two sights. If he was measuring the sun, he had to look through a piece of smoked glass, or he would be blinded. A pointer on the arm indicated the height of the star in degrees on the scale marked around the edge of the disk. The astrolabe was more practical than the quadrant, whose plumb line was so easily thrown off by the rocking of a ship.

Longitude (the distance traveled to the east or west) was at first measured by dead reckoning. In other words, the captain used his knowledge of winds and currents and his own instincts to estimate the distance his ship had traveled from a given point. Eventually, navigators learned to measure their speed to determine how far they traveled in one hour. This was done by tossing a log off the front of a ship and timing with an hourglass how long it took before it passed astern of (behind) the vessel, allowing for currents and cross-winds. In the sixteenth century the log would be tied to a knotted line. The sailors counted the knots that slid through their fingers in an elapsed time to estimate the ship's speed (and thus its longitude) in knots. Even today, the speed of a boat is measured in nautical knots, and the figures recording the progress of a sea voyage are entered in the ship's log.

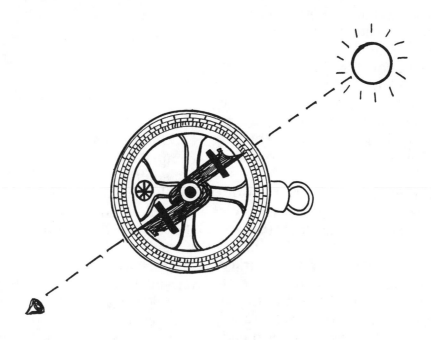

Figure 41: An Astrolabe

REVIEW QUESTIONS:

1. Who was Galen and what were some of his major ideas?

2. Why did physicians sometimes "bleed" their patients?

3. What was Fracastoro's theory about contagious seeds and why wasn't it accepted?

4. How did Vesalius contribute to the understanding of the human body?

5. What is alchemy?

6. What is the geocentric theory?

7. What were the major discoveries of Copernicus?

8. How did the Catholic Church respond to the writings of Galileo?

9. Name one important mathematician of the Renaissance and explain what he did.

10. What were the strengths and weaknesses of Ptolemy's maps?

11. Why is a map less accurate than a globe?

12. What is an astrolabe and how does it work?

FURTHERMORE:

1. During the Renaissance a theory of psychology arose from Galen's theory about the four humors. Each humor was associated with a certain character trait: phlegm was linked with quiet acceptance of things, blood with optimism, melancholy (one of the biles) with high intelligence, and cholera (the other bile) with anger. According to the psychologists of the time, some people have a predominance of one humor. For example, those with an excess of melancholia are intellectually gifted. They are the poets, philsophers, and scholars. Durer's engraving MELANCHOLIA depicts a scholarly figure surrounded by mathematical instruments. In Chapter XV you'll learn about a whole new genre of literature based upon the theory of the four humors.

2. Sixteenth century Nuremburg was a center for invention and manufacture of scientific instruments.

3. Dante was clearly thinking of Ptolemy's view of the universe when he wrote his DIVINE COMEDY. As you will remember, the rings of Hell lay well beneath the surface of the earth and the steps of Purgatory led up to Heaven.

4. A bearded Ptolemy, surrounded by his maps and charts, is portrayed in a relief statue in the Duomo in Florence.

5. In 1590 the microscope was invented by Dutch spectacle maker Zacharius Janssen. This timely discovery led to the discovery of bacteria.

6. Doctors advised Henry II of France to eat snakes and adders once or twice a week each spring. Their flesh, either eaten raw or cooked in a broth, was believed to purify the blood and cause one to perspire more freely.

7. Pope Gregory XIII was responsible for correcting the errors of the Julian calendar which had been in effect in Europe since the time of Julius Caesar. The Julian calendar had a few too many minutes in the year, and by the sixteenth century it was at odds with the natural yearly cycle by ten days. In 1582 Gregory announced that October 4 would be followed by October 15. The Catholics, of course, followed his instructions, and their calendars became more accurate. However, the Protestants were reluctant to do so. England didn't accept the Gregorian calendar until 1752!

PROJECTS:

1. Leonardo Fibonacci was an Italian mathematician who lived in the late twelfth and early thirteenth centuries. Thanks to his efforts Arabic numerals (which we use today) replaced the cumbersome numbers used by the Romans. Write the number 2,479 in Roman numerals. Look at the clock. Then see if you can multiply that number by 462 (using Roman numerals). Did you do it? How long did it take you? Now multiply the two numbers using Arabic numerals. How long did this take you. Can you understand what a tremendous breakthrough the use of Arabic numerals was for mathematicians (and everyone else)?

2. Mercator called his book of maps an Atlas. It is actually named after a figure in Greek mythology. Find out who Atlas was, and why Mercator connected him with maps of the earth.

3. Pretend that Galen meets Vesalius in another life. Write a short script about their encounter.

4. Copernicus, Bruno, and Galileo were all devout Catholics. As we learned, the Church didn't think very much of their discoveries. But just think about what they might have accomplished if they didn't have to worry about pleasing the Pope.

5. The first navigational instrument that could be used in rough seas was the cross-staff. Find out what this was. Then draw a picture of it and explain its use to the class.

Chapter XIII
VOYAGES TO DISTANT SHORES

Given all the advances in navigational devices we've just learned about, it's not surprising that some of the major discoveries of the Renaissance were made by intrepid explorers. With the aid of a compass, chart, and astrolabe, a vessel could leave the coastal waters to find out what lay beyond the distant horizon. But it wasn't just curiosity that motivated their expeditions; a major factor was the need to find better trade routes.

MARCO POLO

As early as the second century, the Silk Road (which was actually a network of roads) had connected China with the West. This route skirted the mountains and deserts and enabled Asian merchants to bring to Europe such luxuries as silk (for which it was named), jewels, gold, and spices. However, the path across central Asia was later blocked by Muslim peoples who refused passage across their land. Early in the thirteenth century the Mongols, nomadic tribesmen led by the legendary Genghis Khan, conquered a vast territory stretching from eastern Europe to China. Khan brought peace to the region and reopened the trade route.

Nicolo and Maffeo Polo were Venetian merchants who traveled east along the Silk Road through the huge kingdom of Kublai Khan, the grandson of Ghenghis. Kublai Khan was a wise leader, and he was eager to learn about other parts of the world. He welcomed the Polos and invited them to his palace, where he asked them all sorts of questions about the land from which they had come. When the merchants later re-turned to Italy, they carried a letter from the Khan addressed to the Pope. It was a request that 100 Christian scholars be sent to his court to teach him more about western culture.

When the Polo brothers made a second trip east in 1271, they were joined by Nicolo's seventeen-year old son, Marco. Remembering the Khan's request, the Pope sent along two preaching friars (a far cry from 100 scholars!), but they lost courage in the first stage of the journey and fled home. The Polos traveled across central Asia by camel, carrying engraved gold tablets issued by the Khan which served as passports. Marco kept a detailed diary of their adventures, carefully describing such unusual sights as a geyser that squirted hot oil and herds of sheep with curly horns that measured four feet. After three years the expedition finally reached the summer palace of Kublai Khan in China, where they were warmly welcomed.

The Polos spent most of the next twenty years at the Khan's court. (When you consider the average man lived only forty years, this was half a lifetime!) Marco became a favorite of the Mongol ruler, who sent him on numerous missions to distant parts of the empire. He continued writing in his diary about the amazing things he observed: exotic birds and ferocious tigers, bamboo forests, paper money (this was unknown in Europe), "black stones" that were burned for heat (coal), and workers making silk cloth. He also described the Khan's horsemen who carried messages long distances, stopping at courier stations to change mounts. It was an early version of the pony express! Marco called the vast territory that stretched between Zanzibar, Africa and Japan the Indies. Later that name would refer only to southeast Asia.

In January 1292 the Polos finally set out for home. They sailed from China along the southern coast of Asia to the Persian Gulf, then traveled by land to Constantinople and caught a boat to Italy. When Marco arrived in Venice, he looked so strange in his eastern flowing robes and baggy silk trousers that at first no one recognized him. (Besides, he had been gone for over twenty years.) Soon afterwards he was captured by the Genoese, who were at war with Venice. While in prison Marco shared the story of his fabulous adventures with a fellow prisoner, Rustichello. Later published as THE TRAVELS OF MARCO POLO, the account vividly describes the riches of Kublai Khan and the exotic marvels of his kingdom. It also includes descriptions of such bizarre creatures as people with thick tails and dogs' heads. (Rustichello was the author of numerous romantic tales, and he embellished some of the descriptions to make a better story.) After Marco's release copies of his book were circulated throughout Europe. Although his journal was enjoyed by many people, few took it seriously and regarded it as a sort of fairy tale. When he was dying, a friend asked Marco if he had told the truth in his diary. He replied, "I never told half of what I saw."

A number of curious adventurers were inspried by Marco's book to travel east. Some of them seem to have had an even greater imagination than Rustichello! They described encounters with all sorts of fantastic creatures - men with ears like elephants, others with faces on their chests, and odd looking fellows who had one huge foot that they held up like an umbrella when it rained! These colorful images simply added to the commonly held belief that the Indies were some sort of never-never land. It was not until later when more serious travelers verified portions of Marco's story

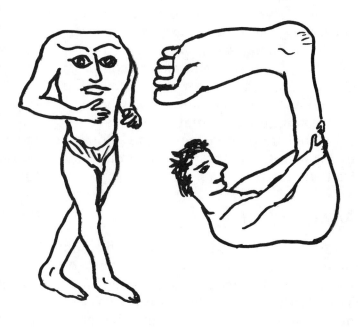

Figure 42: Creatures Supposedly Sighted In Asia

that Italian merchants began to take a lively interest in the possibilities of large-scale trade with the lands of eastern Asia.

THE NEED FOR NEW ROUTES

By the early fourteenth century, large caravans of camels were plodding west along the Silk Road, heavily laden with luxury products from China, while Arab ships brimming with spices sailed from the islands of modern Indonesia to the Persian Gulf or the Red Sea. These exotic wares were brought to Alexandria, Egypt, which was a major trading port of the Mediterranean Sea. Many of them were bought by merchants from Venice or Genoa, who then shipped them north across the Alps. Of course, they made a tidy profit with every transaction.

In 1368 the Chinese overthrew the Mongols and barred foreigners from their territory in eastern Asia. Further west, some of the Mongols became Muslims and refused passage over their land to all Christians. So once again the Silk Road was closed. In the next century Mehmet II and his army of Ottoman Turks captured Constantinople (1453). (Do you remember how this attack caused the city's artists and scholars to flee to the West, enriching the Italian Renaissance?) The conquest of Constantinople put the Turks in control of all the land routes to Asia. Although western merchants were free to trade with their Muslim counterparts, who served as the "middle men" between the West and the East, the prices were exorbitant. An ounce of pepper cost more than an ounce of gold! Not even the seas were free, since Muslim ships now controlled the Black Sea and the eastern Mediterranean. Clearly the Europeans needed to find another route to trade with the East.

HENRY THE NAVIGATOR

Portugal was a tiny outpost at the southwestern edge of Europe. Since medieval times Portuguese sailors had navigated the Atlantic coastal waters transporting local wine, olive oil, and dried fruits to distant markets. Given their location and history of sea trade, doesn't it seem logical that the Portuguese would be the first to seek a water route to the East?

Henry, the third son of Portugal's King John I, was a studious youth who was fascinated by astronomy and mathematics. (Perhaps you've noticed that Henry was one of the favorite names of European royalty.) The prince was an attractive young man with blond hair (his mother was English)

and an athletic build. He was also deeply religious to the point of being an ascetic (a person who practices extreme self-denial) - he always wore a hair shirt beneath his princely clothing to remind himself not to let comfort weaken his faith.

Henry and his two brothers wanted to prove that they were worthy of being knighted, so they led a Portuguese army south and captured Ceuta, a Muslim trading port in Morocco, North Africa. As their army plundered the city, the princes were entranced by the huge amount of gold, silver, pearls, and spices merchants had brought there from the East. And they were intrigued by stories they heard of gold mines that were said to be located beyond the Sahara Desert in southwestern Africa.

After returning home, Henry began wondering whether it was possible to send an expedition south along the African coast to search for the gold mines. He was also curious about the tales of Prester John, a Christian king supposedly living somewhere in Africa, who had tremendous wealth and an invincible army. Perhaps Portugal could form an alliance with this man against the Muslims.

The Arabs called the Atlantic Ocean the Green Sea of Darkness. In those days most people believed that anyone who sailed too far south would reach a point where the water boiled, sailors were burned black (like the natives of Africa) by the sun, ships caught fire, and the air was filled with thick green fog and poisonous fumes. And even worse things lay ahead! Beyond the equator (which was believed to mark the southern tip of Africa) were the Antipodes, an island of horrible monsters.

But Henry didn't believe everything he heard. As we know, he was an intellectual, and he was extremely well read. To learn more about navigation, he started a school on the wind-swept, rocky coast at Sagres, the most southwesterly point in Europe. (The Portuguese referred to Sagres as the "end of the world.") He recruited a community of scholars of many nationalities to train Portuguese navigators in geography, mathematics, chartmaking, and astronomy. Because of his keen interest in exploring the seaways, Henry came to be known as "the Navigator." Thanks to his efforts, Sagres became a center of information about navigation, maps, new lands, and improved shipbuilding techniques. This is where the cross-staff was invented.

Most merchant vessels of the time (called galleons) were rather narrow and had two square sails that enabled them to be pushed forward by the wind. Henry supervised the building of caravels, small (they were about sixty-five feet long) but sturdy and extremely seaworthy vessels, which had two or three triangular sails instead of the two square ones. The triangular sails enabled a caravel to sail against the wind by zigzagging (tacking) into it. The addition of a stern rudder made it easier to steer the ship.

Although Henry never traveled himself, he masterminded the exploration of the west coast of Africa. His first goal was to send ships beyond Cape Bojador, a peninsula jutting out 200 miles south of the Canary Islands. Its red cliffs marked the frontier of the known world. Of the fourteen expeditions Henry sent out, every one turned back at the Cape, fearing the perils that lay beyond in the Green Sea of Darkness. The prince angrily scolded his captains, asking them how they could know if any dangers lay beyond the Cape without venturing south to find out! Finally, in 1434, Gil Eannes convinced his crew to cross the dreaded frontier. He didn't go far, but when he returned unscathed with a cargo of wild flowers that were unknown in Portugal, others were willing to follow his lead.

Gradually, Portuguese ships ventured further south until one explorer, Antao Gonhara, returned home in 1436 with boxes of gold dust and ostrich eggs. He also brought back ten Africans he had captured, including a chieftain named Adahu who told Henry about the rich lands in the African interior. The capture of these natives marked the beginning of a terrible slave trade that would last for centuries. The Prince soothed his conscience by having the Africans baptized and thus "saving their souls."

Henry the Navigator died in 1460 at the age of sixty-six, but the exploratory voyages continued. In 1473 Lopo Goncalves crossed the equator without bursting into flames or turning black. Soon caravels were skirting the coast beyond the equator in search of gold and slaves. In 1483 Diogo Cam discovered the mouth of the Congo River. He erected a huge stone pillar (called a *padro*) there to mark his achievement. (He had carried the pillar all the way from Portugal.) For a long time the Congo was considered a branch of the Nile River, and many believed that by sailing upstream they would reach the kingdom of Prester John. Although such expeditions were later made, no one ever encountered the legendary (and probably fictitious) white ruler. As for Cam, he continued on beyond the river mouth for a few nautical degrees until the coastline seemed to become more easterly. Convinced that he had discovered the southern tip of the African continent he returned home. (He was close, but he wasn't quite there.)

DIAZ ROUNDS THE CAPE

In 1487 King John II of Portugal sent Bartholomew Diaz with three ships to chart the African coast and to find a route to the Indies. A storm blew his ships southwards into the open sea. When he finally saw land

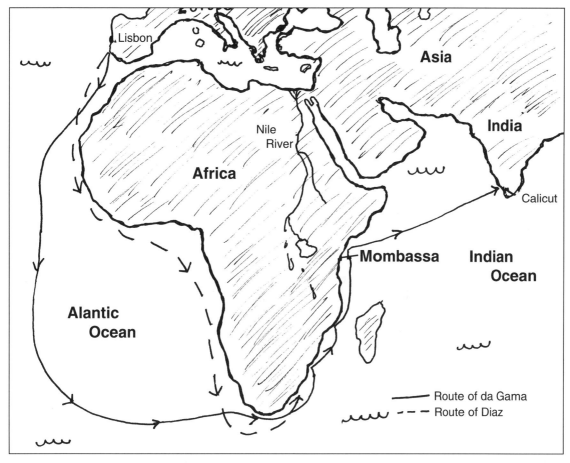

Figure 43: The Routes of Diaz and da Gama

again he realized from the northeastern line of the coast that he had rounded the tip of Africa. He anchored in Mossel Bay, where he and his crew encountered a local tribe called the Hottentots. They sold him an ox, whose fresh meat was a welcome change after the salted beef and fish they had been consuming aboard ship. Dias wanted to follow the coast further, but his men worried about continuing in unknown waters. To avoid a mutiny, he turned back and soon saw for the first time the rocky cliff that juts out into the sea at the southern tip of the African continent. He named it the Cape of Storms, although King John later renamed it the Cape of Good Hope because it held the promise of a new route to the Indies.

Diaz also noted that there was no monster-ridden island to the south!

On To the Indies

In July 1497 Portuguese courtier Vasco da Gama set sail from Lisbon with four ships. (Da Gama was born on the very day Henry the Navigator died.) He followed Diaz's route along the African coast as far as the Cape Verde Islands, but from there he sailed directly south through the open seas. He hoped to take advantage of the prevailing winds and also avoid the coastal storms Diaz had run into. He was out of sight of land for ninety-six long days until he arrived at the coast just north of the cape.

This must have been a frightening experience, since sailors customarily hugged the shoreline in order to keep their bearings.

As usual it was stormy near the cape, and da Gama had to wait a couple of weeks until it was calm enough to proceed. Then he rounded the tip of Africa and continued eastward until the coast turned northeast. When he reached modern Mozambique, he was surprised to encounter a prosperous society of Muslim merchants, nattily dressed in fine linens trimmed with silk and golden thread. Further north he came to the bustling harbor of Mombassa (in modern Kenya), filled with vessels from many parts of the Indian Ocean. This part of Africa was a thriving center of trade, but the Muslims controlled it, and they were not happy to see the Portuguese.

Da Gama crossed the Indian Ocean in May of 1498, arriving in Calicut on the southwest coast of India. Here he encountered yet another prosperous trading community of Muslims, who, like those in eastern Africa, had a cold welcome for the European intruders. Da Gama returned home with a cargo of spices, having blazed the trail to India via the Cape of Good Hope for future generations of European merchants.

PORTUGAL GAINS CONTROL OF THE SPICE TRADE

A few years later heavily armed Portuguese vessels returned to take over the major ports of the Indian Ocean by force, destroying the peaceful system of trade that had thrived there over the centuries. The cities of Mozambique and then Mombassa soon fell into their hands. In 1510 they conquered the Indian seaport of Goa, the chief trading center of Muslims and Indians, making it their own major port in the East. Goa was a

long way from home - a year's journey by sea from Portugal's capital, Lisbon. From Goa other vessels sailed on to the Indies, capturing the port of Malacca in 1511 and thereby gaining control of the spice trade. In 1515 the Portuguese took Ormuz, which controls the Persian Gulf. Now they had in their hands all the major routes of the spice trade except the Red Sea. Portuguese ships later sailed to China, and in 1552 they carried the first Europeans to Japan.

Within a century of the death of Henry the Navigator, Lisbon had became the major European trading center. Portugal now controlled a commercial empire stretching halfway around the earth. Its ships carried home 1,300 tons of black pepper in a single year! The Venetian monopoly of the spice trade was over. The focus of trade had shifted from the Mediterranean Sea to the Atlantic Ocean. Unfortunately, most Portuguese explorers and merchants had little respect for the non-Christian cultures they visited, and they killed large numbers of people who resisted their authority. As we will see, such barbaric behavior was common among explorers from most European countries.

In 1572 Portuguese poet Luis Vaz de Camoes celebrated the discovery of the sea route to India in THE LUSIADS. This lively tale of sea adventures was patterned after such classical epics as Virgil's AENEID, Homer's ODYSSEY, and the Greek myth about Jason and the Golden Fleece. In a curious blending of religious beliefs, de Camoes describes how the Portuguese explorers undertake their mission in the name of Christianity but are aided (and sometimes hindered) in their travels by such pagan deities from Roman mythology as Venus and Bacchus! (You might disagree with the poet's portrayal of the explorers as noble missionaries.) Scattered throughout the poem are descriptive passages of other heroic moments in Portugal's history. Today, THE LUSIADS is considered that country's national poem.

SPAIN LOOKS WEST

Remember how Ferdinand and Isabella drove the Muslims out of Granada and then established the Inquisition to make certain that all Spanish citizens were Catholic? Queen Isabella was an extremely pious woman, and when she heard about the travels of the Portuguese, she began to dream about carrying the Christian faith to the more remote parts of the world. Pope Alexander VI (a Spaniard) sanctioned the conquest of new lands on the condition that the natives be converted to Christianity. So conditions were favorable in the Spanish court for the financing of an expedition to distant shores. This brings us to the story of Christopher Columbus.

COLUMBUS

Christopher Columbus (Cristoforo Colombo in Italian) was born in Genoa, Italy in 1451 and went to sea at the age of fourteen. A red-haired, freckle-faced teenager, he shuddered with excitement when he actually sailed to the exotic destinations he'd heard other sailors rave about, places like Iceland and Ireland. In 1476 the merchant ship he was on was attacked by pirates just beyond Gibraltar, the entry from the Mediterranean to the Atlantic Ocean. The vessel caught fire and began to sink six miles from shore. A quick thinker, Columbus grabbed a broken oar and jumped into the sea. After hours of paddling with both hands, he made it to the Portuguese beach. He eventually settled in Lisbon and opened a shop to sell maps. He married a local woman, Dona Felipa, whose grandfather had served under Henry the Navigator when he and

his brothers conquered Ceuta.

Columbus spent much of his time reading about navigation upon the open sea. He also obtained a copy of Marco Polo's book and became fascinated with the Far East, particularly Japan (known in those days as Cipango) and China (Cathay). He pondered Ptolemy's map of the world and wondered if he could reach the Indies by sailing directly west. Ptolemy, as we have learned, believed that most of the earth was land and that the ocean separating Europe from Asia was relatively small. Columbus wrote a letter to a leading Italian geographer of his time, Paolo Toscanelli, requesting his professional estimate of the distance between the two continents. Toscanelli responded that only 3,000 miles of water lay between the Canary Islands (off the west coast of Africa) and Japan. (He, too, was influenced by Ptolemy. In reality, the distance is 12,000 miles!) Columbus concluded that the earth was one fifth the size that it actually is. Toscanelli, by the way, was Brunelleschi's math teacher. (Isn't it interesting how the many pieces of the Renaissance puzzle fit together?)

The more Columbus thought about it, the more he wanted to sail to Cipango by the western route. He asked King John II if he would finance such a venture, but the Portuguese monarch had no interest in a western route when his rich trading empire was easily reached by sailing around Africa. So Columbus went to Spain. Although Isabella applauded his project, Spain was still fighting the Moors in Granada. Columbus was told to come back when the war was over. After six long years, he was finally given funds by the Spanish monarchs to obtain some ships and a crew. This was in spite of the fact that a commission hired by the Queen found Columbus' estimate of the distance between the continents to be unrealistically short. Ferdinand went along with the plan because he was anxious to use any riches obtained in Asia to pay the expenses of the long war against the Muslims.

Columbus left Spain on August 3, 1492 with 120 men and three ships (the famous Nina, Pinta, and Santa Maria). He carried with him a letter from Ferdinand addressed to "the Great Khan" described in the works of Marco Polo. (Little did the Spanish king suspect that the descendants of Kublai Khan were long gone. China had been ruled for years by the Ming dynasty.)

Columbus stopped at the Canary Islands for provisions and then set sail toward the western horizon. He was certain that no one had ever attempted such a voyage (he didn't know about the Vikings, who sailed to America from northern Europe). His men, uneducated and very superstitious, were uneasy from the start. The open sea was to fifteenth century seamen what space was to the first astronauts - a vast, frightening, and seemingly endless place filled with unknown dangers. Most of the sailors were convinced that the earth was flat and that if they sailed too far they'd simply fall off, landing who knows where. Columbus, of course, knew better and was also convinced that God was guiding his ships; he had everyone attend prayers twice a day. Perhaps this helped calm some of the sailors' fears. But although the ships moved along fairly swiftly because of the prevalent easterly winds and currents at that southern latitude, the time seemed to drag. Columbus often worried about a possible mutiny, so he lied to his men about the distances the ships had covered, hoping they wouldn't realize just how far they were from Europe.

On October 11 they finally sighted an island in the Bahamas, to the great relief of the anxious crew. It is one of history's more fascinating coincidences that the islands now known as the West Indies lay roughly where Columbus estimated the Far East (the East Indies) to be. Stepping boldly ashore the next day, the explorer planted the Spanish flag in the sand and claimed the island, which he named *San Salvador*, for Ferdinand and Isabella. A group of curious natives (the peaceful Tainos) came forward from a grove of palm trees. They were wearing little more than gold bangles and necklaces. Columbus, decked out in a velvet suit and silk stockings (he had dressed for the occasion), quickly concluded that he couldn't be in Japan. (The Japanese were believed to be highly civilized people who dressed in silk.) This, he thought, must be one of the outer islands of the Indies. He called the natives Indians, a name that would be used for any natives of the Americas for centuries. Even today.

Columbus was intrigued by the hammocks the natives slept in and he later had some placed on his ships for his sailors to sleep in. (You don't notice the back and forth movement of a ship as much when you're lying in a hammock.) He also got his first whiff of burning tobacco, a substance that would later addict millions of Americans. Before leaving the island, Columbus coaxed six of the Tainos to sail with him. (Some say he forced them on board.)

From San Salvador the Spanish ships sailed on to several neighboring islands. Cuba seemed so much bigger than the others that Columbus was convinced it was mainland China. And if this was China, then Japan must be nearby! So off he sailed to the east until he sighted an island he named *Hispaniola*.

About this time the Santa Maria hit a reef and sank. Although no sailors were lost, the ship needed to be replaced. So after building a fort on Hispaniola (he named it *Navidad* - Spanish for Christmas - because the ship had sunk on Christmas Day), Columbus left most of his men there to search for gold. Then he sailed back home for more ships, selecting a route to the north of the one by which he had come. Since the winds blow in a circular pattern, this route enabled him to be "pushed home," just as the earlier one had propelled him to America.

When he arrived in Spain, he was greeted as a great hero. Ferdinand and Isabella were pleased that he had reached the Indies, and they were impressed by the Tainos, parrots, tobacco leaves, and gold trinkets that Columbus had brought back with him. But now questions arose over the ownership of the "Asian islands." Spain and Portugal, competing for chunks of the unknown world, appealed to Pope Alexander VI. He obligingly drew up the Treaty of Tordesillas in 1494, which drew an imaginary line from the North Pole to the South Pole in what was considered the middle of the ocean separating Europe and Asia. It was approximately 1,175 miles west of the Cape Verde Islands. All the land to the east of the line belonged to Portugal, while Spain owned everything to the west. Of course, the Pope had no idea how large the landmass to the west of Europe was. (Nor did he realize that it was not part of Asia!) When the Portuguese protested that Spain was getting too much territory in Asia, the line was moved further west. (Look at a map of North and South America in an atlas. Do you see where Brazil bulges out? This is about where the line was. Can you see that Spain was getting the better part of the bargain?)

The following September Columbus left for his second voyage with seventeen ships. Arriving at Hispaniola, he discovered that the fort had been burned to the ground and his men had been killed. A local chief, whom Columbus had met before his departure, explained that the Spanish sailors had attacked the villages, demanding all their golden objects. The natives had done what seemed logical: they killed the greedy invaders.

Columbus established a new settlement on the island, but unfortunately he turned out to be even greedier than his men had been. He demanded tributes of gold from the natives and cut off the hands of any who failed to comply! He sent shiploads of natives as slaves to Spain, many of whom died en route. When his own men rebelled against his tyrannical rule, he executed them for treason. One resourceful group stole a ship and returned to Spain and complained to the King and Queen about Columbus' behavior. Meanwhile, the explorer went back to Cuba and sailed along its coastline. Had he gone further, he would have discovered that Cuba is an island. But he turned back before he rounded its far end. Columbus apparently sensed that he might not be where he thought he was, so he forced his men to sign an oath swearing that they had sailed along the coast of China.

Ferdinand ordered Columbus back home in 1496 to answer to charges of exploiting the people of San Salvador. The explorer was a persuasive man. He not only cleared his name, he obtained financial backing for a third voyage. This time he explored the coast of South America (modern Venezuela). He wondered at one point whether this land might be a new undiscovered continent (it was far south of where China should be), but he foolishly concluded that he had stumbled upon the Garden of Eden, which was often depicted on medieval maps of the world. He came that close to realizing that he had found a "new world!"

When Ferdinand received more reports of Columbus' brutal treatment of the natives, he appointed a new governor of Hispaniola, Francisco Bobadilla, who sent Columbus back to Spain in chains. Again he defended himself so persuasively that he was let off, and in 1502 he made his final voyage. This time he explored Trinidad and sailed along the coast of Central America. After months at sea, his ships became so worm-eaten that he had to return home for repairs. Times had changed. Isabella had died, and no one was interested in supporting any further expeditions.

By now Columbus was in poor health, and, despite his visions of acquiring coffers of gold, his funds were few. He began to feel sorry for himself. Hadn't he been the first to venture across the vast ocean, relying only on his instincts and his excellent navigational skills? He had seen so many wondrous things in the Indies - alligators, flamingoes, parrots, pumpkins, pineapples, sweet potatoes, corn, and tobacco. True, he hadn't made it to Japan and mainland China, but hadn't he reached the outer Indies by sailing west? Yet few people seemed to appreciate him. When he died at the age of fifty-five, Columbus was still convinced that he had been exploring the islands of eastern Asia. In 1542 his remains were transferred from Spain and reburied in Hispaniola.

One person who did appreciate his efforts was his son, Ferdinand. Using the detailed and lively accounts contained in Columbus' log, as well as the descriptions included in his letters, Ferdinand described his father's four expeditions in a long volume entitled HISTORIE. This is an invaluable resource that rivals the lively account of the travels of Marco Polo. Columbus would have liked that.

OTHER ADVENTURERS SAIL WEST

Columbus' voyages inspired other people to explore the lands across the Atlantic. John Cabot (Giovanni Caboto) was an Italian navigator commissioned by the merchants of Bristol, England and backed by Henry VII. He set out in 1497 on his ship, *the Matthew*, taking a northern route. When he reached Cape Breton Island, off the coast of Canada, Cabot was convinced he had arrived in Asia. He claimed the territory for England and returned home in triumph. In 1498 he set out again, this time with five ships. This is where the story becomes muddled, due to contradictory accounts of the time. Most likely some of the ships explored part of the North American continent, possibly sailing as far south as Long Island or Chesapeake Bay before returning home. No one is certain whether Cabot himself survived the trip or was lost at sea.

Pedro Cabral was a Portuguese navigator and explorer who set out with a fleet of ships in 1500. He planned to follow da Gama's route around Africa, but he sailed too far west and the southern equatorial current carried him to South America. (Some authorities believe this "mistake" was premeditated.) Cabral took possession of the region where he landed, calling it "the Land of the True Cross." It lay conveniently east of the line defined in the Treaty of Tordesillas. The territory later became Brazil, the single South American country where Portuguese is spoken today. Cabral sent one of his ships home with news of his discovery and sailed east toward India with the others. During the voyage seven vessels sank, including one captained by Bartholomew Diaz.

Amerigo Vespucci was a Florentine who worked as a shipping agent for Lorenzo de Medici. He became interested in navigation equipment and moved to Seville, Spain, where he met young Christopher Columbus and helped to outfit his ships. When Columbus' role of governor was called into question, Vespucci sailed to Hispaniola as part of a commission of investigation. This aroused his interest in exploration, and he made several more trips to the west. In 1500 Vespucci and Gonzalo Coelho led an expedition down the coast of Brazil, carefully charting and describing everything they observed along the way. The distance they sailed along the South American coast was so great that Vespucci concluded that this was not eastern Asia. It must be an entirely new continent. His long letter, THE NEW WORLD, was the first document to define America as a landmass separate from Asia. It also introduced the term "the New World." (It was new to the Europeans, although people had been thriving there since about 20,000 BC!)

Martin Waldseemuller, the German cartographer we learned about earlier, read Vespucci's account of his voyages. When he produced his own map of the world in 1507, he included a very long, narrow continent between Europe and Asia and named it America (from the Latin *Americus*) in honor of the Italian explorer. The name stuck. But some people think he should have named the continent Columbia. Do you?

CORTES CONQUERS THE AZTECS

Hernando Cortes was the first of the Spanish conquistadors who sailed to America. Unlike the earlier navigators and explorers who were seeking a route to Asia, the *conquistadors* (a Spanish word meaning conquerors) were soldiers and adventurers whose goal was to subdue parts of America and bring treasure back to Spain.

Cortes was ten years old when Columbus made his first trans-Atlantic voyage. In 1504 he sailed to Hispaniola to seek his fortune there. He participated in the conquest of Cuba and became the Mayor of Cuba's capital, Santiago. But he was distracted by rumors of a rich empire on the mainland just to the west. In 1518 Cortes transported an army of 600 well-trained men, sixteen horses, and several cannons to Veracruz (on the coast of modern Mexico). He was welcomed by the trusting local natives, who had never seen light-skinned, bearded Europeans, let alone sailing ships, guns or horses. After establishing a settlement, Cortes burned all his ships but one to discourage his soldiers from deserting. The surviving ship went to Spain to inform the king of the founding of a new colony.

Much of Mexico was ruled by the highly sophisticated Aztecs. These warriors had arrived in the region in the fourteenth century and absorbed the cultures of earlier civilizations, creating their own complex system of law and government. The Aztecs built their capital city, Tenochtitlan, on a group of connected islands in a lake. It was reached by a narrow causeway. (Modern Mexico City is built on the dried-up lakebed.) Nothing in Europe compared to Tenochtitlan, with its magnificent palaces and temples, busy canals crossed by portable bridges, extraordinary floating market gardens, ball game courts, and incredible zoological and botanical collections. Over 200,000 people lived in the city's five square miles. (Spain's largest city, Seville, had only 45,000).

At first the Aztecs believed that Cortes was the god Quetzacoatl. According to their legends, a fair-skinned god of that name had left Tenochtitlan many years earlier and sailed to the east, promising to return one day. As soon the Aztec king, Montezuma, heard about the strange men arriving on "towers floating on the waves of the sea," he sent ambassadors to greet them. They carried the insignia worn by the Aztec high priest when he impersonated Quetzacoatl at religious ceremonies. Montezuma reasoned that if the new arrival was indeed the god, the insignia would prompt him to reveal his divine identity. But he also sent lavish gifts (gold and silver crests with feathered plumes, beautifully wrought golden animals, and an embossed golden sun the size of a cartwheel) that were intended to buy off the new arrivals if they were only mortal trespassers. But Montezuma's strategy failed. Cortes ignored the insignia and took the gifts, but then he proceeded inland to demand more treasures.

When the Spaniards arrived at Tenochtitlan, they were met by Montezuma himself. The richly attired Aztec king was carried in a magnificent golden litter with a canopy decorated with glittering jewels and colorful feathers. Montezuma was distressed that the Spaniards had proceeded inland. By his actions, Cortes had made it clear that he was not Quetzacoatl. The king wondered what he was up to, but to appease the new arrivals he treated them like gods, kissing the ground before their feet and giving them more precious gifts. He even had their food sprinkled with the fresh, bright blood of human sacrifice intended for the Aztec deities (the Europeans shook their heads in disgust), and he housed them in a palace next to his own.

After six days of cordial meetings and lavish banquets, Cortes heard about the king's vast treasury. Blind with greed, he imprisoned Montezuma and demanded a huge ransom of gold for his release. When the natives paid the ransom, Cortes went back on his word and kept their ruler captive. (Wasn't this predictable?) Montezuma was later struck by a stone during a riot and killed. His death inspired the Aztec warriors to unite and drive the cruel Spaniards from Tenochtitlan. Cortes lost two thirds of his men in their charge, many of whom were carried off as sacrificial victims to the Aztec gods.

The following summer the invaders returned and besieged the city. Within three months the Aztecs surrendered. How could a few hundred Spaniards defeat thousands of natives? Partly because the Aztec spears were no match for the Spanish cannons and horses. And partly because of radically different philosophies: an Aztec warrior earned rank by the number of prisoners he took, but the Spanish simply blasted their enemies to bits! A major factor was the smallpox carried by the Europeans. Having no natural immunity to the disease, many of the city's defenders died miserably from its affects. Once Tenochtitlan fell, the Aztec Empire was quickly destroyed. Those natives who survived the Spanish attack became the slaves of their conquerors.

Cortes gathered up vast quantities of gold and silver treasure and shipped it all off to Spain. His boastful account of the conquest of the Aztecs filled five letters to the reigning monarch, Charles I. These were published in 1524, along with the first map of Mexico. Cortes became the ruler of the vast territory that makes up most of modern Mexico. He called it New Spain.

Years later Cortes left Mexico and served with the Spanish forces in the siege of Algiers, Africa. After this victory Cortes met Charles, who didn't remember who he was. The Spanish King (and Emperor) was offended by the conquistador's arrogant manner. "Who is this presumptuous man?" he asked. Cortez replied, "I am the man who has given you more kingdoms than your ancestors left you towns." And yet, when

Cortes died in Spain just a few years later, he was a forgotten man. Just like Columbus.

MAGELLAN'S SHIP CIRCLES THE GLOBE

Ferdinand Magellan was born to the Portuguese nobility, and as a youth he served in the court of King John II. In 1505 he sailed the eastern route to the Indies and learned all about navigation on the journey. From then on, he was always on the move. He helped establish a fort in Mozambique and fought at Goa in a battle that helped confirm the Portuguese supremacy of the Indian Ocean.

In 1512 Magellan was involved in the fighting in Morocco, and when he was wounded, he petitioned the Portuguese king (John's successor, Emanuel) to increase his pension. The king refused, so Magellan left Portugal and went to Spain and offered his services to King Charles I. Vasco Nunez de Balboa had recently traveled across the narrow isthmus of Panama in the New World and became the first European to view the Pacific Ocean (which he claimed for the Spanish crown!). Magellan now proposed to sail west across that uncharted sea to the East Indies (so called to differentiate them from the West Indies of the New World) and then turn around and return to Spain. Magellan assumed that the sea to the west of the New World was smaller than the vast Atlantic. He was in for a big surprise!

In September 1519, Magellan left Seville with five ships carrying 270 men and crossed the Atlantic. When the coast of South America came into view, he veered south and cruised past the region claimed by the Portuguese. When he reached the southernmost point of this territory, Magellan rejoiced, believing that the end of the continent and passage to the Pacific were just ahead. It had not occurred to him that South America might extend further south than Africa's Cape of Good Hope. (In fact, it extends 1,000 miles further.) So as they sailed into the bay of modern Rio de Janeiro, Magellan assured his crew that they would reach the route to the west very soon.

It was now December, which, in the southern hemisphere, is the middle of summer. The weather was balmy, but as the ships continued south, the coastline became more barren. And the continent did not end! The sailors became increasingly uneasy. Finally, the tension erupted as the captains of three of the ships staged a mutiny. Magellan proved his mettle by winning the support of nearly all his crewmen. Then he dealt with the rebellious captains, having one killed and the two others cast in chains. He was the judge at the trial of the surviving captains, whom he found guilty. Their sentences were extremely harsh: one man was beheaded and the other drawn and quartered, his remains hung from a gibbet (a wire cage) above the deck of his ship as a warning to others. A crewman who was a ringleader in the mutiny suffered a punishment perhaps more terrible: he was abandoned on the mainland of South America.

On they sailed. Along the coast of present day Argentina they encountered some very tall natives clad in furs. The natives clomped about, their feet wrapped in animal skins packed with dry grass. Remember, the ships were pretty far south, and this unusual footwear must have provided warmth. The Spanish called the natives *Patagones*, which means "big feet." Today, this region is known as *Patagonia*. The crewmen also observed creatures never seen before by Europeans - penguins and guanocos (a type of llama).

In October, 1520, four ships (one had sunk) entered the passage near the tip of the continent that would later be named the Strait of Magellan. The sailors noticed the fires of the local people along the shores, so they named the area *Tierra del Fuego* (Land of Fire). Crossing the narrow strait required tremendous skill on the part of Magellan. The wind blew furiously, and rocky, ice-topped mountains loomed on either side of the channel. The captain of one ship (the San Antonio) lost his courage and sailed back to Spain, taking most of the expedition's food with him. (He captained a supply ship.) For more than a month the remaining vessels made their way through a maze of islands and treacherous currents, finally emerging into the open sea on November 28. Compared to the stormy region they had just left, the vast ocean seemed relatively quiet, so Magellan named it the Pacific (meaning "peaceful"). Actually, this ocean can be quite stormy, but Magellan first saw it during a period of uncharacteristic calm.

Before setting off across the vast Pacific Magellan stopped at a small island to replenish his food supply and to rest his weary men. Unfortunately, as we have learned, he badly underestimated the distance across the ocean, believing he would cross it in a week or at most two. He took on only a two week's supply of food. As it turned out, the ships would travel over 12,000 miles before finding fresh supplies.

Let's take a moment to consider the typical meals served on board in those early times. It was far from appetizing! Salted pork and beef were the staples, to which were added dried peas, ship's biscuit (dried crackers as hard as a rock, which is why they were also known as hardtack), and cheese. The food was stored with the water in the hold, which was usually filthy. Rats and mice scurried over everything, worms wiggled in the biscuits, the meat slowly rotted, and the drinking water turned green. (The water had to be strained through a cloth to filter off the stinking scum.) No wonder more sailors died from food poisoning, typhus, dysentery, or scurvy than from fighting at sea.

What is scurvy? It's a condition caused by a lack of Vitamin C. This vitamin is found in citrus fruits and certain fresh vegetables, but, of course, these perishable foods were not carried on board the vessels of the sixteenth century. When a sailor developed scurvy his gums swelled, making his teeth fall out. His joints became so weak he couldn't stand, and then he began to bleed internally. Eventually, he died. The Chinese had known about scurvy for centuries, and they routinely carried pots of ginger plants on their ships so the sailors could eat something fresh. This made all the difference.

One survivor of Magellan's long trek across the Pacific described the deteriorating dried biscuit from the hold that "in truth was biscuit no longer but rather a powder full of worm, and in addition it was stinking with the urine of rats." Twenty men died of scurvy, and everyone suffered from malnutrition. Many resorted to eating anything from leather rope covers and their own shoes to the rats themselves.

Four months after leaving the strait they arrived at the island of Guam, where they remained and recuperated for some time before continuing on. How wonderful it must have felt to walk upon dry land and to eat fresh fruits and to drink clear spring water. From Guam Magellan sailed due west until he spied a group of islands on the horizon. He named them the Philippines after Prince Philip of Spain (later King Philip II). At last someone had reached the East Indies by sailing west. Magellan remained in the Philippines for quite a long time and even became involved in local affairs. He arranged for a great Catholic Mass to be held for all natives to observe, and he later convinced the local ruler and his family to be baptized. A large number of their subjects followed suit. (This remarkable conversion established the Philippines as the only predominantly Christian Asian nation, as it remains to this day.)

But there were a number of natives who resented the strangers because they showed no respect for the local religion. An army of indignant warriors ambushed Magellan and a band of his men. Although Magellan was outnumbered fifty-to-one, he allegedly fought with his back to the surf for an hour before being killed by a spear that penetrated his heart. (This happened the very same year Cortes destroyed the capital of the Aztecs. History has a funny way of balancing things out.)

Soon after Magellan's death his subordinate, Juan Sebastian del Cano, brought one ship (the Victoria) and eighteen men through the Indies and then around the Cape of Good Hope and home to Seville. It was now clear that Magellan's original plan - recrossing the Pacific and Atlantic Oceans to return to Europe - was totally ridiculous! The odyssey had taken three long years. Although Magellan did not complete this first circumnavigation of the earth, his skill and great determination had made it possible. Now the Europeans knew just how big the planet really was.

An Italian crew member, Antonio Pigafetta, kept a detailed journal of the many fascinating things they saw as they circled the earth. It was published two years after his return to Spain. Magellan himself had kept voluminous notes, but before leaving the Philippines, del Cano had loaded them onto the Concepcion and torched the vessel. Perhaps he was worried about how the Spanish king would view some of the more sordid events of the mission, but the burning of Magellan's thoughts and feelings is a terrible loss to history.

PIZARRO CONQUERS THE INCAS

The sorry condition of the crew of the Victoria discouraged others from taking Magellan's circular route to eastern Asia for another half century. However, news of the vast quantities of gold Cortes had found in Mexico drew hordes of other Spanish conquistadors across the Atlantic to America. Remember how Balboa discovered the Pacific Ocean in 1513? One member of his expedition was Francisco Pizarro, a soldier who had spent his early years as an illiterate pig-keeper. Pizarro later recrossed the isthmus of Panama and then sailed south along the western coast of South America. On a second expedition he came into contact with the Incas, whose rich civilization rivaled that of the Aztecs.

The Inca Empire stretched for 2,000 miles through the Andes Mountains, which ascend along the western coast of the continent. Its capital, Cuzco, was high in the mountains of modern Peru, more than 9,000 feet above sea level. The Incas had built a vast network of roads and rope bridges connecting mountain to mountain, and they had cut terraces into the mountainsides to grow corn and potatoes. They domesticated llamas, which they used as pack animals and as a source of wool for blankets and clothing. They mined silver and gold, which were melted down to craft beautiful jewelry and other objects. The Inca ruler, Atahualpa, was believed to be descended from the god of the sun.

Despite Pizarro's accounts of the marvelous things he had seen on his journey, including a temple covered in gold, the governor of Panama refused him permission for further exploration. Unwilling to give up his dreams of riches, Pizarro returned to Spain and appealed to Charles I. The king appointed him governor of New Castile (modern Peru) and equipped him with 180 men and thirty horses for a return trip to South America.

In 1531 Pizarro landed and sacked the Incan city of Tumbes. Then he marched inland to meet Atahualpa. Like the Aztecs, the Incas were expecting a god to arrive someday from distant shores (theirs was named Virococha), and many believed that Pizarro was the long-awaited deity. This explains why the Incan emperor warmly welcomed the Spaniards. (But then again, the American natives seem to have been extremely hospitable to anyone who arrived on their shores.) Pizarro responded to this show of kindness by lecturing to the king about Christianity and then demanding that Atahualpa declare himself a Christian as well as a subject of King Charles! Understandably, the Incan refused, flinging the Bible he had been given on the floor. Pizarro then angrily seized the Emperor, while his men attacked the natives who were assembled nearby.

Atahualpa, aghast at this display of hostility, offered to fill a hall twenty feet by sixteen with gold, and another hall of the same size with silver. This would be the price for his freedom. Pizarro, of course, accepted the terms. For two months shining treasures were brought in from all parts of the empire by loyal subjects. When the halls were nearly filled, Pizarro suddenly placed Atahualpa on trial and declared him guilty of worshiping idols (rather than the Christian God). He then savagely strangled the bewildered king. (Does this remind you of what Cortes did to Montezuma?) Cuzco was subdued within the year.

Like the Aztecs, the mighty Incas were easily defeated by a few hundred well-armed European soldiers. (At the time of Pizarro's arrival there were six million Incas!) And like the Aztecs, those Incas who survived the onslaught became the slaves of their conquerors. The Spaniards built their own capital city at Lima (the present capital of Peru) in 1535, and from there they explored further south and east. Francisco de Orellano, one of Pizarro's men, sailed all the way down the Amazon River to its mouth at the Atlantic Ocean. Meanwhile, large numbers of Spanish noblemen grabbed up chunks of South America and enslaved the local people to run their large plantations.

Thanks to the huge amounts of gold and silver stolen from the people of America by conquistadors like Cortes and Pizarro, Spain became the wealthiest country in Europe. Every object seized in the New World was melted down for its metal content. All those beautifully crafted vessels, trays, and articles of jewelry are gone forever. But since business and investments were frowned upon by the Spanish nobility, the vast treasury, which could have improved the prosperity of the nation, was used to fund wars (such as those against the Netherlands). Spain gained little from the conquests of the Aztecs and the Incas. Once the money had been spent, Spain became a one of Europe's poorest countries.

THE NORTHWEST PASSAGE

Like the Spanish, the English and the French were eager to find a means of reaching the Far East by sailing west. But wishing to avoid the long and difficult route around Cape Horn (the tip of South America), they hoped to find a waterway through the northern section of the American continent. This was the elusive Northwest Passage. It never occurred to anyone that ice and frozen seas might make it impossible to sail so far north. Both nations ignored the Treaty of Tordesillas, which unfairly divided much of the newly discovered world between Spain and Portugal.

Their captains had instructions to claim any new lands they found.

In 1534 Francis I commissioned Jacques Cartier to find the passage to the Pacific. Cartier did find the mouth of the Saint Lawrence River, which he hoped might lead to the Pacific Ocean. On a later voyage he met two natives, who led him upstream to the village of Stadacona (later Quebec) and then on through the rapids to another village, Hochelaga. Here Cartier named a prominent hill Mont Royal (Royal Mountain). It later became the site of Montreal, Canada. When France became involved in wars in Europe, the search for the Northwest Passage was put on hold. But this didn't prevent resourceful Frenchmen from establishing a lucrative trade network with the natives of North America. They were particularly interested in obtaining beaver and otter furs, which were soon highly prized by wealthy Europeans.

The English never forgot about John Cabot's pioneering voyage in the late fifteenth century. In 1576 Martin Frobisher set sail for America. He discovered a body of water in northern Canada which he believed would lead to Asia, but it turned out to be only an inlet on Baffin Island. (It's now known as Frobisher's Bay.) He then abandoned his mission.

THE SEA DOGS

Queen Elizabeth was envious of the huge amounts of gold and silver being shipped from South America to her rival, Spain. So when English vessels began attacking the heavily laden Spanish galleons, she gave them her full support. Before long there were many English sailors engaged in these acts of piracy. They came to be known as the Sea dogs (we've heard about them before), the most famous being Francis Drake. He raided vessels and settlements,

Spanish and Portuguese, up and down the coast of South America.

As relations deteriorated between England and Spain (this was the time of the wars in the Low Countries), Queen Elizabeth decided to back Drake's plan to sail around the world. There were many similarities between his voyage and that of Magellan. For example, Drake had five ships, and he had to deal with a mutiny off the coast of Patagonia (where he abandoned two small store ships). While passing through the turbulent Strait of Magellan, one captain lost heart and returned to Spain. Another vessel simply disappeared during a storm, so by the time he entered the Pacific Ocean, Drake had only the ship he captained, the Golden Hind.

He sailed up the western coast of South America, raiding any Spanish ships he met, and then continued as far north as the site of San Francisco (which he claimed for England and named New Albion). From there he set off across the Pacific, his vessel riding low in the water because of all the loot he had stolen from the Spanish. He stopped in the East Indies and picked up some barrels of pepper, cinnamon, and ginger, and then sailed home via the Cape of Good Hope. He reached Plymouth, England on September 20, 1580. Elizabeth was so pleased with his accomplishment (and the treasure) that she came on board the Golden Hind to knight Drake. He later led a raid on Cadiz ("singeing the king of Spain's beard") and played a prominent part in the defeat of the Spanish Armada.

In 1584 Sir Humphrey Gilbert obtained a grant from Elizabeth to colonize all parts of North America not occupied by the Spanish or the French. This vast, uncharted region was called Virginia, after the Virgin Queen, Elizabeth. The following year an expedition organized by courtier Sir Walter Raleigh, arrived at Roanoke Island, off the coast of North Carolina. John White, the leader of the group, returned to England in the spring to obtain more supplies, but his ship was seized to join the fleet attacking the Spanish Armada. When he finally returned two years later, the island was deserted. There were no signs of struggle, no bodies, no clues except for the letters "C R O" carved into a tree. (A local tribe was called the Croatians.) Historians have been arguing ever since about what happened to those first settlers of "the Lost Colony."

In 1607 three ships (the Constant, the Discovery, and the Goodspeed) carried 143 adventurers to the mainland, where they founded Jamestown (Virginia), the first permanent British colony in America. Thirteen years later a group of English families seeking religious freedom landed at Plymouth, Massachusetts. England's domination of North America had begun.

A New Awareness of the World

Between 1420 and 1620 the Europeans learned that all the seas of the earth are really one huge body of water, something considerably larger than the Oceanus described by ancient Greek philosophers. Now a well supplied ship could reach practically any port on the planet. The daring explorers we have studied demolished the geographical theories that had prevailed since antiquity (Ptolemy had never mentioned America or the Pacific Ocean!), and a new breed of professional seaman arose, who were willing to sail anywhere if suitably rewarded. They were the maritime counterparts of the mercenary soldiers, and they carried thousands of Europeans to distant shores. Between the founding of Hispaniola in 1493 and the early seventeenth century, over 200 towns were planted on American soil - from Lima and Buenos Aires in the south to Santa Fe (New Mexico) in the west and Plymouth (Massachusetts) in the north.

Most of the Europeans who swaggered around the globe had one main interest: profit. They wrote little and kept secret what they saw for the men who sponsored them. Unlike the artists and scientists we have studied, they had no thirst for knowledge, no interest in the cultures of distant parts of the world. They were the masters, and the natives they encountered were considered poor devils who needed to be either destroyed or brought into the fold of their own culture, whichever worked best. Those settlers who treated the natives as equals were the exceptions. In 1513 Spanish author Juan Lopez de Palacios Rubios wrote his BRIEF ON THE ISLANDS OF THE OCEAN SEA, using Aristotle's argument that barbarians are natural slaves and "proving" that Indians should serve the Europeans.

When Columbus arrived at San Salvador there were as many as 75,000,000 natives in North and South America, almost one third of the current population of the United States. Within a relatively short time, most of them were dead. Montaigne thoughtfully noted in his essays how much better it would have been if the Europeans had made an effort to establish fellowship and understanding among the people of the New World rather than to simply exploit them.

REVIEW QUESTIONS:

1. Describe some of the things Marco Polo saw in the East.

2. Why did the Europeans need to find new routes to the East?

3. Why did Henry the Navigator want his ships to sail beyond Cape Bojador?

4. Who was the first European to round the Cape of Good Hope?

5. What did Vasco de Gama accomplish?

6. What miscalculations did Columbus make?

7. How did America get its name?

8. Who was Quetzacoatl?

9. Was Magellan the first man to sail around the earth?

10. Describe the Inca Empire.

11. What was the Northwest Passage?

12. What part of North America did the French explore?

13. Why was Sir Francis Drake knighted?

14. What was the main reason for European exploration?

FURTHERMORE:

1. Columbus was named after Saint Christopher, the patron saint of travelers. His parents would never have dreamed what an appropriate decision this was! His scholarly son Ferdinand collected 15,000 books and manuscripts. He received grants from Emperor Charles V to maintain this library. Ferdinand worried about theft and left instructions in his will that the books be kept in cases which were protected by an iron grill. A reader sat on a bench outside the grill and had to reach through a hole that was just large enough for his hand to squeeze through to turn the pages!

2. Columbus set sail from one of Spain's smaller ports because the main port of Cadiz was too crowded with Jews escaping the Inquisition and sailing to a new life in such Islamic lands as Morroco, Turkey, and Egypt.

3. The explorers brought many American products never before known in Europe. These included potatoes, corn, wild turkey, green and red peppers, avocados, pineapples, lima beans, peanuts, vanilla, sunflowers, and squash. Tomatoes were introduced as golden apples (they must have been the yellow variety), but few people dared to eat them, fearing they were poisonous. Tomato plants probably first grew as weeds between the rows of maize (corn) in early America. Cocoa beans were brought to Spain by Columbus. They were crushed, mixed with sugar and milk, and served as a drink. Chocolate milk!

4. The Aztecs believed that their sun god, Huitzilpochtli, died each night and could only be reborn in the morning if he received a sufficient sacrifice of human blood. Every day Aztec men, women, and children pricked an ear with a cactus spine and offered drops of blood to sun god. Larger sacrifices involved prisoners of war. Priests cut open their chests with a special sacrificial knife and offered the still-beating hearts to the sun god. Then they ate the limbs of sacrificed prisoners, believing that they would gain the strength and fighting power of their victims.

5. In 1562 Sea Dog John Hawkins sailed to western Africa and bought a shipload of black slaves for a few trinkets, then proceeded to the islands of the Carribbean and sold his prisoners to Spanish sugar plantation owners there. (The slave trade would make England the richest country in Europe by 1800.) On another voyage, when he was joined by his kinsman Francis Drake, he became involved in a major battle with the Spanish fleet off the coast of Mexico. Only the ships commanded by Hawkins and Drake escaped to return to England. Hawkins later commanded a unit in the

English fleet that defeated the Spanish Armada.

PROJECTS:

1. Find a copy of Marco Polo's book. Pick out several interesting sections and read them to the class.

2. Look at a map of the world. Run your finger around the part that was "known" in the time of Columbus. Compare that to the rest of the world. Think about how much of the world came to be known to Europeans during the Renaissance.

3. Ibn Batuta was a Muslim raised in Morocco in the fourteenth century. He spent thirty years traveling through Asia. When he returned, the Sultan of Morocco ordered him to write down his story. Find out more about this early world traveler.

4. Cheng Ho was a Chinese explorer. In 1405 he began a series of voyages that took him from China to the Persian Gulf, the Red Sea, and even the Cape of Good Hope. Find out more about his adventures.

5. The Spanish were later lured to the land that became Venezuela by the legend of of *El Dorado*. Check out this story in the books in your library and then tell it to your classmates. Explain why the Spanish became so interested in the story.

6. Columbus was not the first explorer to reach America. Some historians believe that Egyptians sailed to South America 2500 years ago. We know that the Vikings arrived in North America around 1000. Find out more about the voyages of one of these groups and write a short report.

7. When the Incan king (known as the Supreme Inca) died, his body was mummified and kept in the palace. Once a year the mummies were carried out on golden biers to the temple of the sun god. This was followed by a big religious festival. Find out more about the Incan mummies. How were they preserved? How do they compare with the more famous Egyptian mummies? Write a short report based upon your findings.

8. We've been hearing so much about the spices of the East, such as pepper, nutmeg, cinnamon, and cloves. Today these are available in jars in any grocery store. But what do they look like when they are growing? Some spices are derived from roots, others from leaves, and others from bark. Make a list of five common spices and consult a book in your library to determine how each one is grown and harvested. Also, explain what types of food each one is used to flavor.

9. It has been said that the Spanish sailed to the New World for Gold, Glory, and God. What does this mean? Write a short report explaining your views.

10. Most historians believe the letters carved into the tree on Roanoke Island spelled the first part of the word "Croatians," a tribe of native Americans living near the island. Check out the encyclopedias and see what you can learn about the "Lost Colony." Then write a short play based upon events leading up to its final hours.

Chapter XIV
NEW DIRECTIONS IN MUSIC

Music is an important part of any culture. It expresses a wide spectrum of emotions - everything from pure delight to darkest despair. A musician blends notes, rhythms, and lyrics to create a mood, just as an artist employs color and form to depict a moment in time. Music draws us together and helps us to share our joys and sorrows.

Even primitive people living in caves during prehistoric times must have expressed their happiness after a good hunt or the birth of a child by whistling a lively tune or rhythmically clashing some sticks together. Ancient societies like the Egyptians used the sounds of flutes and cymbals to add drama to their religious festivals. The Greeks believed that the god Apollo inspired mortals to compose pleasing melodies. Another deity, Orpheus, played the lyre (an ancient harp) so beautifully that he charmed Cerberus, the three-headed dog who guarded the entrance to the Underworld. Roman armies marched to the sound of a hundred trumpets. In the Middle Ages most music was, of course, religious, but there were also traveling minstrels, who entertained the public with songs of love and adventures.

The music of the Renaissance reflects the refined elegance of the courtiers, as well as the religious fervor of Catholics and Protestants alike. At first the composers copied earlier styles of music, but then they began to come up with some really original forms. New instruments appeared, and compositions were published and widely distributed. A piece of music, like a painting, was now valued for itself, not for its function.

THE HERITAGE OF MEDIEVAL MUSIC

Medieval music strongly influenced that of the Renaissance. The earliest sacred music of the Middle Ages was composed by monks who spent their lives in cloistered monasteries. They attended numerous prayer services each day (as many as eight!), and it became the custom to rhythmically chant in unison the words of the psalms (lyrical poems of the Old Testament). (Think about it. Isn't singing a passage more interesting than simply reciting the same words time after time?) The monastic chant was known as the plainsong. It was monophonic, which means it had a single melody, and was sung *a cappella* (without the accompaniment of an instrument). Occasionally soloists chanted particular phrases, thus adding some variety to the piece. Every monastery slowly developed its own chants until the sixth century, when Pope Gregory had most of them codified. From then on, all the monks same the same songs, which came to be known as Gregorian chants.

In the ninth century the monks began to experiment with polyphonic music. Polyphonic means "many sounds," and the new chants called for two or more melodies to be sung by soloists or groups of monks at the same time. This created a more intricate and harmonious sound. The earliest form of polyphony, called the *organum*, consisted of an existing piece of plainsong to which new melodies were added.

The plainsong had been easy to learn and remember because of its simplicity, but the more complex songs were more difficult to commit to memory. In the eleventh century music, theoretician Guido d'Arrezo devised a system of musical notation (the writing down of notes of music). He drew horizontal lines (called staffs) to represent the musical scale and then drew the individual notes of a piece of music on or between the appropriate lines. The notes had different shapes to indicate how long they should be held. This added rhythm to the piece. Now the brothers could read their musical parts during services.

In the twelfth and thirteenth centuries, composers who were not monks created many new forms of polyphony for regular church services. One type, known as the *motet*, consisted of a plainsong melody (sung by a tenor), plus two or more additional voices, each with different words. (The motet gets its name from *mot* which is French for "word.") The added parts were faster-moving than the main melody and contrasted with it. This type of musical arrangement is known as counterpoint (meaning melodies sung against, or counter to, the primary one). Now ordinary people could enjoy the new music every Sunday.

Although most music was written for the Church, some pieces were written strictly for fun and entertainment. In medieval France courtiers, known as troubadours, composed original songs about romance and chivalry. These were performed at court by hired musicians called minstrels. Meanwhile, other musicians traveled from castle to castle and from town to town. In those days before radio and television, everyone would gather together in the evening to hear the stories of a minstrel, sung to the accompaniment of a harp or lute.

MUSIC AT THE DAWN OF THE RENAISSANCE

In the fourteenth century music grew even more complex, as composers experimented with unusual variations of tones and rhythms. The evolving trend in music was known as the *ars nova* (Latin for "new art"). This term actually comes from a treatise written in 1320 by Philippe de Vitry, and its innovations in rhythm and counterpoint mark a break with older, simpler melodies (referred to as the *ars antiqua* or "old art"). Individual musical parts were becoming more independent of one another, and greater use was made of instruments.

Guillaume de Machaut (1300-1377) was a composer and poet who served in the court of the French King Charles V. He wrote twenty motets, as well as an entire Roman Catholic Mass (MASS OF OUR LADY). He also composed many pieces in the tradition of the troubadours. Machaut's interest in secular music led to the development of a new genre - the French *chanson*. This polyphonic love song became immensely popular at the royal court.

Francesco Landini (1325-97) was the most celebrated Italian poet-musician of the fourteenth century. Blinded at an early age by smallpox, he turned to music for solace, and he later became the leading organist in the Church of San Lorenzo in Florence. He wrote over a hundred compositions, mostly ballads (simple love songs) and madrigals. (The early madrigal was a love song of eight to eleven lines for two voices.)

By the end of the fourteenth century, many composers were setting lyrical poems to polyphonic music. Clement Janequin was a court musician in the time of Francis I. He is noted for his witty chansons, but he also composed a small number of motets and two Masses. (Interestingly enough, the Masses are closely based upon two of his chansons.) The growing trend in secular music spread to other lands. In Germany the equivalent of the chanson was the *lied*, while Spanish composers produced love songs called *vallancicos*. Although the texts of sacred music continued to be in Latin, the secular pieces were written in the vernacular. This, of course, added to their popularity among the middle classes (who often couldn't understand Latin).

THE INFLUENCE OF PYTHAGORAS

Just as poets and artists of the Renaissance looked to the ancients as sources of inspiration, so, too, did the musical composers. The most important ancient authority on music was a Greek mathematician named Pythagoras. He lived in the sixth century BC and wrote several short treatises about his theories of music. Like most of the ancient writers we have studied, Pythagoras had a passion for balance and order, and he was convinced that harmony was an essential component of nature. This harmony ought to be reflected, he reasoned, in music. The humanists were drawn to his theory, which fit in so well with their own vision of a unified and orderly universe.

Pythagoras was intrigued by the way musical sounds are produced. When he plucked the strings of a simple lyre, he discovered that there is a numerical ratio between the length of the string of an instrument and the note it produces. A shorter string delivers a sound of a higher pitch than a longer one. This is because tone is made by the vibrations of the strings, and the faster the vibrations, the higher the pitch of the tone. (A short string vibrates faster than a long one.) Then he noticed that if two strings are of the same length but one is thicker or looser, the second will vibrate more slowly, producing a lower tone.

Pythagoras found that the notes produced by two strings are especially harmonious if their lengths are in certain simple proportions, such as three to two, or four to five. His observations show that by varying the tension and weight of the strings, a musician can create a variety of notes. The same principles can be applied to wind instruments by substituting air columns for strings.

The humanists studied the writings of Pythagoras and wondered what the music of his age sounded like. Although there were no surviving ancient songs, commentaries written in those early times indicate that they were simple, monophonic melodies.

THE INSTRUMENTS OF THE RENAISSANCE

Although Gregorian chants were sung *a cappella*, later sacred music often called for the accompaniment of a pipe organ (a Roman invention). Secular music usually involved a variety of musical instruments. The most popular instrument of the Renaissance was the lute, a stringed instrument shaped like a mandolin. The lute was brought to medieval Spain by the Moors. They, in turn, had obtained the instrument from the East, where it had existed in different shapes for over three thousand years. (Did you know that all of our modern stringed instruments are descended from those of the ancient Asian world?) The classic Renaissance lute had six strings, although in later times more strings were added.

Another popular stringed instrument was the viol, which was also pear-shaped (like a modern bass fiddle) and came in many sizes. The dulcimer was a type of zither, an instrument with metal strings that

Figure 44: A Courtier Plays A Lute

sackbut (a medieval form of trombone), cornett, hautbois (oboe), recorder, and flute. And, of course, there were drums, cymbals, and tambourines to provide a lively rhythm.

The oldest keyboard instrument is the clavichord (*clavis* means key), which appeared in the twelfth century. Two centuries later the first two-keyboard pipe organ was built. During the sixteenth century the clavichord evolved into the harpsichord and its smaller models, the Italian spinet and the English virginal. The keys of these instruments activated a mechanism that plucked a set of strings. Nicola Vicentino of Ferrara constructed a harpsichord that had not twelve but thirty-one tones for each octave. It must have been extremely difficult to play.

MAJOR COMPOSERS OF THE FIFTEENTH CENTURY

But let's return to the music itself. Guillaume Dufay was a very influential composer of the mid-fifteenth century. He was born in Cambrai, France, where he sang in the cathedral choir as a boy. He later joined the papal choir in Rome and met many of the leading musicians of his time. He soon began composing his own original works and was recognized for his beautiful sacred music. Dufay abandoned the plainsong as the melodic backbone of his religious pieces and used popular tunes instead. (As you can probably imagine, many clergymen thought this most inappropriate!) He also wrote intricate motets for special occasions. For example, he composed a piece *(NUPER ROSARUM FLORES)* for the dedication of Brunelleschi's dome in Florence.

John Dunstable was an English contemporary of Dufay, whose music became famous both in England and on the Continent.

were struck with light hammers. It was held in a horizontal position on the musician's lap. The guitar was a popular Spanish instrument, as it is today. The violin, the most commonly used member of the modern string family, was introduced into Europe in the sixteenth century. However, this descendant of the medieval fiddle was originally considered more suitable for dance music and country festivals than for the church or the court. Its great versatility and wide range were not generally acknowledged until the seventeenth century. Wind instruments of the Renaissance included the trumpet (another Roman invention),

Most of his surviving works are sacred pieces written for three voices, the plainsong often appearing as the basic melody. (He did not go the route of Dufay.) Dunstable wrote many motets as well as two Masses. Gilles de Binchois was a Flemish composer who is remembered mostly for his sacred music, although he wrote fifty-five chansons for one voice and two instruments.

In 1477 Johannes Tinctoris, a Flemish music theorist and composer, dismissed all music that had been written more than forty years earlier, claiming it was not worth listening to! He went on to list those composers of recent years who had achieved a state of perfection: Dufay, Dunstable and de Binchois. Tinctoris also wrote the first printed music dictionary, which defined 299 musical terms.

NEW FORMS OF MUSIC

In the late fifteenth century, a new style of music known as imitative counterpoint became popular. It involved different voices or instruments which followed one another and repeated (imitated) the original melody with slight variations. This genre, later known as the fugue, was the major form of composition in the High Renaissance.

Josquin des Près (1440-1521) of Flanders was the most celebrated musician of the generation after Dufay. He was employed by Duke Galeazzo Maria Sforza of Milan in 1474, and when the Duke was assassinated two years later, he joined the service of his brother, Cardinal Ascanio Sforza. Des Près traveled to Rome with his new patron and sang in the papal choir. He later became court composer for King Louis XII of France, then served Duke Ercole d'Este before finally returning to Flanders in 1516. He was a master of polyphony and a prolific composer. Twenty Masses, a hundred motets,

and seventy-five secular works written by him have survived. He developed many techniques of composition which would later be copied by other composers, such as the canon (a form of imitative counterpoint in which two or more parts enter in succession at different points).

In Italy an enthusiasm for imitative counterpoint led to the development of the madrigal from a simple song of two voices to a complex polyphonic piece with from three to six parts sung by men and women, usually *a cappella*. Each part consisted of several voices that sang in harmony, each voice being as important as the others. This was a very different concept from the earlier songs, in which the additional melodies simply embellished the main one. Music was certainly getting more complicated. The newly expanded madrigal became extremely popular in Italy and England. Many of the lyrics were inspired by the sonnets of Petrarch.

THE PUBLICATION OF MUSICAL SCORES

At the dawn of the sixteenth century, a Venetian named Ottaviano Petrucci invented movable type for printing polyphonic music. He had to run the paper through his press three times - first for the lines (staves), then for the words, and finally for the notes. His notes were diamond-shaped, in imitation of the notes in a manuscript made by a scribe using a quill pen. The round-headed notes familiar to us were not printed until 1550.

Petrucci's first published work was a collection of French chansons. He spent most of the rest of his life printing music, and thanks to him people could gather together to sing the "latest hits." Petrucci was directly responsible for the great popularity of the works of such composers as

Josquin des Près. Other presses followed his lead. One of the most popular collections of madrigals written by Jacob Arcadelt was reprinted forty times. Some publishers responded to the growing interest in music by producing "how to" manuals for playing various instruments.

MUSIC AT THE COURT

Renaissance princes patronized musicians just as they did artists. Federico da Montefeltro supported a fine choir of boys, as well as many skilled musicians in his court of Urbino. Duke Ercole d'Este backed the organization of a group of "lady singers" in 1480 to entertain the members of his court in Ferrara. His daughter Isabella carried her love of music to Mantua, where the court musicians invented the *frottola*, a polyphonic song for soprano, alto, tenor, and bass. Isabella ordered a clavichord from instrumentalist Lorenzo Gusnasco, requesting that the keyboard respond to a light touch, "for our hands are so delicate that we cannot play well if the keys are too stiff." Among the musicians she patronized was Marchetto Cara, the leading lutanist of the day, and Bartholomeo Tromboncino, a widely-acclaimed composer of beautiful madrigals. Isabella so esteemed the talents of Tromboncino that she protected him from punishment after he murdered his unfaithful wife!

Competition raged among the Italian courts to offer their visitors the most memorable musical experience. The composer, like the artist, was now esteemed as a creator of great works, and the most talented musicians were in tremendous demand. They signed contracts for their performances and received very high salaries. Francis I offered French citizenship to the most gifted Italian musicians, hoping to keep them in his royal court.

As we know, the model Renaissance prince could play a number of musical instruments. Henry VIII of England played the lute, the recorder, and the virginal with great skill, sang pleasantly, and composed an impressive amount of music, including several Masses. According to legend, he also composed the well-known English song, "Greensleeves." Mary Queen of Scots played the lute and wrote madrigals, while her cousin Elizabeth I played the virginal. (Isn't that an appropriate instrument for the Virgin Queen?) Even Pope Leo X dabbled in musical composition. He appointed fifteen composers to the papal court and he hired lute player Gian Maria Giuldeo, whom he paid twenty-three ducats a month (a very high wage). He even gave him the rank of count!

Paintings of the times reflect the courtly interest in music, particularly Titian's THE CONCERT and Raphael's ST. CECILIA. Jan Bruegel's THE SENSE OF HEARING, painted in 1600, displays the rich variety of musical instruments commonly used at the end of the sixteenth century.

The courtiers and ladies of the Renaissance loved formal dance routines, which were accompanied by a lute and other instruments. They spent much of their time learning the latest steps from professional dancing masters *(balletti)*. Catherine de Medici introduced Italian dances and spectacles to high society in France. (A spectacle was a lavish musical play acted out by costumed courtiers and their ladies.) Among the most popular court dances were the fast-paced *gavotte*, the bouncy *galliard* (danced in triple time), the stately *pavane*, and the lively *volta*. The *branle* was a French dance accompanied by a chorus rather than an instrument. (Its English translation is "brawl"!)

Thoinot Arbeau was a dancing master, who wrote an instruction manual

(ORCHESOGRAPHY) for his fashionable patrons. It describes the various steps to popular dances of the day and gives tips about proper manners associated with the dance. For example, a gentleman always bowed to his partner before and after a dance, and he made an effort to say amusing things while they were doing the various steps. The book is still used today to teach Renaissance dances.

Wealthy people often hired musicians to play appropriate melodies for each of the courses of their banquets. A spicy dish called for a lively tune, while the pudding course required a slow, plodding beat! This was known as "table music." What do you suppose would be played for vegetable stew?

PROTESTANT MUSIC

Martin Luther thought it was important for worshipers to take an active part in church services by singing hymns in their own language. He once remarked that a piece of music was "a gift from God, and not from men, which causes anger, impurity, and other vices to be forgotten." He even composed his own hymn, which it still sung in modern Protestant services: A MIGHTY FORTRESS IS OUR GOD. The Reformation led to the creation of a new type of German sacred music known as the chorale - a simple, yet emotionally uplifting song derived from secular music (including folk tunes) as well as Catholic songs.

Other leaders of the Reformation responded in varying ways to the idea of congregational singing. Calvin permitted the unison singing of psalms, but Zwingli forbade music of any kind in church. In England the anthem, similar to the German chorale, evolved in the newly established Anglican churches. During Elizabethan times Thomas Tallis and William Byrd composed many beautiful anthems that are still popular in Protestant churches today. Byrd is believed to have invented the multi-verse anthem.

PALESTRINA

Giovanni Pierluigi da Palestrina (1525-94) was by far the most talented composer of religious music in the sixteenth century. In 1554 he wrote his first book of Masses, the earliest by an Italian composer. He dedicated them to Pope Julius III, his patron. A prolific composer, he left us hundreds of sacred pieces of music as well as madrigals.

Much of Palestrina's output was a direct result of the Counter Reformation. The Council of Trent declared that many of the words of contemporary religious music were unintelligible, since different voices were singing different verses at the same time. It called for new pieces whose words could be easily heard and understood. (This assumes that you know Latin!) In 1564 Pope Pius IV appointed a commission of eight cardinals to oversee the reform of Italian church music.

Palestrina met this challenge by writing polyphonic pieces, in which the words of the various voices come together more often than they did in earlier works. He also attempted to avoid any secular elements in his music. (Remember how the earlier pieces often contained melodies derived from folksongs?) His goal was to restore a sense of splendor and of spirituality to the music of the Church. He submitted three of his Masses to the commission. One of these, the Mass of Pope Marcellus II, was his masterpiece. It became the model for all Masses written in the following centuries. Palestrina composed music of such beauty and elegant harmony that he was called "The Prince of Music" by the grateful Catholic Church.

EMPHASIS UPON THE INSTRUMENT

As new types of music appeared in the sixteenth century, instruments often replaced one or more voice parts. No longer limited to the role of accompanying singers (or dancers), the instruments were appreciated for their own unique sounds, and compositions were written for them alone. The *fantasia, ricecari, canzoni,* and variations on themes are types of music for groups of instruments. Other genres were developed for specific instruments, such as the *toccata* for the keyboard.

Andrea Gabrieli of Venice was the first composer to write sonatas for keyboard instruments. His organ music formed the basis of Italian organ music for the following centuries. He was also one of the first to write music for a specific combination of instruments without voices and, in choral works, to ally groups of instruments against contrasting vocal groups. Gabrieli composed Masses, motets, and madrigals as well as organ music. His nephew and student, Giovanni Gabrieli, wrote the first concerto - a piece in which a single instrument is accompanied by an entire orchestra. The *concerto* is the form that would dominate the baroque music of the seventeenth century.

A RETURN TO SIMPLICITY

Every major movement in art, politics, and just about every other area inevitably offends certain people, who long for the good old days before everything changed. So it was in Italy, where every important city had an academy devoted to the performance and discussion of music. Not surprisingly, many of the discussions centered on ancient music. In 1570 a group of Florentine musicians formed the *Camerata Florentina* -

a literary and artistic society whose most pressing goal was to develop a simpler form of music reminiscent of the classical past. One member, Vicenzo Galilei (father of the famous astronomer) published A DIALOGUE ON OLD AND NEW MUSIC in 1581. This became the Bible of a new generation of Florentine music lovers. It renounced polyphony and counterpoint in favor of the simplicity of the single voice. It also reflected the ideas of Greek philosopher Plato, who wrote that musical notes should be subservient to the words of the text.

The Camerata's attempts to revive the principles of ancient music led to the development of the *aria* - a melody, often with a dramatic text, for a single voice accompanied by instruments. They also helped to create the recitative, in which a person half sings and half speaks a part.

THE BIRTH OF OPERA

In the 1590's the Camerata met at the house of Jacopo Corsi, a gifted amateur poet and musician. The new emphasis on the dramatic expression of verse with musical accompaniment paved the way for the birth of opera. The breakthrough occurred when poet Ottavio Rinuccini and composer Jacopo Peri adapted many of the inventions of the Camerata (namely the aria and the recitative), added an orchestra, and created a musical play - DAPHNE. This first *opera* (a word derived from the Latin term for works) combined singing, acting, dancing, and instrumental music with elaborate stage designs and costumes. It was produced in 1597, but unfortunately the music was later lost. Peri's EURIDICE, produced in 1600, is the oldest surviving opera.

Opera reached greater even heights early in 1607 when Italian composer Claudio Montiverdi set to music the Greek myth of Orpheus and produced his ORFEO in Mantua with a forty-piece orchestra accompanying the singers. It created a sensation and was followed by other grandiose open-air productions. The first public opera house would open in Venice in 1637. By mid-century opera was Italy's favorite dramatic form. It still is!

THE MUSIC OF THE COMMON PEOPLE

Although the ordinary people of the Renaissance had an opportunity to hear beautiful music during church services, they had little contact with the madrigals and pavanes enjoyed by the members of the court. Nonetheless, secular music played an important part in their lives. May Day was celebrated with dancing and lively instrumental music throughout much of Europe. Many towns had publicly paid bands that played on summer evenings and for special occasions, and there was always a fife and drum to provide music at weddings and fairs.

REVIEW QUESTIONS:

1. Why were the first monastic chants written?

2. What is monophony and what is polyphony?

3. What is a Renaissance chanson?

4. How did Pythagoras influence Renaissance music?

5. What were four instruments commonly used during the Renaissance?

6. What is imitative counterpoint?

7. Where were most chansons and madrigals performed?

8. What is the chorale?

9. How did Palestrina redefine sacred music?

10. Name three types of music written for instruments.

11. What was the purpose of the Camerata Florentina?

12. What was the first opera?

FURTHERMORE:

1. Greek philosophers Plato and Aristotle believed that music had emotional qualities and influenced human behavior. For example, a person who listened to a certain type of music acquired qualities associated with it. A slow, steady melody created a sense of calm, while a lively tune would agitate the individual.

2. Building on the growing reputation of Florence as a center for music, Lorenzo de Medici (The Magnificent) founded the School of Harmony, which attracted musicians from all over Italy.

3. Most later Renaissance instrumental music was written down in a form known as tablature. Letters, numbers, and other marks indicated the string, finger hole, or key to play. This system of notation did not indicate the actual musical notes as modern scores do.

4. Music was very popular in Elizabethan England. Customers waiting in barbershops were often provided with lutes, upon which they could play for themselves and their friends. And after dinner, songbooks were often passed around so that everyone could sing together.

PROJECTS:

1. Listen to the recordings of Gregorian chants that have been made in recent years. One CD is simply entitled CHANT.

2. One of the most beautiful canons ever written is Pacabel's Canon. Find a recording and listen to it.

3. Find a CD of Renaissance music. There are many available today. Listen to the various genres. Then play some of the pieces for your classmates, explaining to them what they are listening to.

4. Choose one of the composers mentioned in this chapter and do a research project on his life.

5. Look at the illustrations in a book about Renaissance art or simply Renaissance culture. Find some that have references to music (singing, dancing, or playing an instrument). Bring them to class and discuss what is depicted with your classmates.

6. Listen to a Mass by Palestrina.

Chapter XV
HUMANITY TAKES CENTER STAGE

"All the world's a stage," William Shakespeare once wrote, "and we are all merely players." That famous playwright of Elizabethan England saw drama in the most ordinary events, and he considered a humble gravedigger just as fascinating as a king. Shakespeare did not share the humanist belief that every man can carve his own destiny, if only he makes the effort. Didn't bad things happen to good people, in spite of their efforts? He wondered what forces *did* determine a person's fate. Did the makeup of his character decide which roads he would take in life? Or did events simply occur without "rhyme or reason?" These are a few of the thoughts that were running through Shakespeare's mind as he composed thirty-seven memorable plays.

As has been the case with so many of the creative geniuses we have studied, Shakespeare's achievements represent the pinnacle of a craft that had its origins in medieval times.

MEDIEVAL DRAMA

The priests of the Middle Ages often wrote plays to teach their illiterate parishioners about the lives of the saints and the stories of the Bible. These plays were called miracles (the lives of saints) and mysteries (the biblical stories). But since the priests insisted upon writing their plays in Latin, the audience (who, of course, didn't understand that ancient tongue) had to depend upon the actions and gestures of the actors to understand what was happening.

In later years the priests wrote allegories, known as morality plays, to demonstrate how easily a person can be tempted by such "enemies" as Greed or Vanity to lead a sinful life. The most famous of these, entitled EVERYMAN, was written by an unknown Flemish author around 1500 and was quickly adapted into English. It focuses upon the moment when Everyman (who represents the typical parishioner) is summoned by Death to account for his sins. Death was usually portrayed by a priest dressed in a hooded black robe, his face whitened with chalk to make it look ghostly. Abandoned by his companions (Beauty, Worldly Goods, and Fellowship), Everyman realizes that the joys of the earthly life are fleeting. Then, with the aid of Knowledge and Good Deeds, he repents for his sins. Now he is prepared to face Death, knowing that his soul will reside in heaven. The play was obviously intended to make everyone in the audience think twice before letting material comforts interfere with his piety!

The early medieval plays were performed in the churches, but when the productions became more elaborate, they were taken outside to the church steps. In the fourteenth century secular themes began to mingle with religious ones (some of the morality plays became quite bawdy), so the Church forbade the use of the steps for their presentation. This is when traveling troupes of actors took their plays to the market squares and performed on carts, balconies, or wooden platforms. The plays were now written in the vernacular, so they were easy to follow. Theater was becoming a popular form of entertainment.

COMMEDIA ERUDITA

It was in Italy, of course, that classical drama was rediscovered. Inspired by the descriptions of ancient plays in Aristotle's POETICS and Horace's ART OF POETRY, the Italian humanists began seeking out the great dramas of the past. In the elite settings of scholarly academies and ducal courts, they revived the comedies of such classical playwrights as Plautus, Terrence and Seneca. A comedy was a light play about the foibles of human nature, while a tragedy portrayed the sufferings of noble characters. Aristotle wrote that comedy "depicts people as worse than they are," while tragedy "makes them appear better." The humanists, whose attitude tended to be more optimistic than pessimistic, were drawn to the lighter form of drama.

Before long, Italian authors were creating original comedies in imitation of the ancient ones. These were written in the Italian vernacular and took place in contemporary urban settings. Known as *commedia erudita* (learned comedy), the new plays usually contained an elaborate love intrigue spiced with comic episodes involving mistaken identities and disguises, conniving servants, and other clever, shady, or gullible characters.

Intermezzi were short skits that were performed between the acts of a play. They often drew humorous parallels between mythical characters and well-known figures in contemporary society, often someone sitting in the audience. Gradually, as music and elaborate scenes were added, the intermezzo became a distinct type of play that might be presented between the courses of grand banquets or as a source of amusement at court. (Many were written by the courtiers themselves.)

EARLY THEATERS

The discovery of Vitruvius' ancient work, ABOUT ARCHITECTURE, in the monastery of Saint Gall in 1414 (Book V dealt with theater design), coupled with the growing interest in classical drama, led to the creation of the Renaissance theater. Ludovico Ariosto, a talented poet and the first major comic writer of the period, supervised the construction of the theater at Ferrara in which his plays were performed. Toquato Tasso succeeded Ariosto as court poet of Ferrara and produced his own pastoral play, AMINDA, there in the summer of 1573. (A pastoral play is an idealized story about country life.) By the late sixteenth century, there were several theaters in Italy. The year 1585 marked the opening of Andrea Palladio's impressive *Teatro Olimpico* in Vicenza, the first large public theater. The opening play performed there was an ancient Greek tragedy, *OEDIPUS REX*.

COMMEDIA DELL'ARTE

The aristocratic plays of the *commedia erudita* had, of course, a limited audience. But troupes of professional players often obtained copies of the plays and rewrote them in a more "down to earth" style. Eventually they developed a new genre, known as *commedia dell'arte* (comedy of the actor's craft), which appealed to the common people. These plays were boisterous three-act comedies, in which actors improvised (made up) words and actions around a basic story line as they went along. The plot usually consisted of young people in love outwitting their narrow-minded parents or guardians. The emphasis was upon broad comic action, which included acrobatics and a stock of verbal and visual jests. Actors specialized in particular roles of stereotyped characters, whose costumes and masks made them readily recognizable to the people in the audience. These characters included Pantalone, an old, greedy Venetian merchant; Graziano, a pompous Bolognese lawyer; the *miles gloriosus* (braggart soldier), who was often a Spaniard; the lovers; and the *zanni*, comically coarse female servants (such as Columbine). The most popular characters were the buffoons, or clowns, named Arlecchino and Pulcinella. Arlecchino was a slow-witted servant. When he ran out of things to say, he would hit the other actors with his stick! This is the origin of slapstick comedy, often connected with "The Three Stooges" of more modern times. The actor playing Arlecchino had to be an excellent acrobat, able to execute handstands and backflips whenever he felt like it. Arlecchino and Pulchinella survive today as Harlequin and Punch in the traditional English Punch and Judy puppet shows.

The *commedia dell'arte* was the first theatrical genre to allow women to perform. (Since ancient times, only men had performed in the theater.) The beautiful and talented actress Isabella Andreini belonged to a troupe known as the *Gelosi*. People flocked to the theaters just to see her act. She was also a gifted dramatist and poet.

Because the *commedia* players traveled widely and were extremely popular outside Italy, they had a considerable influence on the theatrical productions of other nations. In Paris, where they were known as *La Comedie Italienne*, they were given a theater of their own.

Spanish Drama

Medieval religious drama flourished longer in Catholic Spain than in any other European country. (Can you explain why?) Most Spanish plays of the early Renaissance were known as *autos sacramentales*. They featured odd combinations of human and supernatural characters, who mingled with such allegorical figures as Pleasure, Sin, and Grace. The plays were presented in public theaters, which were owned by religious brotherhoods and city governments. These were set up in *corrales* (empty yards between houses) on large platform stages. The spectators sat on benches in the street or viewed the play from rooms (boxes) in the adjacent houses. All roles were played by men until 1587, when a few women appeared on the stage. The actors were under contract to managers *(autores de comedias)*, who purchased costumes and plays and hired out their troupes to the owners of the corrales.

In the sixteenth century, a number of secular plays appeared in Spain, which dealt with historical events or dramatized social intrigue among the aristocrats. Bartolome de Torres Naharra wrote several romantic comedies and introduced the "cape and sword" action play (with the emphasis on swordsmanship). Not surprisingly, his works were outlawed by the Church in 1559. The following century Lope de Vega and Pedro Calderon de la Barca would write hundreds of secular and religious plays of such high quality that their times are known as the Golden Age of Spanish Theater.

English Drama

The English drama of the Renaissance had its roots in several sources: Greek and Roman historical writings, the bawdy Italian romances of the *commedia dell'arte*, the chronicles of English kings and warriors, and folk traditions. These elements merged in the late sixteenth century, when university students began writing plays for professional actors to perform. Their early plays had such colorful titles as RALPH

ROISTER DOISTER, GAMMER GURTON'S NEEDLE, and FERREX AND PORREX.

Late in the sixteenth century a group of Oxford and Cambridge students formed a drama society, known as the University Wits, and produced a series of their own clever original plays. Among the group was John Lyly, who composed elegant prose comedies that blended mythological themes with English subjects. Robert Greene drew upon the Italian comedies to create light-hearted romances. His heroines are noted for their wit and charm. Thomas Kyd brought the classical influence to popular drama when he wrote THE SPANISH TRAGEDY in blank (unrhymed) verse, a form he is credited with inventing. Inspired by the ancient works of Seneca, his play is very melodramatic. In its violent finale a father avenges the murder of his son. Kyd's play set the tone for Elizabethan tragic drama, while creating the revenge tragedy as a literary genre. The greatest playwright in the group was Christopher Marlowe. He is admired for his mastery of blank verse and his talent for creating a powerful central character. His series of tragedies, including DR FAUSTUS and TAMBULLAINE THE GREAT, focuses upon the agonies of heroes (or anti-heroes), who become caught in a web of dire circumstances.

Ben Jonson was among the most learned dramatists of his day. He displayed his familiarity with classical comedy and satire in scathing plays that ridiculed the greed and folly of contemporary English society. He created a new genre, the "comedy of humors," that attributed extravagant character traits (such as being moody or lazy) to an imbalance of the four bodily humors. (Remember Galen's theory of the four humors, the essential fluids of the human body?) Too much bile, for example, was supposed to make a person melancholic. In

his witty satires, EVERY MAN AND HIS HUMOR and THE ALCHEMIST, Jonson gleefully pokes fun at foolish characters who are dominated by obsessive traits like greed, jealousy, or religious fanaticism. While attributing these tendencies to an excess of a particular humor, he is, in fact, mocking anyone silly enough to believe in the humors theory. His main intent was to make his contemporaries aware of the consequences of obsessive behavior.

Many of the Elizabethan playwrights led lives at least as colorful as the works they wrote. Greene spent much of his time attending parties and drinking heavily, supported by his highly profitable writing talent. Marlowe was an atheist, and at the time of his death (he was stabbed in a tavern brawl) a warrant was out for his arrest. (Atheism was not tolerated by Anglican England.) Ben Jonson was imprisoned for killing an actor and barely escaped hanging.

THE EARLY THEATERS

In the early sixteenth century, English plays were performed by small companies of actors in the houses of the nobility or (under the control of the Lord Chamberlain) at the royal court. In time, some of the companies set up public playhouses (theaters). The first playhouse, appropriately named "The Theater," was built by the actor James Burbage. It opened in 1576 in the London suburb of Shoreditch. The University Wits wrote plays specifically to be performed at The Theater. Other playhouses were built soon afterwards. These included the Rose, which opened in 1587 in Southward (nearer the center of London), and the Swan, opening in 1595. (The Swan was the biggest theater, holding 3,000 people.)

The typical theater was circular and consisted of a three-story thatch-roofed structure (called the frame), which surrounded an open-air courtyard (called the pit). Spectators who could afford the price sat in boxes or galleries within the frame, while the common people stood below in the pit. Those in the pit were called the "groundlings" and were known for their boisterous behavior. A portion of the pit was occupied by a platform stage several feet high, which was partially protected by a "shadow" or roof supported by wooden pillars. The performers were thus in close contact with the standing spectators, and this must have made the plays seem all the more realistic. There was no curtain. At the rear of the stage was the "tiring house," where the actors dressed and stored their property.

The galleries that hung over the back of the stage often served as a balcony or even the top of a castle wall in a play. Trap doors built into the stage floor allowed for "sudden departures" or appearances of ghosts and spirits, while a system of ropes and pulleys enabled a god or goddess to "fly down" from the heavens. Although there was no scenery on stage, there were many props, such as thrones, tables, rocks, and trees. Special effects were sometimes used to enliven the drama. For example, cannons were exploded behind the building to create the illusion of thunder. (This must have jolted a number of people in the audience!)

Watching a play was certainly a pleasant alternative to cockfights and bullbaiting as a form of public entertainment. Perfor-

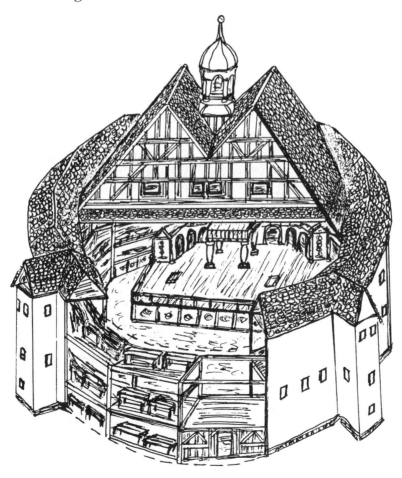

Figure 45: An Elizabethan Theater

mances were given every day but Sunday, beginning around two and concluding with a song-and-dance act three hours later. Refreshments were sold during the show. In the winter months, plays were often presented in smaller, indoor playhouses (known as "private theaters").

The actors wore sumptuous costumes of contemporary styles; only rarely was there an attempt at historical accuracy in the dress of the characters. (Does this remind you of some of the Italian paintings?) The audience would shout and clap to express their approval or throw a barrage of apple cores to show their dismay! No women appeared on the English stage. Following the ancient tradition, the roles of women and children were played by boys (aged between eight and thirteen). The acting company of Saint Paul's consisted entirely of choirboys.

SHAKESPEARE

William Shakespeare (1564-1616) was the greatest literary figure of the English Renaissance and probably the greatest playwright of all time. His plays have been translated into more languages than any book except the Bible. They are at once entertaining and thought-provoking, blending popular appeal with profound human and intellectual qualities. Shakespeare had a genius for probing character and portraying in a single situation elements of humanity that apply to all times and all places. Because of his interest in questions of morality and virtue, his plays often focus upon the consequences that arise from such human vices as greed and envy. Gone is the medieval concern with the hereafter. What matters in a play by Shakespeare is how people cope with the dilemmas of "the here and now."

In HAMLET the playwright expresses his high regard for the power of human rea-

son: "What a piece of work is a man, How noble in reason! how infinite in faculties!...in apprehension how like a god!" Isn't this the essence of humanism? And yet, Shakespeare was also a realist. Life is not always pleasant or easy. Perhaps his message is that man's ability to reason offers the only hope of surmounting the pains and sorrows of everyday existence.

The playwright was the son of a glovemaker. He left school at the age of twelve, the same year The Theater was built. As a young man he joined a drama company known as the Lord Chamberlain's Men. The name refers to the member of the royal court who served as its official patron. However, the company was owned and run by eight of the actors, including Shakespeare. It consisted of about twenty actors (including the young apprentices who performed the female roles). They performed a variety of plays, and since the success of a play depended upon the skillful delivery of the lines, each actor spent much of his "free" time memorizing his part.

Shakespeare somehow found time between acting and memorizing parts to rewrite some of the old plays, adding extra scenes or changing lines to bring them up to date. Then he started writing his own original plays for the company at the astonishing rate of two a year. Half of his plays were written for the Lord Chamberlain's Men. Sometimes he created roles for members of his troupe, in particular Richard Burbage (son of James Burbage, who built The Theater), the leading tragic actor for many years, and Will Kempe, a celebrated comedian. His new schedule was a hectic one. He would rehearse in the morning, act in the afternoon, then write and revise his plays at night.

Since earliest times, stories had been told in verse because it was easier to remember lines that way. Shakespeare's plays are similarly written in poetic rhythmical patterns, with rhymed couplets at the end of each scene. They reflect the playwright's absolute mastery of the dramatic blank verse first used by his contemporaries, Christopher Marlowe and Thomas Kyd. Shakespeare's keen ear for language enabled him to convincingly reproduce the speech of the loftiest lord or the humblest peasant, making these characters "come alive."

Special features of the plays are *soliloquies* and *asides*. In a soliloquy, an actor speaks directly to the audience, or to himself, expressing his innermost thoughts. This is often one of the highlights of the play. (Hamlet's speech about mankind is a good example.) In an aside, the actor says things to the audience that others on the stage are not supposed to hear. Shakespeare saw to it that the contemplative moments of his plays were mixed with sword fights, slapstick comedy, and general mayhem in order to appeal to every level of society. Since there was no scenery, he incorporated into the dialogue such things as the time of day, the setting, and the weather conditions. For example, a character might remark what a fine spring day it was in such and such a town, or mention an episode that has supposedly just taken place. Besides his keen insights about human nature, Shakespeare was knowledgeable about a wide range of subjects, including law, politics, history, music, war, sports, hunting, and the sea. In fact, his expertise in so many areas led certain incredulous scholars to claim that no single person could possibly have written all thirty-seven plays!

THE EARLIER PLAYS

Shakespeare's earliest plays reflect the influence of the classical playwrights, in particular Seneca and Ovid. His first tragedy, TITUS ANDRONICUS (1592), is now considered a somewhat coarse melodrama, although it was popular in its day. His first comedies, TWO GENTLEMEN OF VERONA and COMEDY OF ERRORS, appeared at about the same time and were clearly inspired by the works of Plautus and Terence. Some of the basic ideas of COMEDY OF ERRORS - the dispersal and reunion of a family, time's destructive passage and its potential for renewal, and the imagery of ocean water, strange lands, and voyages - appear again in his last play, THE TEMPEST (1611). In that play, the character Caliban is a strange, fish-like monster inspired by the often outlandish accounts reported by overly imaginative world explorers.

Shakespeare drew upon the rich chronicles of English history to write the three parts of HENRY VI and then KING JOHN and RICHARD III. (Richard was the man defeated by Henry Tudor of Lancaster, who became Henry VII, grandfather of Queen Elizabeth.) These plays reflect the Elizabethans' horror of civil war (remember the Wars of the Roses?) and bring into question the responsibilities of the monarch. Shakespeare's histories and tragedies include comic scenes, which offer some relief from the emotional intensity. This mix of elements represents a Renaissance innovation: the tragicomedy.

In the last five years of the sixteenth century, Shakespeare wrote some of his most memorable plays, including ROMEO AND JULIET, A MIDSUMMER NIGHT'S DREAM, MUCH ADO ABOUT NOTHING (the two last plays were written for comedy actor Will Kempe), AS YOU LIKE IT (written for Kempe's successor, the more intellectual comic Robert Armin), THE MERCHANT OF VENICE, and the history plays RICHARD II, HENRY IV (parts I and II), and HENRY V. Shakespeare's greatest comic character, Falstaff, appears in the plays about Henry IV. He is the playwright's version of the braggart soldier first depicted by Plautus and later seen in the plays of the *commedia dell'arte*.

THE GLOBE THEATER

In 1596 the Lord Chamberlain's Men were forced out of The Theater, where they had been performing, by a greedy landlord who demanded a higher rent. In revenge, members of the troupe made a midnight raid on the playhouse and carried away parts of the stage. These were eventually incorporated into a new theater called the Globe, built in 1599 on the south bank of the Thames River. At this time Shakespeare was at the peak of his profession - as an actor and playwright.

The Globe would become the most famous theater in Europe. It could house over 2,000 people. The theater's name was represented on a wooden sign near the entrance, which depicted the classical hero Hercules holding a globe on his shoulders. Like the earlier theaters, the Globe was a round structure built of wood and plaster, with timber-framed galleries rising to a height of thirty feet. The raised stage, which jutted out from the frame into the pit, backed toward afternoon sun so that the actors could perform in the shade and not be blinded by the bright rays. In the middle of the stage was a tall tower supported by columns painted gold and bright colors. The lower level represented a palace and was the setting of scenes involving royalty. Balcony scenes (such as the famous one in ROMEO AND JULIET) took place in the second story of the tower. At the back of the stage were two doors for the actors to make their entrances and exits.

Plays were presented at the Globe throughout the year except during Lent, times of plague, or bad weather (especially in winter). A yellow silk flag flying above the theater meant that a play would be performed that day. The crowd began to gather by noon, because popular plays were nearly always sold out. Admission was cheap (a penny) for those prepared to stand in the central pit beneath the open sky. The more affluent, of course, paid a few pennies more and sat on benches in the galleries or in the highly prized private boxes of the frame. There were even seats placed on the side of the stage where fashionably dressed young people often sat, as much to be observed and admired as to watch the play. The start of a performance was signaled by three successive blasts by a trumpeter, standing in the balcony of the tower above the stage.

With the opening of the Globe, Shakespeare wrote his seven great tragedies: JULIUS CAESAR (this was the first play presented at the new theater), HAMLET (in one production Burbage had the role of Hamlet and Shakespeare played the ghost of Hamlet's father), OTHELLO, KING LEAR, MACBETH, ANTONY AND CLEOPATRA, and CORIOLANUS. He also wrote the comedy, THE TWELFTH NIGHT (with the major role for Robert Armin, the comic actor who succeeded Will Kempe). Among his later works, MEASURE FOR MEASURE, ALL'S WELL THAT ENDS WELL, and TROILUS AND CRESSIDA are excellent examples of the new genre, the tragicomedy.

LATER YEARS

From the beginning, Shakespeare's plays were well received by the literary world of London (and loved by the more boisterous lower classes). By 1595 he was the most famous playwright in England. In 1603 King James succeeded Elizabeth to the throne. He became the official patron of

Shakespeare's company, which then became known as the King's Men. Five years later, Shakespeare purchased the fashionable Blackfriars Theater, so that his company could perform in winter. (Of course, they continued to present their plays at the Globe and at court in the summer.) On this occasion Shakespeare wrote the romantic comedies PERICLES, CYMBELINE, THE WINTER'S TALE, and THE TEMPEST (which is generally viewed as the playwright's farewell to the stage).

OUR GREATEST PLAYWRIGHT

Because Shakespeare wrote his plays strictly for performance, he had no interest in printing the scripts. However, during his lifetime nineteen of the plays were published by others as *quartos*. Some quartos were derived from texts recalled from memory by an actor or group of actors, while others were supplied to a printer by the company. The first type of quarto was, of course, far from accurate. (Who could possibly remember an entire play?)

Seven years after Shakespeare's death, all of his plays (except PERICLES) were gathered together and published as the FIRST FOLIO. The sources of the collection were the quartos just described and promptbooks. (A promptbook was an original copy of a script with detailed directions for the production of the play.) Since Shakespeare never oversaw the printing of any of his plays, it is somewhat difficult to establish exact dates for them and to be absolutely accurate about their content. We can only make a "best guess estimate."

One thing is certain: Shakespeare's acute understanding of human nature gave his works a timeless quality. His characters could easily have lived in any century and in any setting. The kings in his plays face many of the same choices modern presi-dents do, while the ditch diggers and washer women bemoan the same miseries as today's manual laborers. Ben Jonson wisely described the playwright as "not of an age, but for all time."

William Shakespeare died at age the age of fifty-two. Despite his renown, we cannot be certain about what he looked like. Only two authenticated likenesses exist: a memorial bust in his native parish church in Stratford-upon-Avon and an engraving by Martin Droeshout on the frontispiece of the FIRST FOLIO. In these he appears as a pleasant-faced, balding fellow with a moustache and dark hair curling under just above his stiff, Elizabethan collar. But his physical appearance matters little. It is his poetic genius that lives on through his masterpieces.

REVIEW QUESTIONS:

1. Describe a typical medieval play.

2. What was the *commedia erudita*?

3. What were *intermezzi*?

4. How did *commedia dell'arte* differ from *commedia erudita*?

5. Describe Arlecchino (Harlequin).

6. Where were the Spanish plays performed?

8. Who were the University Wits?

9. Describe a typical Elizabethan theater.

10. List five factors that made Shakespeare's plays popular.

11. What was the symbol of the Globe Theater?

12. What is the First Folio?

FURTHERMORE:

1. Pantalone was a thin, foolish old man (a greedy Venetian merchant) in the *commedia dell'arte*. He wore trousers with long fitted legs that were loose at the hips. They came to be called Pantalones, which in English translated into pantaloons. This is the source of our present word, "pants." (The French still refer to trousers as *les pantalons*.

2. The Elizabethans lumped together actors with all other entertainers, including bearbaiters, bullbaiters, and acrobats. Even in the days of Shakespeare they were at the bottom of the social ladder, along with rogues and vagabonds.

3. Shakespeare added more than 1700 words to the English language. He invented such terms as frugal, dire, lapse, barefaced, bump, countless, courtship, critic, critical, disgraceful, dishearten, dwindle, eventful, exposure, fretful, gloomy, hurry, impartial, lonely, monumental, recall, and suspicious. And these are just a few! Many expressions in common use today date back to the English bard: a foregone conclusion, elbowroom, fair play, foul play, tongue-tied, vanished into thin air, dead as a doornail, the long and the short of it, don't budge an inch, having seen better days, as good luck would have it, a tower of strength, and to catch a cold.

4. Some scholars insist that Shakespeare didn't really exist, and that his writings were penned by Christopher Marlowe or Sir Walter Raleigh or Sir Francis Bacon or someone else. However, most people believe that Shakespeare lived and wrote the plays.

5. Shakespeare's main resources for his history plays were CHRONICLES OF ENGLAND, SCOTLAND AND IRELAND by Raphael Holinshed and PARALLEL LIVES OF NOBLES GREEKS AND ROMANS by the Roman biographer, Plutarch.

6. Music played an important in Shakespeare's works. He used over fifty songs in his plays and wrote hundreds of stage directions calling for music. THE TWELFTH NIGHT might be categorized as a Renaissance "musical comedy," and there are many dances included in THE TEMPEST, A WINTER'S TALE, and ROMEO AND JULIET.

7. London's newest theater is the Globe, a replica of the sixteenth century building where Shakespeare' plays were presented. The original Globe was demolished in 1644. Actors avoid wishes of "good luck," which they consider unlucky, and instead use the term "break a leg." George Innes was playing dual roles in Shakespeare's TWO GENTLEMEN OF VERONA in a pre-opening production in the new theater when he fell from a rope ladder and literally broke his leg!

8. Marlowe and Shakespeare both made allusions to Machiavelli. In Marlowe's play THE JEW OF MALTA the ghost of "Machevil" says, among other "scandalous" remarks, "I count Religion but a childish Toy, And hold there is no sinne but Ignorance." In Shakespeare's MERRY WIVES OF WINDSOR a tavern keeper asks, "Am I subtle? Am I a Machiavel?"

PROJECTS:

1. Find out more about the comic figure, Harlequin. Then write a paper tracing his evolution from the clown in early Italian comedies to the Punch and Judy shows.

2. Read a play by Ben Jonson and write a review of it as it might appear in a modern newspaper.

3. In the summer of 1592 a plague struck and killed 11,000 people in the London area alone. Everything came to a halt, and, of course, the theaters closed. To occupy himself Shakespeare turned to writing sonnets and narrative verse. These were published after his death. One hundred and fifty-four sonnets have survived to our times. Read ten of them.

4. Today there are many versions of Shakespeare's plays written for young people. Select one, read it (using a good dictionary), and give a report about it to the class.

5. Look at #3 above in FURTHERMORE. Make a list of the expressions mentioned and then explain what each one means.

6. Make a timeline of the life and works of William Shakespeare.

Epilogue
THE RENAISSANCE LIVES ON

Whew! As we conclude our study of the Renaissance, aren't you amazed by how much a relatively small number of talented Europeans accomplished in just a couple of centuries? That extraordinary time was one of the most creative periods in the history of mankind. The achievements of the artists, poets, philosophers, playwrights, scientists and adventurers we have learned about not only enriched western civilization, but also altered it immeasurably. Things would never be the same again. Europe had emerged from the "dark times," and the torch of knowledge that was reignited continues to burn brightly.

Although other ages have succeeded the Renaissance, the spirit of Shakespeare, Michelangelo, Machiavelli, Palestrina, Martin Luther, Montaigne, and all the others is still very much alive today. Take architecture, for example. The arches, pillars, and domes of Roman times that so inspired designers like Brunelleschi and Palladio can be seen in buildings in every major city. The White House and the Capitol building in Washington, DC are striking examples. Many of the latest "hit movies" have been adaptations of the plays of Shakespeare, and people continue to flock to the opera. CD's of Gregorian chants recently ushered in a revived interest in "early music," and Renaissance melodies are now "big sellers."

Mythical figures are ever popular, as modern advertising will testify: a winged Mercury is the logo for FTD Florists, and Botticelli's Venus (from BIRTH OF VENUS) often appears in ads for shampoos and face lotions. And what about those Ninja Turtles named Donatello, Raphael, and Michelangelo? But apart from the popularization of Renaissance faces and symbols, the art of the masters we have studied remains one of the high points in the history of western culture.

Good manners are important in today's world, and so are practical politics. Success in business and government often depends, sadly enough, upon manipulating people and doing what works best rather than what is most honorable. Machiavelli would have heartily approved. The Italian city-states were the first to appoint diplomatic envoys to foreign courts; today's world diplomacy owes much to those early international networks of communication. The spirit of inquiry is still very much alive. Just think of how far science has advanced since the days of Copernicus! And the successors of intrepid explorers like Columbus and da Gama now look toward the planets and stars, not as navigational guides, but as future destinations.

Protestant sects have followers in most parts of the world, and they are no longer "at war" with the Catholics. A small elite of society no longer establishes the standards of dress and behavior for the rest of the population, although celebrities like film stars are "trendsetters". And the women of the western world have emerged from the shadows to claim an equal role with men in modern society. It's no longer surprising to hear about a woman who has written a novel, run a business, or supported herself and her family. Today's woman has come a long way, and a major source of her inspiration lies in the humanist belief that a person can and should be all that he or she can be. Perhaps that's the greatest legacy of the Renaissance.

GUIDE TO PRONUNCIATION

(Note: In Italian when c is followed by i or e it is
pronounced "ch"; otherwise it sounds like "k."
Also, ch is pronounced like "k.")

Apollo - uh **poll** oh

Aristotle - Ar is **tot** ul

baroque - bar **oke**

Boccaccio - Bo **cotch** ee oh

Cesare Borgia - Chay **zah** ree **bor** gee ah

Hieronomous Bosch - Her **on** amus **bosh**

Botticelli - **bot** a **chel** ee

Tycho Brahe - **tee** koe **bra**

Bramante - Bra **mon** tay

Bruegel - **broy** gul

Brunelleschi - **broon** el **es** kee

Budé - **boo** day

Byzantine - **biz** an teen

Castiglione - Cas tee **yon** ee

Cellini - Chee **lee** nee

chiaroscuro - kar oh **skur** oh

Cimabue - **Chee** ma **boo** ay

commedia dell'arte - com **ed** ee yah del **ar** tay

commedia erudite - com **ed** ee yah er yoo **dee** tay

condottiere - Con **dote** ee **yer** ee

Copernicus - Cop **er** nuh kis

Cortes - Kor **tez**

Dante - **Don** tay

Josquin des Près - **jos** kwin day **Pray**

Duomo - Du **oh** mo

Durer - **Dur** er

Donatello - Don uh **tel** oh

El Greco - **El grek** oh

Erasmus - Er **ras** mus

Fugger - **Foog** er

Galen - **Gay** len

Giotto - Gee **ot** oh

Gutenberg - **goot** en berg

Guillaume de Machaut - Guy **ome** duh Ma **show**

Machiavelli - Mak ee uh **vel** ee

Magellan - Muh **jel** an

magi - **mah** gee

Masaccio - Mah **sach** ee oh

Medici - **Med** uh chee

Michelangelo - Mi kul **ang** el oh

Montaigne - Mon **ten** yuh

palazzo - pal **otz** oh

Palestrina - Pal es **tree** na

Palladio - Pal **ah** dee oh

Petrarch - **Pet** rark

Petrucci - Pet **roo** chee

Pisano - Pee **zan** oh

Pizarro - Pee **zah** roe

Plato - **Play** toe

priori - pree **or** ee

Ptolemy - **Tol** mee

Pythagoras - Pith **ag** or as

Rabelais - Rab ul **aye**

Raphael - Ra fiy **yel**

Savonarola - Sa **von** ar **oh** la

Sforza - **Sfor** tza

Signoria - Seen **yore** ee ah

Tintoretto - Tin tor **et** oh

Titian - **Tish** in

Urbino - Ur **bee** noh

Valois - Val **wah**

van Eyck - van **Ike**

Vasari - Va **sah** ree

Vesalius - Veh **sale** ee yus

Amerigo Vespucci - Ah **mer** i go Ves **piuu** chee

Leonardo da Vinci - Lay on **ar** do da **vinch** ee

Visconti - vis **kon** tee

Zeus - **Zoos**

INDEX